**Awarded by
The Percy Dares Memorial Prize Society**

Along the Cole Harbour Road
A journey through 1765–2003

HARRY CHAPMAN

COLE HARBOUR RURAL HERITAGE SOCIETY

Front cover: Long Hill on the Cole Harbour Road ca. 1918 by Ian Forsyth, tinted in 2003 by Nancy Roberts. (Courtesy of Mary Forsyth)

Back cover: Cole Harbour marsh at sunrise, Rosemary Eaton, 1975.

Endpaper maps: Compiled by Dawn Reiss based on NTS maps.

Cole Harbour Rural Heritage Society
471 Poplar Drive, Dartmouth NS B2W 4L2 Canada
farmmuseum@ns.sympatico.ca

© 2003 Cole Harbour Rural Heritage Society
All rights reserved. No part of this book may be reproduced, stored in a retrieval system or transmitted in any form or by any means without prior written permission from the publisher except for brief quotations embedded in a critical article or review. For photocopying or other reprographic copying, request permission from The Canadian Copyright Licensing Agency (Access Copyright). For an Access Copyright licence, visit www.accesscopyright.ca or call 1- 800-903-5777

Editors: Paula Sarson, Nancy Roberts
Designer: Nancy Roberts Design
Indexer: Virginia MacIsaac

National Library of Canada Cataloguing in Publication

Chapman, Harry, 1937-
    Along the Cole Harbour road : a journey through 1765-2003 / Harry Chapman.

Includes bibliographical references and index.
ISBN 0-9733624-0-5 (bound).—ISBN 0-9733624-1-3 (pbk.)

    1. Cole Harbour (Halifax, N.S.)—History. 2. Cole Harbour (Halifax, N.S.)—Biography. I. Cole Harbour Rural Heritage Society II. Title.

FC2345.C74C42 2003   971.6'22   C2003-905144-7

To Rosemary Eaton

whose work for the Cole Harbour Rural Heritage Society
has contributed greatly
to recording and preserving the area's
history and heritage

ACKNOWLEDGEMENTS

Over the past few years, the Cole Harbour Rural Heritage Society has received donations in memory of people who had passed away. Donations that were not designated for a specific purpose we have used toward the cost of this book. We are grateful to the donors and pleased to help keep the memory of the following people alive in this way:

Bernice Settle	Sarah Barker
Helen Horne	Ken Giles
Ira Settle	Gwen Brunelle
Renee Lee Orichefsky	Barbara Bell
Danielle Orichefsky	Barbara Mackintosh
Gerald Kent	Molly Campbell

Thank you to the following for their generous donations toward publishing this book:

    CIBC   Harry McInroy   The CHRHS Craft Group

Author's Note

A good many people assisted me in the publication of *Along the Cole Harbour Road* by providing photos, reference material, files, and other information. I would particularly like to thank Elizabeth Corser and Terry Eyland, the Heritage Farm Museum staff, for making available their files of material and photos, plus other background information; Gary Gibson for supplying several of his files of collected material on Cole Harbour and its past; Rosemary Eaton for the numerous audio tapes of interviews with older Cole Harbour and area residents; Paula Sarson for editing the manuscript; and Nancy Roberts for the cover and overall design and layout of the book.

CONTENTS

MAPS/KEY TO PHOTO CREDITS 9

FOREWORD 11

INTRODUCTION 13

I
EARLY SETTLEMENTS 17
1 *Wampawk* – The Peaceful Waters 19
2 The Acadians 26
3 The Governor's Town 31
4 Cole Harbour Land Grants 35

II
THE ARRIVING PEOPLE – 1700S 39
5 European Protestants 41
6 United Empire Loyalists 48
7 Black Loyalists and Maroons 51

III
BUILDING COMMUNITY – EARLY 1800S 59
8 Early Farm Families 61
9 The First School 70
10 Methodist Chapels 74
11 The Census of 1827 83
12 Diary of a Farmer's Daughter 86
13 Support Industries 95

IV
YEARS OF GROWTH – MIDDLE AND LATE 1800S 99
14 To Market, To Market 101
15 Spreading the Word 106
16 A Temperate Anchor 115
17 Dyking the Harbour 123

18 County Poor Farm 133
19 Goodbye Nineteenth Century 142

V

HELLO TWENTIETH CENTURY 159
20 Dawn of a New Century 161
21 War in Europe 166
22 The Decade that Roared 180
23 The Dirty Thirties 189
24 The Home Children 196
25 World War Two 202
26 Farming – A Cole Harbour Tradition 209

VI

CHANGES AND CHALLENGES –
MID-TWENTIETH CENTURY TO 2003 227
27 Post-war Years 229
28 A Decade of Change – 1960s 240
29 The Royal Commission 252
30 Mr. Cole Harbour 256
31 The Cole Harbour Rural Heritage Society 260
32 Voices from the Past 281
33 The Bulldozing Era 286
34 Politics Then and Now 292
35 A Century Ends 299
36 Postscript – The Twenty-first Century 314

TIMELINE OF COLE HARBOUR AND AREA HISTORY 321

SELECTED SOURCES 323

ENDNOTES 325

INDEX 326

MAPS

Maps are for illustration purposes only.

1 – Captain Cook's 1759 chart of Cole Harbour 25
2 – The initial six 1765 land grants in Cole Harbour 37
3 – Part of Collyer's 1808 map showing Bissett farm 47
4 – Turner's farm and Colin Grove circa 1808 67
5 – Cole Harbour with dyke, early twentieth century 131
6 – Plan of the Cole Harbour Mi'kmaq reserve 153
7 – Cole Harbour circa 1960, showing railway 173

KEY TO PHOTO CREDITS

All images, regardless of their provenance, now also reside in the archives of the Cole Harbour Rural Heritage Society, and the society may be able to provide more information about them

CHR-SU   Cole Harbour residents – series unidentified, an archival classification of the Cole Harbour Rural Heritage Society
DHM   Dartmouth Heritage Museum
NAC   National Archives of Canada
NSARM   Nova Scotia Archives and Records Management
RE   photographed by Rosemary Eaton from a photo album in private hands
RE (date)   contemporary photograph by Rosemary Eaton
RIMS   Registry Information Management Service, a division of Service Nova Scotia and Municipal Relations

"Courtesy of" designates the provider of a photo. A name without this phrase designates a photographer. Date is not given in credits if the most accurate date available is already in the caption or if the date is unknown.

FOREWORD

If early Cole Harbour is described, the road is the way to do it. When I first heard the title *Along the Cole Harbour Road* it sounded exactly right. The road was the artery that linked the farms and their lanes, lanes that were often marked by milk stands, the icons of many rural farming communities. The road had natural features, such as Long Hill, Beck's Hill, Bell's Hill, Breakheart Hill, and Clifford's Meadow – names that held real meaning for the people who travelled by horse-drawn wagon or sleigh and by foot.

Names are important. The older names link us to our past; they make us ponder and question their origin. New names are important too, and those that withstand the test of time will find their place in history. Cole Harbour, as well as the communities of Preston, Lawrencetown, Musquodoboit, and Chezzetcook, have helped preserve their heritage by naming streets, schools, parks, and public buildings from their researched and remembered past.

Along the Cole Harbour Road is the story of a community's development. In the early years it was necessary to build roads, mill logs, raise crops, and in general colonize new land. The community was shaped by its proximity to the garrison at Halifax and the military presence. It continues to be influenced by the cities of Halifax and Dartmouth as centres of commerce, industry, research, and education.

Growing up and living in Cole Harbour in the 1900s provided at once a wonderful perspective on farm life that was my heritage and a view to the future of Cole Harbour. The two views were vastly different. The future of farming was under pressure long before the housing developments came on the scene. The marketplace called for farming techniques well beyond the mixed farming format that was the norm in Cole Harbour. Opportunities for education and careers away from the farm were beginning to take their toll. The community was ready to change. The vision of a rural community populated by farms and woodlots becomes fainter as we make the turn to the new millennium.

The Cole Harbour Rural Heritage Society's mission is to encourage awareness of, interest in, and protection of our natural surroundings and cultural resources and to foster appreciation and respect for the community as a unique and valuable trust. To carry out this mission the society promotes the preservation of Cole Harbour's history and that of the surrounding areas, and maintains a collection of artifacts, buildings, and records of the people and lifestyles of the area.

The society has undertaken many important projects over the years. Issues relating to the Cole Harbour Salt Marsh, view planes from Long Hill, the impact of power line corridors across the community, and advocacy for the Coastal Heritage Park were addressed and remain active concerns. Refurbishing the Meeting House and the relocation of the Giles "Salt Box" House were major projects. The preservation of natural history and historic buildings and sites was the rationale to establish the Cole Harbour Heritage Farm Museum. It is arguably the largest and most visible project of the society.

The Society is remarkably fortunate to have Harry Chapman write this book. Harry brings to the task a wealth of local knowledge, sensitivity to the story, and the ability to lay it out before us in a logical, informative manner.

This book by Harry Chapman is a testament to the work of a dedicated society and to its many valued supporters.

H. Scott Morash
First president (1973)
Cole Harbour Rural Heritage Society
June 2003

INTRODUCTION

Cole Harbour Road measures a mere 4.5 kilometres (2.5 miles) in length, but its story stretches back to 1765, winding through several generations of families that farmed the land and built the community to today. The earliest Cole Harbour Road was little more than a dirt track, a condition imposed by the governor of the province on the first six land grantees, who required a road from Dartmouth to their land grants located around the inlet of water called Cole Harbour. The original road left Dartmouth, branched off from the Lawrencetown Road at Woodlawn and continued through the pristine wilderness past a large lake that was later named for one of the early settlers – Nathaniel Russell. The road crossed the flat unbroken wilderness and climbed the torturous hill that was later given the appropriate appellation "Breakheart Hill." After the summit was crested, the road rolled across the rich, undulating farmland to the harbour. Eventually, the road reconnected to the Lawrencetown Road.

The early settlers from Protestant Europe, Great Britain, Jamaica, and the newly established American states travelled this road with their families and their dreams for a better life in a new world. Along this road the early settlers toiled from dawn to dusk, clearing the land of trees, stumps, and rocks to develop prosperous farms. They built homes, barns, and other outbuildings, and dug wells. The homesteaders established a farming community that became the food basket for Halifax and Dartmouth. Along this same road, long before the sun popped over the eastern horizon, farmers began their weekly pilgrimage with horse and wagon to sell their produce at the Halifax Market.

The spring rains changed the road into a muddy soup, the hot summer sun made it dry and dusty, and the winter months choked the roadway with snow, forcing the farmers to exchange their wagons for smooth-running sleighs. The scene was ever changing along the Cole Harbour Road. Farmers worked in the fields to open the land

Cole Harbour Road in the 1930s was still little more than a dirt track that cut across a wilderness landscape connecting the farming community to Dartmouth and Halifax. Some workers with an early horse-drawn grader smooth out rough spots on the road. (James Albert Giles album)

for spring planting. They cut and stacked hay at the end of the summer, and in the autumn reaped the harvest of their labour.

Once public education was introduced in 1814, children walked along Cole Harbour Road first to a one-room school then to a two-room school near Bissett Road for their early education. Along the same road, families travelled to Sunday services or other church-related activities. The road was also an avenue for quiet evening strolls by young courting couples.

Victoria Hall, a prominent landmark from the late 1920s to the 1960s, was the locale for many meetings and social gatherings such as church suppers, teas and sales, community meetings, and credit union activities. Toe-tapping music could be heard from the small building when couples gathered for dances.

Cole Harbour developed into a close-knit community with most of its residents related by either blood or marriage. The farms and land passed from one generation to the next. Neighbours came together for barn raisings, crop harvesting, or fighting ruinous house or barn fires in the years before the fire department was established.

Of course, Cole Harbour Road has changed since the days when farmers themselves kept it clear of snow during the winter months. The government assumed that task long ago. The road was widened to accommodate increased traffic. In 1954, it received its first coat of asphalt for the benefit of the automobile, which debuted in Cole Harbour in the early years of the twentieth century.

Cole Harbour Road is much shorter than it was, beginning now at Caldwell Road instead of Gaston Road; however, it's still important to the life of a much larger community with a new breed of homesteaders. In the last half of the twentieth century, Cole Harbour was transformed when bulldozers replaced farm tractors to convert the open fields of fertile farmland to residential subdivisions. Commercial venues – gasoline outlets, shopping centres, banks, strip malls, and fast-food outlets – overtook the quiet pastoral scene along the road.

Residents now band together to build parks, recreation areas, and playing fields, and to stop intrusive governments from polluting the harbour and building ring roads through the community. Residents also joined their efforts to create the Cole Harbour Rural Heritage Society and the Cole Harbour Heritage Farm Museum in order to preserve the area's past.

This book, commissioned by the Cole Harbour Rural Heritage Society on the occasion of its 30th anniversary, is the story of Cole Harbour Road and its evolution from clusters of small rural farm communities to a sprawling suburb of nearly 30,000 people and one of the largest growth centres in Nova Scotia.

Just as the Cole Harbour Road traverses the rise and fall of the terrain, so does *Along the Cole Harbour Road* travel from the past to the present, taking in triumphs and tragedies through the evolution of a community.

I
EARLY SETTLEMENTS

1
Wampawk – THE PEACEFUL WATERS

2
THE ACADIANS

3
THE GOVERNOR'S TOWN

4
COLE HARBOUR LAND GRANTS

I

Wampawk – THE PEACEFUL WATERS

At the dawn of history, a thick mantle of ice blanketed what is now Cole Harbour as the great glaciers moved down from the Arctic Region and covered most of what are now Canada and a good part of the United States. When the glaciers melted and retreated northward, they left in their wake a rocky and barren landscape with hills, valleys, lakes, rivers, and harbours. Over time, trees and other forms of vegetation covered the land.

The marshy estuary deeply indenting the coast was an excellent feeding ground for all manner of waterfowl, especially the Canada goose and the great blue heron. The soil on the eastern side, from Upper Lawrencetown throughout the Lawrencetown area, is mostly rocky debris left behind when the great glaciers melted and is generally unsuitable for farming. The land on the western side, however, is more fertile and better suited for agriculture. This did not matter to the Mi'kmaq, but it mattered later.

At the head of the inlet, a large tree-covered point of land juts into the harbour creating eastern and western arms. The inlet is also dotted with several small islands – Fly Island is the largest on the eastern side and Glasgow Island the largest on the western arm.

Located about 12 kilometres (7 miles) east of present-day Halifax Harbour, the inlet is 2.9 nautical miles from its headwaters at Upper Lawrencetown, where it is fed with the fresh water from Little Salmon River and Smelt Brook, to its mouth at the Atlantic Ocean. It is 3.1 nautical miles at its widest point.

The Mi'kmaq called what we know as Cole Harbour *Wampawk*, meaning "still or peaceful waters." They were members of the Algonquian language family and lived by the shores of what we know now as the Great Lakes in Central Canada before migrating east to

The "peaceful waters" of Cole Harbour taken at sunrise by Rosemary Eaton. The harbour's salt marshes have played an important role in the long history of the community. (RE 1975)

the Atlantic region. Their ancestors, the first inhabitants of North America, were nomadic hunters who crossed the land bridge that once joined the Siberian region of Asia to North America at the time of the first ice age 15,000 to 20,000 years ago. When the glaciers melted, the water levels rose and covered the land bridge with the Bering Sea, trapping the hunters and their families on the North American continent. As the ice slowly retreated northward, more land on the continent opened up, allowing these hunters to travel east and south in search of food.

The Mi'kmaq came to Nova Scotia about 11,000 years ago, settling first in the Debert area, near Truro. Excavations in recent years have unearthed numerous artifacts: fireplaces, crude tools, and implements used in preparing animal skins. Over time, a Mi'kmaq population of approximately 100,000 occupied most of the eastern Canadian land mass that included the Gaspé Peninsula and the Maritime provinces. The Mi'kmaq territory was divided into seven districts. A district chief and a council consisting of elders, village chiefs, and other distinguished members of the community governed each district. The Mi'kmaq districts were part of a larger body known as the Wabanaki Confederacy, formed by the tribes living along the North American coast as a defence against possible invasion by the Iroquoian tribes. The Wabanaki Confederacy remained in force until the early 1700s.

Cole Harbour was part of the district called *Eskikewa'kik*, meaning "skin dressers' territory." Headquarters for the district chief and the Mi'kmaq people was the Shubenacadie area, where they lived and hunted deer, moose and rabbit during the cold, bleak winter months. In the spring, they paddled up the Shubenacadie River through the chain of lakes in their great birchbark canoes to their summer camping grounds along the Dartmouth lakes, Halifax Harbour, Bedford Basin, Eastern Passage, Cow Bay, and Cole Harbour.

For generations before Europeans arrived in the area, Native people made the shores around this sheltered saltwater inlet their summer home. The forest offered them bountiful wild game and fowl plus fruit and berries. The harbour teemed with salmon, mackerel, sea trout, smelts, eels, and clams.

The Mi'kmaq were primarily hunters and fishers, so their quest for food dictated their nomadic lifestyle. Male members of the tribe hunted, fished, took part in war raids, made and repaired the equipment and weapons needed for these activities. The women were the caregivers and food-gatherers. They prepared and cooked the food, collected firewood, looked after the wigwam, made clothes from animals skins, and mats and baskets from reeds.

The religion of the Mi'kmaq was based on respect for nature and mother earth, the giver of the necessities of life. The sun and the moon, both heavenly bodies, were regarded as manifestations of the Great Spirit, the Supreme Being responsible for all existence. They prayed daily at dawn and again at dusk.

The Mi'kmaq had no written language before the arrival of the Europeans, but a rich oral tradition passed their legends and history from generation to generation.

The word *mi'kmaq* means "my kin friends." It was a form of greeting, which became associated with the people themselves. Eventually, the word was anglicized to "Mikmah," "Micmac," and other variations.

The Cole Harbour summer encampment is believed to have been located near Little Salmon River. For hundreds of years, the Mi'kmaq occupied the land around Cole Harbour in peace and freedom. The arrival of the Europeans – first the French and later the English – drastically changed their way of life forever.

The harbour has had several names applied by the various groups of people who have owned or occupied the surrounding land. No one today knows for certain how it received its present name, Cole Harbour. Unlike nearby Halifax and Dartmouth, which were named for a person or a place in Great Britain, the name Cole Harbour appears on some early maps without any factual information to support its origin. While there may be no documented evidence about the source of the present name, there is considerable speculation as to how it may have evolved. The inlet was also called the Inner Harbour of Mouscoudabouet, a name that appears on an old land grant given to Mathieu de Goutin, formerly of Port-Royal, on August 4, 1691, by Comte de Frontenac, governor of New France. This land grant along the Atlantic coast comprised an area from present-day Chezzetcook to the western shoreline of Cole Harbour.

Much later, in a 1752 report of English land surveyor Charles Morris, the Mi'kmaq and French names and a new English name appeared together. A long chain of events had led to Morris' survey. The great French fortress at Louisbourg had been captured from the French by a rag-tag New England expeditionary force of mostly militiamen in 1745, but the terms of the Treaty of Aix-la-Chapelle returned it to France three years later. The deal was brokered in London, offering the French the return of their Nova Scotia possession if they ended support for Bonny Prince Charlie, the Young Pretender, in his quest to seize the British throne. France jumped at the opportunity to regain their military toehold on the Atlantic coast. With French troops and a fleet restored at Louisbourg, New Englanders feared renewed hostilities and demanded an English military and naval presence on the eastern coast of Nova Scotia. Governor William Shirley of Massachusetts demanded that Great Britain create a military fortress along the Atlantic side of Nova Scotia to counter possible attack from the French at Fortress Louisbourg.

Britain's answer to Shirley's demand was Halifax, settled in 1749 by Governor Edward Cornwallis and 2,500 eager but unsuitable colonists. The following year, a settlement named Dartmouth was created on the eastern side of the harbour. The 1751 arrival of additional settlers from Germany, France, and Switzerland to the area created an urgent need for suitable land for new townships. Capt. Charles Morris, Chief Surveyor of Lands in Nova Scotia, was commissioned to survey land along the Atlantic seaboard from Liverpool on the South Shore to Chezzetcook on the Eastern Shore, examining possible sites for new townships in which to settle the 1,500 new arrivals from continental Europe.

Captain Morris had arrived in Nova Scotia from Boston in 1746 with a company of reinforcements for the defence of Annapolis Royal. In addition to his duties as chief surveyor, he held other important public offices until his death at Windsor in 1781. He received numerous land grants in Dartmouth and the Cole Harbour area in the course of his life. Captain Morris went to the Musquodoboit area in 1752 to examine the former Acadian lands as possible sites for settling the new European arrivals. Captain Lewis and a troop of 20 rangers for protection against the Mi'kmaq escorted him. In his report to the governor, Captain Morris mentioned the ruins of Acadian buildings in the present-day Lawrencetown and Chezzetcook area and identified today's Cole Harbour by French and Mi'kmaq names: next to the sketch of the harbour is written "Inner Harbour of Muscodoboit or *Wampawk*, or by some Cold Harbour."

The new arrivals from France, Germany, and Switzerland settled first in Halifax but were subsequently relocated to Lunenburg on the South Shore. Over the next 50 years, some of these Lunenburg and Halifax settlers made their way to the Cole Harbour area. They came with such surnames as Ott, Bissett, Kuhn, Beck, Conrad, and Morash. Even an English or New England family by the name of Gammon, who had once settled in Lunenburg, also came to Cole Harbour.

In his *History of Nova Scotia*, Beamish Murdock wrote that the Inner Harbour of Musquodoboit, identified by Captain Morris, was the present Cole Harbour. The historian also stressed that the "Township of Lawrence Town [*sic*]," which was granted in 1754, was the "same place" that had been previously granted to Mathieu de Goutin's

"Seigneury at Mouscoudabouet." The boundaries extended from the Head of Chezzetcook westward to Smelt Brook at the bottom of Long Hill, Cole Harbour.

The grant map indicates that the harbour was called *Wampawk* by the Native people and known by others as Cold Harbour. One explanation for the Cold Harbour name may have been because the Township of Lawrencetown and the French land grant contain three major bodies of water – Porters Lake, Lawrencetown Lake, and Cole Harbour. Anyone who has ever swum in these bodies of water in the summer will readily agree that Cole Harbour is by far the coldest.

Another tenuous name claim to the harbour was "Cope's Harbour." District chief Jean Baptiste Cope and his council of elders were upset with the English over the founding of Halifax in 1749 and of Dartmouth in 1750. With the aid of a French priest, he wrote a strong letter of protest to the governor. In September 1752, Cope, sometimes called Major Cope, came to the Governor's House in Halifax with a proposal for peace and friendship. Cope, in addition to being district chief of *Eskikewa'kik*, was also grand chief of the Council of Mi'kmaq Chiefs. Since Cope's district included the harbour that became Cole Harbour, and it may have been loosely referred to as Cope's Harbour.

However, the peace treaty signed in late 1752 lasted only six months, until two English soldiers attacked a group of Native people. Once the peace was broken in 1753, Cope took up the cause for his Native people and became a hated enemy of the British. It's most unlikely the English would have assigned Cope's name to the harbour or continued any casual association of the name and harbour.

Captain Lewis, who accompanied Morris on his surveying expedition to the area, also prepared a map about 1755 and called the body of water Cole Harbour.

When Capt. James Cook of the Royal Navy charted the waters around Nova Scotia with surveyor Samuel Holland in the winter of 1759, he also labelled the inlet Cole Harbour on a map he prepared in about the same year. He noted that most of it was "dry at low water."

Some have believed that the harbour might have been named for a person surnamed Cole. If the harbour were named for a person, it probably would be for someone living in the general area at the time.

EARLY SETTLEMENTS

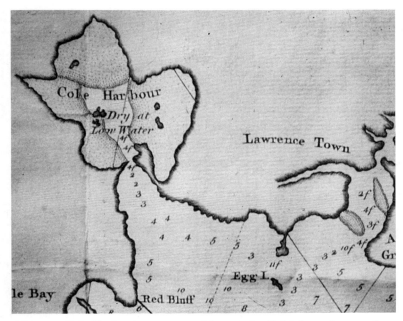

Map 1 – Cole Harbour was mapped in 1759 by British mariner and explorer Capt. James Cook during a charting expedition around Nova Scotia. Captain Cook used the name Cole Harbour on his map. (NAC)

Records indicate that the only person with that name was Joseph Cole, who lived in the area between 1749 and 1757. Cole arrived in Halifax in 1749 on the *Alexander*, one of the vessels that carried the founding settlers. Listed as a private in His Royal Highness' dragoons, Cole was given a land grant in the new settlement. He sold it the following year and bought land across the harbour in the new settlement of Dartmouth from John McDonald. He later sold his Dartmouth property and again acquired property in Halifax in 1753.

Cole became embroiled in a bitter lawsuit with John Williams, a trader and retailer, over the balance owing on his account from November 1751 to October 1753. Cole had a contract to supply provisions to the government sawmill in Dartmouth and made purchases from Williams. When Cole reneged on his debt, Williams took the matter to the Inferior Court of Common Pleas. The jury ruled in Cole's favour, but Williams and his lawyer appealed the decision to the

General Court. On May 6, 1754, three arbitrators reversed the earlier verdict and ruled in Williams's favour. Cole apparently then refused to pay his debt with the result that the Provost Marshal sold Cole's property at public auction on November 20, 1757. Williams was the highest bidder, acquiring the property for £6 and 7s, a bargain considering that Cole had purchased the property four years earlier for £9.

No record of Joseph Cole's stay in Nova Scotia has been found after 1756. He and his wife may have left before his property was sold to square his debt. It's most unlikely that a harbour would be named for an army private in trouble with the law over non-payment of his debts.

Former Dartmouth Museum director Syd Gosley offers another explanation for the name, pointing out that "cole" was an old English word meaning "sea kelp," and a place of its abundance might be called Cole Harbour. The inlet has also been referred to as Coal Harbour on some older maps and documents.

How the harbour acquired its present name becomes less important as time passes; it has now been called Cole Harbour for more than two centuries. What is important is the story of the people who farmed the land and how the community evolved from a rural agricultural society to a modern suburb of residential subdivisions, modern schools, churches, and commercial shopping areas.

2

THE ACADIANS

Pierre Du Gua de Monts and Samuel de Champlain established the first European settlement in Nova Scotia in 1605 on the Annapolis Basin. De Monts was granted a charter by King Henry IV of France in 1603 to "Christianize and colonize all the land then called L'Acadie." [1] He and Champlain, his navigator, left France the following year with four ships and sailed along the Atlantic coast of Nova Scotia, where they explored numerous coves and inlets before entering the Bay of Fundy and the Annapolis Basin. They crossed over to the New

Brunswick side of the Bay of Fundy and sailed down the Atlantic seaboard from the Saint John River to Cape Cod. They returned to the Bay of Fundy, where they spent a disastrous winter on the Ile Sainte-Croix on the New Brunswick side. The following year they returned to the Annapolis Basin, which they named Port-Royal – "Royal Harbour" – and founded a settlement there.

Additional French settlements were established throughout the area, and by 1689, there were approximately 900 French settlers living in communities from Port-Royal along the Bay of Fundy to the Minas Basin, Cobequid Bay, and around Cape Chignecto to Beaubassin near present-day Amherst.

A military expedition from Massachusetts led by William Phipps attacked and captured Port-Royal in 1670 in retaliation for a number of attacks on New England by French troops and their Native allies. The English subsequently returned the fort to the French. One of the prisoners captured during the attack was Mathieu de Goutin, lieutenant-general of Acadia, administrator of the King's accounts, munitions, supplies, and inspector of Crown works. Upon his release, he immediately made his way up the Saint John River to Quebec, where the Comte de Frontenac, the governor of New France, awarded him a grant of land on August 4, 1691.

The grant, located "at a place known by the Indians as Mouscoudabouet," [2] roughly comprised an area from the head of present-day Chezzetcook to the western shore of Cole Harbour and included all the islands, beaches, and the rights for hunting, fishing, and trading with the Native people. The grant was registered at the Sovereign Council of Quebec on September 10, 1692. Governor de Villebon, in a dispatch of October 1699, referred to the number of forts in the area, including the one at Mouscoudabouet. It is listed as one of those individual enterprises that was supposed to come to Port-Royal for supplies. "These posts are only kept for trading with the savages. Port Royal [sic] is the general store of the country."

The name Chezzetcook, sometimes pronounced "Chezzencook," comes from a Mi'kmaq word meaning "running water that divides into many channels." Native people had occupied parts of the area long before the Acadians took up residence.

It is doubtful that de Goutin himself ever spent much time at Mouscoudabouet, but he probably kept it in case he was unable to return to Port-Royal or if the English captured it again. He may also have intended it as a business venture in partnership with his wife's relatives. Following the surrender of Port-Royal in 1710 to Francis Nicholson, de Goutin returned to France with his family. Four years later he was appointed King's Writer at Ile Royale (Cape Breton Island), where he died on Christmas Day 1714.

Another Acadian associated with the Chezzetcook area was Claude Pettipas, a schooner captain and interpreter known for his collaboration with the English. He was born in Port-Royal in 1663, the third child of 15. His youthful voyages and activities brought him in contact with the Mi'kmaq in the area of Port-Royal, where he lived with his father. He married a Native woman, Marie Thérèse, and they had at least seven children. They lived at Mouscoudabouet, where Boston fishermen were active, and complaints arose about Pettipas's association with them. Marie-Thérèse died in 1721, and at about 57 Pettipas married 17-year-old Françoise Lavergne. They had four children. Pettipas eventually went to live at Ile Royale, where he died in 1731 or 1733.

After the fall of Louisbourg in 1745, a dispatch sent from Quebec reported a man and his three children living three leagues (9 miles) east of the entrance of Chibouctou (Chebucto), which might have been Chezzetcook. In 1748, seven or eight families were reported living in the area.

Very few documents mention the existence of Chezzetcook before the expulsion of the Acadians. There are documents mentioning a few French families in the area in the 1740s. Abbé de l'Isle Dieu mentions 10 French families at "Cheggekouke" in a letter written in 1750.

When Charles Morris surveyed the area in 1752, he found only the ruins of an Acadian establishment, and the only building left standing was the chapel. It's possible the families may have felt threatened by the establishment of an English settlement at Halifax in 1749 and decided to leave. It's unlikely they would have remained in the area following the Acadian deportation from 1755 to 1762.

Two separate events led to permanent settlement at Chezzetcook by Acadians after the deportations. The British had incarcerated about

2,000 Acadians who escaped deportation. Most of the prisoners were kept at Halifax, Fort Edward in Windsor, and Fort Beauséjour near Amherst. Approximately 335 Acadians were captured by the British near Bathurst, New Brunswick, and sent to Halifax, adding to the number of prisoners already there.

French historian Edme Rameau de Saint-Père described the origins of Chezzetcook when he first visited Nova Scotia in 1860.

> Chezzetcook is the name of this village, originated with a certain number of Acadian families who had been captured at various times after their banishment. They were led to Halifax where they were held captive for a long time on an island in the middle of the south harbour that is called ile [sic] Rouge. There they lived at times on prison rations and at other times from the fruit of their labour when they were permitted to work for the townspeople. Finally 10 or 12 years after the catastrophe they were permitted to settle a few leagues north of Halifax at the little harbour of Chezzetcook.

According to historical maps Ile Rouge is today known as Devils Island.

The second event that brought a group of Acadian settlers to Chezzetcook arose from the efforts of L'Abbé Pierre Maillard. After the fall of Louisbourg in 1758, he was able to convince Governor Lawrence to free several families who were prisoners on Ile Royale (Cape Breton Island) so they could join him in Halifax. Among the names mentioned in the letter were four brothers: Louis, Joseph, Jacques, and Jean (Baptiste) Pettipas and their half-brother Abraham Levandier. All were originally from Port Toulouse on Cape Breton Island. After making their way to Halifax, they settled at Chezzetcook.

By the end of the 1760s, there were at least a dozen families in the area and at least half were former prisoners released from Halifax, Fort Edward, and Fort Beauséjour. Most of the families remained in the area, but a few left for other destinations. The families that arrived in the 1760s formed the nucleus of Chezzetcook's present-day population. Five communities eventually developed around the six-mile Chezzetcook Inlet: Grand Desert, West Chezzetcook, Head of Chezzetcook, East Chezzetcook, and Lower East Chezzetcook.

Diana Murphy of West Chezzetcook shows off two sets of twin goats she helped bring into the world at the Cole Harbour Heritage Farm Museum in 1987. Ms. Murphy worked at the farm as a summer student in 1986 and 1987. A Chezzetcook native, she is descended from Acadians who returned to settle the area following the 1755 expulsion. (Joe Robicheau 1987)

3

THE GOVERNOR'S TOWN

Charles Lawrence was born in England about 1709, but little is known of his early life before his arrival in Halifax. When he was 18 years old, he was commissioned in the 11th Regiment of Foot and stationed in the West Indies from 1733 to 1737. When he returned to England he was posted to the War Office and promoted to lieutenant in 1741. He made captain the following year. He saw action and was wounded at Fountenoy in Belgium in 1745, during the War of Austrian Succession. Lawrence was promoted to major in the 45th Regiment and joined it at Louisbourg in 1749. He became a company commander in the 40th Regiment in December 1749 and was sent to the new settlement at Halifax. The popular officer was known to be both energetic and direct in his methods.

Governor Peregrine Hopson, who replaced Cornwallis at Halifax, gave Lawrence the responsibility of relocating the new arrivals from Europe to a new settlement named Lunenburg on the South Shore. Lawrence returned to Halifax in August 1753 as the acting president of the council and administrator of the province for Governor Hopson, who was returning to England. Lt.-Col. Charles Lawrence, military commander of Nova Scotia and soon to be governor, decided in 1754 to establish a new settlement on the eastern flank of Halifax. He offered 20 prospective applicants 1,000 acres each on the condition they provide 20 settlers for the new community, which would be located approximately 9 miles east of Dartmouth. He gave his own name to the new colony – Lawrence Town, spelled today as one word.

In spite of his popularity as a soldier, Governor Lawrence was responsible for writing one of the cruelest and darkest chapters in Nova Scotia's history – the expulsion of the Acadians.

In order to connect Dartmouth and Halifax to his new settlement, it was essential to build a road through the wilderness. Soldiers

EARLY SETTLEMENTS

On the Lawrencetown Road at the junction with the West Lawrencetown Road circa 1915 is the Temperance Hall (foreground) where evening church services sometimes were held. (Lynda Conrad collection)

stationed on the Dartmouth side of the harbour were conscripted as road-builders and given the task of constructing a road to the new community. The road began at the Dartmouth Cove, continued up present-day Portland Street through Woodlawn towards Preston, then down towards Cole Harbour and the new settlement of Lawrencetown. It was a labour-intensive task, chopping down trees, clearing the land by uprooting stumps and prying up boulders. The road was little more than a track barely passable for horse-drawn wagons carrying the settlers and their belongings to their new home. In time the road was improved and widened.

The most influential of the original landowners of Lawrencetown was Richard Bulkeley, who came to Halifax with Cornwallis and stayed on as the aide-de-camp and director of public works for Governor Hopson. When Hopson returned to Britain, Lawrence retained Bulkeley's services and the two men became close friends. Another prominent man to receive a Lawrencetown land grant was Benjamin Green Jr., whose father was a member of the Governor's Council and the provincial treasurer. William Morris, the son of Charles Morris, the chief surveyor for the province who surveyed the land for the new community, also received a grant of land.

The Rev. John Breynton, rector of St. Paul's Church in Halifax and later a Supreme Court judge, received a land grant in the new settlement, as did ship captains John Barker, William Drake Spike, and John Taggart. Other citizens to receive Lawrencetown land grants were John Collier, Justice of the Peace; Robert Grant, surgeon; William Nisbett, one of the governor's clerks and later Attorney General; and Robert Ewer, a lieutenant in the army. John Hussey, George Saul, Arthur Price, William Neagee, David Lloyd, Robert T. Walker, Richard Wenman, Matthew Barnard, and John Beseter were the other recipients.

The 20 grants covered an area that began by the Chezzetcook River and stretched westward to Smelt Brook at the head of Cole Harbour. The settlers travelled to the new community in May 1754 accompanied by 200 regular troops and a detachment of rangers. In spite of a blockhouse and picketed perimeter for protection, the Native people and Acadians constantly harassed the new settlement. In one attack, four settlers and three soldiers were killed and scalped. Joseph Broussard, an Acadian better known by his pseudonym "Beausoleil," led the raiders. An indomitable foe of the British, he was later captured and deported to Louisiana in 1763, where he became a Cajun folk hero. The town of Broussard, Louisiana, was named in his honour.

After the beginning of the Acadian expulsion 1755, English settlers began to return to the area to farm the land in order to provide a badly needed food supply for Halifax. When the troops were withdrawn in 1757, the Native people's harassment intensified to the point that the settlers also packed up and left, turning Lawrencetown into a ghost town.

In 1762, the original Lawrencetown grants were resurveyed and subdivided into more lots by Charles Morris. The minimum lot size was 300 acres, with some as large as 1,200 acres. The original landowners carried out a draw in May 1762 to allocate 19 of the lots, the first division of the Township of Lawrencetown. Two lots numbered five and six were not included in the draw, as Benjamin Green Jr. had already made improvements on them for himself and his brother Francis Green.

Fourteen of the lots went to some of the original grant-holders: Richard Bulkeley, John Barker, and William Drake Spike each received two lots, suggesting they may have bought the rights from three of the original proprietors. Benjamin Green Jr. bought the rights of another proprietor to provide his brother with a lot. Among the new names in the draw were Charles Lyons and Charles Morris Jr. The latter probably obtained the rights from his brother William.

On December 1, 1779, the landowners of the Township of Lawrencetown met and agreed to a new division of the township involving the back lots, which was laid before them by the surveyor general. Again 19 lots were selected, with 12 lots going to the 1754 landowners. New names appearing on the lots were Richard Fritton, John Story, John Willis, and the estates of Joseph Gerrish and Joseph Collins. Benjamin Green Jr. acquired another lot for his brother Francis Green, who was living in New York at the time. Benjamin Green Jr. subsequently acquired Joseph Collins's share in 1783.

The maps that outline the 1754, 1762, and 1779 grants contain basically the same notes describing locations reserved for fishing, shipbuilding, and other public uses. Since Charles Morris prepared the newer maps and laid out the lots, he was probably responsible for the unsigned 1754 map. The older map showed the boundaries of the grant, but the interior features such as lakes and rivers were not shown.

The map showing the locations of the first and second land divisions is not dated and appears to have been revised several times. Lot number three in the second division is shown as "now John Gammon." John Gammon purchased the lot in 1819 from his brother George, who in turn had bought it from John Collier in 1817. The undated map also shows some lots in the first division near Grand Desert originally granted to McGee, Green, and Bulkeley and coming into the possession of Acadian families such as Bonnevie, Roma, Bellefontaine, and others.

The undated map showing lot ownership in the "Township of Lawrence Town" changes the wording of Cold Harbour on the earlier map in 1754 to Cole Harbour. But the date when the change was made is not known. Lake Porter, now Porters Lake, was named for United Empire Loyalist William Porter, who arrived in the area in 1783.

After the Lawrencetown land grants had been assigned and divided, and a settlement established, the governor decided to make another allocation of land grants, this time on the western side of Cole Harbour.

4

COLE HARBOUR LAND GRANTS

With a small settlement underway in the Lawrencetown-Chezzetcook area, the authorities in Halifax turned their attention to developing the vacant land on the western side of Cole Harbour. Unlike the Lawrencetown land grants, which gave 20 people 1,000 acres each, the first Cole Harbour land grant comprised 3,000 acres and was divided among 6 people.

Six influential Halifax men – George Frederick Ott, Thomas Newell, Benjamin Green Jr., Benjamin Bridge, James Wakefield, and Benjamin Wakefield – were given the grants of 500 acres each on October 5, 1765, on the condition "that they were to occupy and cultivate the land over a period of time or find others to do the work for them." [3] One family with proper stock and materials for the improvement of the land was to be settled on every 500 acres on the granted land before October 31, 1767, or the grant reverted to the Crown. The grantees were also charged with the responsibility of building a road "of four rods width" to connect the new settlement with Dartmouth. Eleven years earlier a road had been built from Dartmouth to the settlement at Lawrencetown.

The land grant encompassed the western half of Russell Lake, all of Bell and Settle Lakes, and a portion of Bissett Lake down to the shore of Cole Harbour. Unlike the settlement on the eastern side of the inlet, which was named for the governor, no formal name was given immediately to the community on the western shore. Over time the community became known as Cole Harbour.

Among the original six to receive the land grants, George Frederick Ott, a butcher from Württemburg, Germany, had come to Halifax in 1751 on the *Gale* when he was 24 years old. According to St. Paul's Church records, he married Margaret Mary Mason, widow of Charles Mason, on April 24, 1764. The following year he received his Cole Harbour land grant on the south side of Long Hill, fronting on Cole Harbour itself.

Benjamin Green Jr., another land grant recipient, came to Halifax with his parents in 1749. His father, Benjamin Sr., was the provincial treasurer. The younger Green succeeded his father in the role in 1761 and held the post for the next 30 years. He was also a Justice of the Peace for Halifax and a major in the Volunteers. In 1773, he married Susannah Wenman, the daughter of Richard Wenman, another early landowner. She acquired some of her father's property. Benjamin Green Jr. died on December 5, 1793, at the age of 53 without a will, creating considerable hardship for his widow.

Born in England in 1738, Benjamin Bridge was listed on some legal documents as a land surveyor and coppersmith. He was a commissioner of peace, a magistrate for Halifax, and a member of the House of Assembly. Bridge married Elizabeth Ingols in 1763 or 1764 and after her death married Mary Phippens. He died on February 10, 1815. Some of his children were baptized in St. John's Anglican Church in Lunenburg, while others were baptized at St. Matthew's Presbyterian Church in Halifax.

Little is known of James and Benjamin Wakefield. They were probably the sons of Joseph Wakefield, who came to Halifax in 1749 as a lieutenant in the British army and was appointed as one of the surveyors of cordwood in 1754. James Wakefield, who was listed in public records as a painter and glazier, married Ann Giffin on May 12, 1760. After her death, he married Ann Fitzgerald on October 27, 1773. He sold off a portion of his land in 1783 to Nathaniel Russell, Josiah Richardson, and Ephraim Wyman of Halifax. Benjamin Wakefield also sold part of his land grant to Nathaniel Russell.

Thomas Newell, the sixth man to be granted land in Cole Harbour, is virtually unknown. His grant bordered the harbour next to George Frederick Ott's.

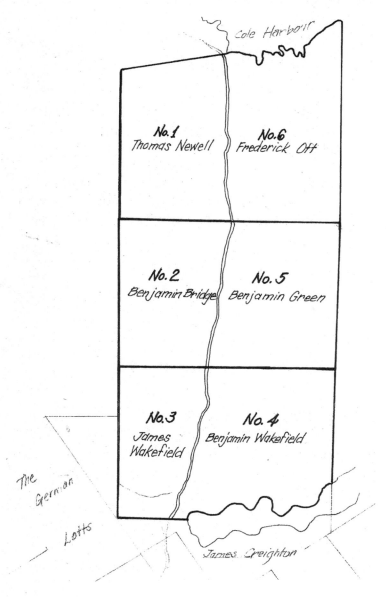

Map 2 – This old map has been retraced to highlight the six original 1765 land grants. The Cole Harbour Road runs up the middle and veers sharply to the left at the harbour shore at top. Russell Lake, near present-day Portland Estates in Dartmouth, forms part of Benjamin Wakefield's boundary. (RIMS, retraced by Dawn Reiss)

For the most part, the early grantees did little to settle or cultivate their lands under the condition of the grant. The road that they promised as a condition of the grant was little more than a trail cut through the forest, and for years after most of the settlers in Cole Harbour continued to use the Lawrencetown/Preston road to travel to Dartmouth and Halifax.

The Cole Harbour area was not properly developed until years later, when settlers from continental Europe moved to the area looking for a new start in life and settlers from the Thirteen Colonies to the south came in search of relief from political upheaval and war.

II

THE ARRIVING PEOPLE ❦ 1700S

5

EUROPEAN PROTESTANTS

6

UNITED EMPIRE LOYALISTS

7

BLACK LOYALISTS AND MAROONS

5

EUROPEAN PROTESTANTS

The 2,500 English settlers who arrived at Halifax with Edward Cornwallis in June 1749 were anything but successful. They were not the industrious, resourceful people Cornwallis had hoped for. In fact they were the opposite. To the aloof and aristocratic Governor Cornwallis they were a collection of adventurers, former soldiers, and misfits, who quickly proved to be utterly unfit for the rigours of pioneer life in the new British colony. In one report to his superiors in England, Cornwallis characterized the group: "[Y]ou know what an English rabble is, you know that they are generally tumultuous, refractory, full of discontent and murmerings, [sic] capricious in demanding favours, and not long satisfied with present concessions." [4]

Among his new settlers, he did find a few honest, dependable, hardworking Swiss colonists who possessed the favourable skills and qualities apparently lacking in his English settlers. In a letter to the Board of Trade and Plantations, dated July 24, 1749, Cornwallis wrote:

> There are among the settlers a few Swiss who are regular, honest, industrious men, easily governed, and work heartily. I hope your Lordships will think of a method of encouraging numbers of them to come over. A proposal was sent to me when at Spithead, which perhaps might answer the purpose to make known throughout Germany that all husbandmen, tradesmen, or soldiers being Protestant should have the same rights and privileges as were promised in His Majesty's Proclamation to natural subjects.

Great Britain was enjoying fairly prosperous conditions, and her North American colonies were having difficulty attracting British immigrants. Several colonies offered subsidies and other inducements to attract new settlers. European Protestants appeared to be the logical choice to counter France's growing strength at Louisbourg. Protestants were good farmers distinguished by their indomitable industry and independence together with a relatively high degree of intelligence. It was from Protestant France, Germany, and Switzerland that England recruited settlers for her new colonies in Nova Scotia.

The British considered the Germans their cultural cousins since King George II, who was also the German Elector of Hanover, ruled Britain at that time. Germany consisted of a number of feudal states, which had existed for hundreds of years. By the middle of the eighteenth century, Germany like most countries in Western Europe had an extremely complicated and inefficient system of government controlled by feudal princes and wealthy landowners whose land was worked by tenant farmers. The landowners issued grants to pay for expenditures such as war, of which there were several throughout the seventeenth and eighteenth centuries. Landowners were extremely powerful in eighteenth-century Europe, for if landowners withheld their approval for expenditures, the princes were unable to act.

By the middle of the eighteenth century, the personal bond between serfs and landowners was supplanted by a more restrictive legal contract from which a peasant could free himself if he had the desire as well as the financial means. European Protestants wanted safety and freedom after many years of suffering with war, famine, overpopulation, religious and political intolerance and persecution. The idea of owning land was appealing and many risked everything. They sold their belongings and left familiar hardships in the Old World to embrace unfamiliar hardships in the New World. Romantic and exaggerated accounts of life in Nova Scotia wouldn't have enticed these tenant farmers to leave their homes in Europe and face a long and treacherous voyage across the Atlantic to unknown territory if they were happy in their respective countries. However, freedom from servitude and free land of their own were strong inducements to encourage them to emigrate.

The British Board of Trade and Plantations hired John Dick as an agent to recruit new settlers from Europe. The proclamation that circulated throughout parts of Europe was essentially the same as the one that recruited English settlers in 1749, except it didn't offer free passage to the Europeans. The proclamation also carried a deceptively attractive description of Nova Scotia.

Although the Europeans were required to pay their own passage, the British government gave those without the necessary financial resources an interest-free loan to cover their fare plus other incidental costs they might incur while waiting to board their ship in Rotterdam. The loan could be paid off at a daily rate working on public works projects, building roads and fortifications.

The new settlers were offered sufficient land for a farm, basic farming implements, and the material to build a house. During their first year in Nova Scotia, they were housed and fed by the government.

During the next three years, approximately 2,200 settlers arrived in Nova Scotia from continental Europe. They came from the Palatinate, Württemberg, and Baden-Durlach in Germany; from Montbéliard, a Protestant enclave in western France; and from Switzerland. Some of these early settlers eventually ended up in the Cole Harbour area.

The first ship *Anne* sailed from Rotterdam in the summer and arrived in Halifax on September 13, 1750, with 321 immigrants after a 12-week voyage, during which 17 passengers died. The following year agent John Dick sent out four more ships during the summer sailing season with 1,004 German immigrants. Eighty-seven died en route.

In 1752, John Dick's representatives visited the Montbéliard region of France, where the German, French, and Swiss borders meet near the city of Basel, Switzerland, to recruit more settlers. Montbéliard was governed by the German Duchy of Württemberg, but its inhabitants were predominantly French speaking. Two ships, *Betty* and *Speedwell*, left Rotterdam on May 16, 1752, with 450 Montbéliardians on board in 135 family groups. They arrived in Nova Scotia in August. At the end of the 1752 summer sailing season, Britain discontinued its German recruitment program.

When the 1752 settlers arrived in Halifax, they discovered that little had been done by the British to establish permanent settlements for the German colonists who had arrived in 1750 and 1751. The earlier settlers were still lodged in barracks at Halifax. The 1752 arrivals, after a period of quarantine on the ships, were housed in crude temporary barracks on Georges Island in the harbour. They complained about their housing, their food, and the fact that earlier settlers were able to pay down their loans at the rate of $30 a day, while they only received credit at the rate of $20 per day.

Governor Peregrine Hopson promptly moved the French-speaking Germans off Georges Island and into better accommodations on the mainland. The winter of 1752–53 was extremely harsh for the European settlers because of severe weather conditions and an epidemic that swept through the community, resulting in many deaths.

In the spring of 1753, British authorities decided to move the German immigrants to an abandoned French settlement about 50 miles down the coast south of Halifax. Before leaving the area, the French had cleared more than 300 acres, which were suitable for growing crops. They changed the name of the settlement to Lunenburg, after one of King George's ducal titles.

The initial plan for the new settlement was to provide each family with a small plot of land 40 by 60 feet on what was intended to be the town centre plus sufficient building material to construct a one-room shelter. Each family was also assigned a small garden plot to grow vegetables to supplement the government's food rations. By the following spring, 30 acres of uncleared land were given to each family where they could build a larger and more comfortable farmhouse.

The German settlers at Halifax were assembled on the parade ground next to St. Paul's Church on Monday, May 21. The plans for the settlement were announced and lots were drawn for the town plots. About 500 able-bodied men were organized into a militia unit.

On Tuesday, May 29, half the settlers loaded their belongings and boarded ships to travel to Lunenburg. In order to minimize the number of ships required, they would leave in two separate groups about a week apart. The settlers were to be accompanied by a small flotilla of warships and a detachment of rangers for protection against Native and French guerillas, who were hostile to the British settlement program. While the vessels were being loaded, the winds changed and the fleet was pinned in Halifax Harbour for almost a week. They finally left on June 7.

Colonel Lawrence, who was in charge of the expedition, kept the settlers on the ships when they arrived in Lunenburg Harbour while his troops secured the area and the work parties assembled the building material. The plan did not sit well with the settlers, who had been cooped up on the ships for more than two weeks and were anxious to go ashore to start building and planting. A temporary blockhouse was built and a palisade was placed around the settlement. Colonel Lawrence returned to Halifax in September 1753, leaving behind a small garrison of British troops and the militia under the command of Colonel Sutherland.

In spite of the hardships endured by the early settlers, the Lunenburg settlement flourished. One of the new Lunenburg settlers was 23-year-old Jacob Conrad, who was born in Oosthoven, Hesse, Germany, on August 3, 1727, where he was baptized in the Reformed Church. He sailed for Halifax from Rotterdam on the *Pearl* with 85 other families in 1751. After his arrival, he had spent two years in Dartmouth doing picket duty around the fences protecting the community against attacks from the Native people. As partial compensation for his work, he was given small land grants outside the picketed area at the present-day corner of Dartmouth's King and Portland Streets.

In 1753, Conrad moved to Lunenburg, where he married Anna Catherine Weigle (or Weagle), a woman about 12 years his senior. He drew two lots of land on the LaHave River, and the following year he was given additional livestock based on his more favourable marital status. When his wife Catherine died in 1774, Conrad took a second wife named Elizabeth. He bought and sold more than 100 town lots in Lunenburg from 1763 until 1781, when he sold off most of his land holdings and moved to Cole Harbour. At Cole Harbour he bought 500 acres from Thomas Newell for £75. He also bought land in the Lawrencetown Township.

Jacques (Jean) George Bizette (also Biset, according to different documents, but now Bissett in Cole Harbour area) was a Huguenot farmer from Montbéliard. In April 1752, Bizette and his family set out for Rotterdam carrying the few personal possessions they were allowed on-board. They sailed on the *Betty* on May 16, 1752, and ar-

Florence Bissett, wife of Stewart Bissett, finds her husband's ancestors on the Foreign Protestant Monument during a visit to Lunenburg, Nova Scotia, in 1990. (courtesy of Stewart Bissett family)

rived in Halifax on July 24 after a voyage of nine weeks and five days. Bissett was 43 years old when he settled in Lunenburg with his wife Anna Catherine, his 14-year-old son Jean George Jr., and daughters Eleanor and Claudine. Both daughters died during an epidemic that hit the community during the winter of 1752–53.

Col. Joseph F. W. DeBarres of the British army persuaded Jean George Bissett Jr. and 18 of his compatriots to leave Lunenburg in 1771 and move to the Tatamagouche area. Tatamagouche, originally an Acadian settlement, was an important location along the supply route to Louisbourg. Cattle and produce were transported overland to Tatamagouche from farms around the Minas Basin then loaded on ships and sent to Fortress Louisbourg. After the Acadians were expelled, the British built a blockhouse in the area in 1768, which they named Fort Francklin. Colonel DeBarres, a Huguenot whose family had also came from the Montbéliard area and settled in Lunenburg, acquired a plot of 2,000 acres stretching from Tatamagouche to what we know today as Brule Point. In order to entice this group to leave Lunenburg for his land in Colchester County, DeBarres offered lower rents than his competitors and supplied livestock and seed in exchange for a portion of the produce.

Ten years after settling in Tatamagouche, Bissett and his son-in-law George Harper, who was married to Catherine Bissett, were granted a licence by Governor Hughes to occupy 750 acres of land in the Cole Harbour area. In his application for the land, Bissett stated that he was married and had seven sons and five daughters. In addition to lumbering and farming, Bissett and his two sons built wooden boats (shallops) at Cole Harbour. By 1795, they were operating at least two ships in the coastal trade.

Map 3 – Part of 1808 watercolour map by Lt. G. Collyer showing the original Bissett farm on the western shore of Cole Harbour (NSARM)

The Otts, Conrads, and Bissetts were the first of the European Protestant families to move into the Cole Harbour area. (Ott, unlike most of the German immigrants, never settled in the Lunenburg area.) They built homes and began the back-breaking task of clearing and farming the land. The European Protestants were soon joined by another group of displaced people, known later as the United Empire Loyalists, who moved to Cole Harbour after a long and somewhat hazardous journey following a bitter war in the Thirteen Colonies to the south.

6

UNITED EMPIRE LOYALISTS

Storm clouds of dissent had been gathering throughout Britain's Thirteen Colonies along the Atlantic seaboard since the 1760s, when Britain imposed a stamp tax to help pay for its costly wars in Europe. The tax was repealed and replaced with taxes on tea, glass, and paper. The colonists' dissent broke into open rebellion on April 19, 1775, in the villages of Lexington and Concord, Massachusetts, near Boston, when gunshots were exchanged between the villagers and British soldiers. Within a year the war between the colonists and British army had spread like brush fire throughout New England and as far south as the Carolinas.

Many settlers throughout the colonies opposed taking up arms against Britain, believing that the problems between the government in London and the colonies could be resolved through peaceful negotiations. A break with Britain and independence would be a grave mistake, they argued. They also believed that the poorly trained and poorly equipped Continental Army under Gen. George Washington was no match for the best-trained and best-equipped fighting machine in all of Europe. They hoped the Continental Army would be defeated and the hotheads who preached rebellion would be arrested and tried for treason. Hopes for the Thirteen Colonies remaining under British rule were dashed at Yorktown in 1781, when Gen. Charles Cornwallis surrendered his army to General Washington, ending the war that became known as the American Revolution.

Once the Thirteen Colonies gained their independence from Britain, life for the United Empire Loyalists changed drastically. The victors did not simply "forgive and forget." Those who had stayed loyal to Britain paid a horrendous price. Their homes and plantations were looted and torched; their lands and businesses were confiscated. Some were thrown in prison, some were killed, and others were tarred and feathered. In the early years of the rebellion, many fled the New England colonies for Nova Scotia or England. Among them was John Wentworth, the last Royal Governor of New Hampshire, who later played a starring role on the stage of Nova Scotia history.

The United Empire Loyalists took whatever possessions or money that they could salvage and headed for New York City, the last British stronghold, to await deportation to Nova Scotia, Quebec, or Upper Canada. The Loyalists spanned all age groups as well as ethnic and religious backgrounds. There were wealthy merchants and plantation owners, doctors, lawyers, educators, clergymen, tradesmen, farmers, governors, government officials, soldiers, and bankers. Most were born in the Thirteen Colonies of English, Irish, or Scottish descent, but there was also a mix of German, French, Swiss, and some Dutch lineage. Included among the group was a large contingent of Black people who either escaped slavery to fight for the British or were set free by their owners.

The Loyalists generally came from the wealthy class, businessmen and plantation owners who were accustomed to a life of ease and comfort. They had lived in large well-furnished mansions and were attended by hired servants or slaves. Now with little or no money and few possessions, they were forced to flee as refugees to a new land to begin life over again.

The exodus north began in April 1783 with a fleet of 20 ships and 7,000 emigrants. The following month, 3,000 left, followed by 12,000 in August, and 18,000 in September. Among them, with their wives and families, were Lawrence Hartshorne, Nathaniel Russell, Ebenezer Allen, Michael Wallace, Jonathan Tremain, Joseph Giles, Francis

Green, Titus Smith, Thomas Boggs, and Theophilus Chamberlain. These men and their families would play leading roles in the development of lands in and around the Cole Harbour area. Many Loyalists were settled in the Shelburne area along the province's South Shore. Another group settled in Halifax, and others on the vacant lands east of Dartmouth.

Although most of the new arrivals survived as small farmers on the land grants they received, others struck it rich and regained their lost prosperity. One who amassed a new fortune was Lawrence Hartshorne. Hartshorne was born in 1755 to a prominent Quaker family in the Sandy Hook area of New Jersey. Twenty-two years later he moved to New York City and entered business. He advanced his business career but compromised his political neutrality three years later by marrying Elizabeth Ustick, whose father William Ustick violated the colonial boycott of British manufacturers. With family and business links to the United Empire Loyalists and the British military establishment forged during the war, Hartshorne had little choice but to join the Loyalist exodus for Nova Scotia in 1783.

Shortly after his arrival, he opened a hardware business in partnership with Thomas Boggs, another Loyalist from New Jersey. During the 1780s, Hartshorne became active in the cause of agricultural improvement both as treasurer of the pioneering agricultural society and as an owner of a model farm, which he established in the Cole Harbour area. At the urging of the province's current governor, John Wentworth, he formed a new partnership in 1791 with Loyalist Jonathan Tremain, and together they established a prosperous gristmill in the Dartmouth Cove. The mill required large amounts of wheat and grain, and Hartshorne's model farm in Cole Harbour was an ideal place for producing wheat and other crops. In addition to his business affairs, Hartshorne entered the political arena first as an elected member of the legislature and later as an appointed member of the Governor's Council.

When his first wife died, he married Abigail Tremain, the daughter of his business partner, in September 1802, and moved from Halifax to a three-storey mansion in Dartmouth known as Poplar Hill. Hartshorne had three sons and six daughters from both marriages.

Although he remained a Quaker all his life, his children were christened in the Church of England.

Ebenezer Allen, whose community burial ground gave its name to the Woodlawn area, established a farm and a tannery in that area. Several other Loyalists also settled on farms in the Woodlawn area.

Nathaniel Russell immigrated to Nova Scotia from Boston and began farming in the Cole Harbour area near present-day Russell Lake.

Joseph Giles (or Gyles), whose family name would be associated with the Cole Harbour area for the next two centuries, arrived in Nova Scotia in September 1783 with Theophilus Chamberlain. Although Giles received a land grant in the Preston area, he settled in Cole Harbour the following year. Two years later he married Anna Catherine Conrad, the eldest daughter of Jacob Conrad, one of the German settlers.

Chamberlain, another prominent Loyalist who prospered from his move to Nova Scotia, played a leading role in the development of the Preston area and in the settling of the Maroons.

7

BLACK LOYALISTS AND MAROONS

The end of the War of American Independence, also called the American Revolution, had a pivotal effect on another group of people living in the Thirteen Colonies, the Black Loyalists, who had been slaves living and working on plantations throughout the southern states. Their journey to Nova Scotia was just one milestone in a long and turbulent history that had begun in Africa, where they had lived as a free people before being captured by white Europeans and brought to the New World to be sold into slavery.

Black Africans were considered better suited for agricultural work in the southern states, the West Indies, and South America than the white Europeans and local Native people due to their high tolerance for diseases such as malaria and yellow fever. Slave trading was an extremely lucrative business during the seventeenth century, and it enhanced the colonial economies of Spain, Portugal, and Great Britain at the expense of the African people.

Ghana was the centre of the slave trade, where 36 of the 42 slave fortresses were located. Other centres for slave trading were Ivory Coast, Gold Coast, and the southeast coast (from the Cape of Good Hope to the Cape of Delgado). Men, women, and children were taken from their villages, marched in chains to these centres, where they were crowded onto ships and transported to the New World. Many died en route. Their bodies were merely tossed over the side and swallowed up by the ocean. At the end of their sea journey, they were bought and sold like farm animals and forced to work on plantations for only basic shelter and barely enough food to stay alive. Family units were often sold off in different directions at the whim of their owners.

During the American Revolution, John Murray, Lord Dunsmore, the Royal Governor of Virginia, issued a decree in November 1775 to indentured servants and Black slaves living in Virginia, Maryland, and the Carolinas, offering them their freedom in exchange for service in the British army fighting against the rebels. Thousands of slaves escaped the plantations and flocked to the British banner and the promise of freedom.

When the war ended with Britain's defeat, the Black Loyalists who had participated in battle had two options: return to slavery or journey north to a new and uncertain future. They elected to move north. In all, 3,000 Blacks boarded ships for exile in Nova Scotia. Some went to the Shelburne area on the South Shore and formed the Birchtown community. Some went to the Digby-Annapolis area. Others went to Halifax-Dartmouth, where they were settled on land in the Preston area a few miles east of Dartmouth.

The man charged with the task of surveying and laying out this new township was another United Empire Loyalist Theophilus Chamberlain, a man of many talents who made the best of every opportunity that came his way. He was an ordained clergyman, a soldier, a Justice of the Peace, a merchant, a teacher, and a land surveyor. Chamberlain was born in Northfield, Massachusetts, in 1737, the fourth son of blacksmith Ephraim and his wife Anne. After his father was killed in the

New England expedition against Fortress Louisbourg in 1745, his uncle adopted him and provided his early education. During the Seven Years War with France, Chamberlain joined Burke's Rangers and fought with them at Fort William Henry in upstate New York. When General Montcalm captured the fort, Chamberlain was taken prisoner and marched off to Quebec, where he was later exchanged for French prisoners. He eventually made his way to Halifax in 1757 and worked at an inn for a year to earn enough money to book passage back to Boston. From there he joined his uncle and aunt at South Hadley, Massachusetts. A year later, he entered Yale College to study theology.

Theophilus Chamberlain was ordained as a Congregationalist minister in 1765 and went to the settlements of the Six Nations in upstate New York. Two years later he was back in Boston teaching in a private Latin school. At this time he became interested in the teachings of Robert Sandeman, a Scottish churchman who stressed personal salvation, that church establishments were unscriptural, and each congregation should be self-governed. Chamberlain was re-ordained as a Sandemanian bishop in 1768. In the same year he married Editha White and moved to Danbury, Connecticut, where he opened a clothing store.

Theophilus Chamberlain, a United Empire Loyalist who came to the area following the American Revolution, was given the task of laying out the township of Preston for other Loyalists arriving in the area. (NSARM)

When Chamberlain and his congregation were persecuted in Danbury for their beliefs, they moved to New Haven, Connecticut, where he returned to teaching. Chamberlain and his followers refused to contribute to the American war fund and were imprisoned. They were eventually released and allowed to go to the British-controlled territory in New York.

Chamberlain's infant son died in 1776. Just three years later his wife died. By 1782, Chamberlain was again teaching in a private school in New York and had married Lamira Humpraville. When the British occupation of New York ended, he accepted a commission in the militia and was given the responsibility for the transfer of refugees to Halifax.

Immediately after his arrival in Halifax, he was commissioned as a Justice of the Peace, named deputy surveyor for the province, and appointed to lay out the new township of Preston and act as the agent for the distribution of the land within the township. All Loyalists, black or white, were promised grants of free land in the province. Chamberlain himself managed to obtain a 1,000-acre grant in the area.

He named the new settlement Preston, but the exact reason for his selection is uncertain. There is one suggestion that it was named for Preston, England, a seaport town on the west coast. The other suggestion is that it was named in honour of Robert Preston, a British officer in charge of the troops during the Boston Massacre in 1770. Preston was tried for murder and later acquitted.

When the land grants in Preston were issued a year after their arrival from New York, the white Loyalists received grants averaging 100 to 200 acres while the 29 Black Loyalist families each received only 50 acres of land. Life for the black settlers proved extremely difficult. Their land was rocky and unsuitable for farming. The harsh Nova Scotia climate was a drastic change from the warmer weather of the southern states. Their leaders loudly expressed the group's disenchantment with their life, not only in Preston but also throughout Nova Scotia. The most vocal of these was Thomas Peters. When his efforts to obtain land for himself and his people in Nova Scotia and New Brunswick went unanswered, he travelled to London, England.

Peters arrived in London in 1790, carrying a petition signed by more than 200 black families, which described a litany of broken promises and shattered dreams. Peters and his petition came to the attention of Granville Sharp, a prominent member of the British movement for the abolition of slavery. One aspect of the abolitionists' efforts was the establishment of the West African colony of Sierra Leone to be settled by free Blacks. To the African-born Peters this suggestion was an excellent alternative to living in Nova Scotia. He returned to the province and convinced many Black Loyalists to make yet another sea voyage, this time to Africa. Resettlement in Africa met with stiff opposition from some white Nova Scotians, who objected strongly to the loss of cheap and easily exploited labour.

Michael Wallace was given the task of arranging the transportation for the Black Loyalists to Sierra Leone. Wallace, a Loyalist from the southern states, also played a leading role in the province's history as a businessman, politician, and one of the key figures in the early construction of the Shubenacadie Canal.

On January 15, 1792, 1,196 Black Loyalists in 15 ships set sail from Halifax Harbour for a new home in Africa. Of those who remained behind, many left Preston for larger centres and better employment opportunities. For a time, the Preston settlement was virtually deserted.

In 1796, the land in Preston was reoccupied, this time by a group of Black people from the British West Indian colony of Jamaica. These new settlers, who came to the area involuntarily, were called Maroons.

The original Maroons were taken as slaves from West Africa to the islands of the West Indies by the Spaniards, who called them *Cimarrones,* meaning "wild" or "untamed." From the Spanish name came the French word *Marrons* and eventually the English name, "Maroons." Over the years some of the slaves escaped and formed roving bands that attacked their former masters' mule trains carrying gold, silver, and other commodities. The Maroon attacks began in 1520 in the colonies of Hispaniola, New Spain, and Panama. In spite of several attempts at peace and even a treaty, the Spaniards never really succeeded in stopping the raids.

When the British took Jamaica from the Spanish in 1655, the Maroons continued the guerrilla war against the new owners, attacking their plantations and settlements and refusing all offers of clemency and freedom in exchange for a cessation of hostilities. In the 1720s, the Maroons' raids forced several British plantation owners to abandon their sugar estates.

A truce, signed in 1738, finally brought the Maroons out of hiding to live as a free community. The largest Maroon community was in Trelawney. One condition of the truce was a requirement to return runaway slaves to their so-called owners if they made their way to a Maroon community. The Trelawney group refused to accept this condition.

War broke out again between the Maroons and the colonial government in 1795. Fierce fighting continued for about six months before the Maroons were finally forced to surrender. To rid themselves of the problem finally, the British authorities decided to send some of the Maroons out of Jamaica and far from the sea to remove any temptation to escape and return home. Upper Canada was selected. London approved the scheme. The Jamaica government promised financial support until the Maroons were settled in their new home.

On June 26, 1796, three ships – the *Dover*, *Mary*, and *Anne* – sailed from Port Royal Harbour, Jamaica, with 543 men, women, and children, and two commissioners, Col. William Quarrell and Alexander Ochterloney. They arrived in Halifax a month later.

Governor John Wentworth was in favour of keeping them in Nova Scotia, and military commander Prince Edward saw them as a labour pool to help build the new fortifications at Citadel Hill. Britain was at war with France and desperately needed to improve the fortifications at Halifax in case of a French invasion. In the end, both the governor and the military commander were served by the Maroons. Governor Wentworth also employed them to work on his own farm and estate in Preston and on his new residence on Barrington Street in Halifax.

Wentworth believed he could "civilize" the Maroons through Christianity, a notion quite common in the eighteenth century, when officials used Christianity to make non-Europeans conform. He appointed the Rev. Benjamin Gray to minister to their spiritual needs as well as their secular education. Attendance at church was only one part of a larger scheme to convert the Maroons. Ending their practice of polygamy was another goal since it went against the practice of both the church and society in the province. The governor's attempts failed.

The Maroons, like the Black Loyalists before them, did not adapt easily to life in Nova Scotia. Climate was one source of discontent. The winters of 1797 and 1798 were extremely harsh. The government's efforts to break up their community and alter their culture were also offensive. The farming they were expected to undertake was servile to them. They were accustomed to the untamed freedom of the Jamaican hills and growing indigenous crops. One of them reportedly told

It is believed that the Maroons constructed this dyke on Lawlors Point in Cole Harbour during their occupation of the area from 1796 to 1800. (RE 1977)

Governor Wentworth that "yams, bananas, and cocoa would not grow on his farm and there were no wild hogs to hunt." [5]

On April 13, 1797, a detachment of 50 soldiers from the Nova Scotia Regiment was sent to Preston, where the Maroons were threatening to destroy their property because provisions were withheld when they refused to work the land.

The Maroons asked the British government to be resettled in Sierra Leone. London agreed due to the increasing costs of providing for them in Nova Scotia. On August 7, 1800, most of the Maroons boarded the ship *Asia* and sailed out of Halifax for their new homeland in Africa. They arrived in Freetown, the capital of Sierra Leone, on October 1. Two years later, word was received in Nova Scotia that the Maroons had settled peacefully into their new home, where they were respected for their courage, fighting prowess, and independence. The small number of Maroons who remained in Nova Scotia continued to live and farm in the Preston area.

There are many negative accounts of the Maroons' years in Nova Scotia and much has been made of their unwillingness to work, but those years were not unproductive and their legacy remains. In Halifax, it includes Government House and Maroon Bastion on Citadel Hill. In Cole Harbour it is a stone dyke. Built to protect a few acres of salt hay meadow on Lawlors Point, this first dyke in Cole Harbour was constructed by the Maroons in the eighteenth century. In addition to their own modest homes, they built several structures in Cole Harbour and Westphal on the 6000 acres purchased for their resettlement. None remain. The Lawlor House, at the bottom of Long Hill remained until 1979, when it was demolished. Still structurally sound, it had been constructed of vertical timbers standing side by side. (See photo page 125.)

In the last half of the eighteenth century, new farming communities were established east of Dartmouth at Preston, Lawrencetown, and Cole Harbour. In the next century these communities would expand with the arrival of new settlers who established more farms as well as industries, churches, and schools.

III
BUILDING COMMUNITY ❦ EARLY 1800S

8
EARLY FARM FAMILIES

9
THE FIRST SCHOOL

10
METHODIST CHAPELS

11
THE CENSUS OF 1827

12
DIARY OF A FARMER'S DAUGHTER

13
SUPPORT INDUSTRIES

8

EARLY FARM FAMILIES

At the beginning of the nineteenth century, Great Britain and most of continental Europe were at war with France. War between France and Britain was nothing new; the two countries had been fighting throughout most of the previous century. These wars often involved their North American colonies. France was just beginning to extricate herself from a bloody revolution in which most of the aristocracy, including the king and queen, had been executed. The newly minted French republic – led by Gen. (soon to be Emperor) Napoleon Bonaparte – was rampaging across Europe, leaving death and destruction in its wake.

As the first decade of the 1800s ended, Britain found herself embroiled in war with the United States. The War of 1812 was mostly fought around the Great Lakes and the Niagara Peninsula, with some incursions by the British onto American soil, and lasted until 1814. However, Great Britain would not know peace until, a year later, Napoleon was finally defeated and captured at Waterloo and exiled to St. Helena.

Both wars brought an influx of troops and naval ships to Halifax to protect the harbour against possible invasion and keep the sea lanes open against French and American warships and privateers. The increased military muscle required additional food and supplies to aid the local war effort. The farms of Cole Harbour, Woodlawn, Preston, and Lawrencetown became the food baskets. The surrounding forests supplied the timber to build and repair ships.

The early years of the nineteenth century also brought dramatic changes to the Cole Harbour landscape. The original six land grants were subdivided into smaller parcels to accommodate the increasing number of settlers moving to the area. While most of the original European and Loyalist settlers were slowly dying out, their farms and land passed to their children, who continued the farming tradition and intermarried with families living within the area.

The second generation continued the back-breaking work of their parents, clearing the land, planting crops, raising livestock, building barns and homes. Of course, some left the rugged and isolated farm life of Cole Harbour and moved to Halifax and Dartmouth for better employment prospects and a more comfortable lifestyle. As they moved out, others moved in, buying land and establishing their own farms in the Cole Harbour settlement.

Frederick Ott, one of the original six to receive a land grant in the area, had become very prosperous by the time of his death 1783. In addition to his Cole Harbour land, he owned the market wharf in Halifax and other commercial properties, yielding annual rents of £750. He left the bulk of his estate to his stepdaughter Amelia (Mason) Beamish, her husband Thomas, and their seven children. Amelia had been 10 years old when her widowed mother had married Ott. Amelia a married Thomas Beamish in 1770, and they lived in Cole Harbour. Bissett Lake, originally known as Beamish Lake, appears by that name on the property deed of the Bissetts when they arrived in 1781.

When Thomas Beamish was appointed port warden for Halifax in 1782, the family moved from Cole Harbour to the city. Each of the Beamish children had the surname Ott as one of their names. The children named in Frederick Ott's will were Margaret Ott, Frederick Ott, Charles Ott, Elisabeth Ott, and Sarah Catherine Ott.

Thomas Ott Beamish (1781–1860) married Louisa Collins (1796–1869), the daughter of Stephen and Phebe Collins. (See Louisa's Diary, chapter 12.) Elisabeth Ott Beamish married Andrew Murdoch and had one son, Beamish Murdoch, who became a lawyer and a Member of the Legislative Assembly for Halifax. He is best remembered as the author of the three-volume *History of Nova Scotia or Acadie*, which was published between 1865 and 1867.

Margaret Ott Beamish married Thomas Akins. They had one child, Thomas Beamish Akins, who became a lawyer and in 1857 was appointed the first commissioner of Public Records, the forerunner of the Nova Scotia Archives and Records Management. He was a founding member of the Nova Scotia Historical Society in 1878. He published *History of Halifax* in 1895.

Thomas Beamish died about 1860, and his children later sold 500 acres of their Cole Harbour land for £300. Amelia Beamish died in 1844 at the age of 84 and was buried from St. George's Anglican Church, Halifax.

Jacob Conrad, another early settler, gave his son-in-law Joseph Glascow a piece of land in Cole Harbour. No money exchanged hands in this transaction; the land was an outright gift. Ebenezer Shelton and Theophilus Chamberlain witnessed the deed. The following year, Conrad sold 100 acres of his Cole Harbour land for £25 to Joseph Giles, the husband of his oldest daughter Anna Catherine by his first wife.

The fact that he made a gift of his land to one son-in-law and a year later accepted payment for land from a second son-in-law appears strange on the surface, but it was an attempt by Conrad to provide for individual family members fairly and equitably. In the tradition brought from Germany, the oldest daughter received more financial support upon marriage than her younger siblings. The custom was to build her a home. If the oldest daughter's wedding gift were a home, then Conrad could provide his second daughter with a gift of land.

In 1800, Jacob Conrad, Lawrence Hartshorne, Lieutenant-Governor Sir John Wentworth, and Charles Morris jointly purchased the land that previously had been granted to Frederick Ott. Conrad also bought a 200-acre oceanfront estate in 1808 from Benjamin Green's widow for £170. The property abutted the Ott land that he had bought with three others eight years earlier. Conrad sold the estate mostly in half parts to his son Thomas in 1812 for £20. Conrad was 86 years old when he died at Lawrencetown on October 7, 1813. His obituary stated that he was the father of 13 children, 42 grandchildren, and 14 great-grandchildren.

Loyalist Joseph Giles came to the Cole Harbour area following the American Revolution. It's uncertain whether he came to the province with Theophilus Chamberlain on the *Nancy* or as a disbanded British soldier who met Chamberlain after he arrived in Halifax. It is known that he was a member of the Cole Harbour community from 1786 to 1836 and that he married Jacob Conrad's eldest daughter. Giles,

The Giles House, photographed on its original site, is thought to have been a wedding gift from Jacob Conrad, one of the early settlers in the Cole Harbour area, to his eldest daughter, Anna Catherine, when she married Joseph Giles, a United Empire Loyalist who came to the area in 1783. Conrad may have brought the house to Cole Harbour by ship from Lunenburg. The house has since been moved from its original Cole Harbour site and is now part of the Heritage Farm Museum. (RE 1974)

either as a civilian Loyalist or a disbanded British soldier, received a 200-acre land grant in the Preston area as well.

On his death in 1836, Giles left his wife 50 acres in Cole Harbour and all his possessions. His son Samuel received 100 acres of his Preston lands plus the 50 acres on the death of his mother. His other son Joseph Jr. also received 50 acres in Cole Harbour. His daughter Louisa Bissett received the other 100 acres of the Preston land grant. There were two other daughters, Catherine, who married William Osborne, and Mary Ann, who married John Hawkins. Each of these daughters received one shilling, although the will indicates that they had been given some of their inheritance previously.

Nathaniel Russell, another Loyalist who settled in the Cole Harbour area near present-day Russell Lake, was a member of the Sandemanian sect. Russell and his wife Mary shared the horrific experience of witnessing the murder of their daughter Mary in their own home on the evening of September 27, 1798.

Earlier in the day, young Mary had accompanied a group of other young people to Dartmouth to see the damage caused by a hurricane-force storm two days earlier. Thomas Bambridge, an ardent admirer of Mary, had heard that "the love of his life" was seen in the company of another young man, William Bell, who worked at the lower ferry. Bell had escorted Miss Russell to her home.

Nathaniel Russell was entertaining some friends, Moses Pitcher and John Phelon, in the kitchen, when the door to their home burst open and in stormed Bambridge, demanding to speak to Mary outside and alone. When she refused his request he came towards her, pulled a knife from under his coat and stabbed the young woman to death. Before the young man could turn the knife on himself, Moses Pitcher leaped at him, wrestled him to the floor and took away his weapon.

A coroner's inquest was held the following day at the Russell home by coroner Daniel Wood. Serving on that jury were Moses Pitcher, Alex Farquharson, Ebenezer Allen, Alexander Creighton, Henry Wisdom, William Fishon, John Allen, Mark Jones, Henry Runt, Donald McDonald, John Collins, and John Phelon.

Bambridge was tried almost immediately for his crime in the Supreme Court, where another jury returned a guilty verdict. Bambridge was hanged on October 16 at the Common behind the Citadel in Halifax, near present-day Sackville Street and Bell Road.

Mary Russell was buried in the Woodlawn Cemetery, but the exact location of her grave is unknown. Her father, Nathaniel Russell, died in 1831 at the age of 85 and was also buried in the Woodlawn Cemetery.

Nathaniel Jr. lived in Cole Harbour for a time and became an active member of the Methodist denomination. His first wife Mary died about 1804. Four years later he married Almy (Green) Elliot, the widow of Jonathan Elliot and the daughter of Quaker preacher Thomas Green of Rhode Island and Dartmouth. The Russells moved to Dartmouth, where Nathaniel played a leading role in establishing Grace Methodist Church, now Grace United Church.

The Kuhns were another of the early families to settle in the general area of Cole Harbour. The first of the Kuhns was Jacob, who was born in 1775 and moved to Cole Harbour from McNabs Island. Jacob's father, Henry Kuhn, had come to Dartmouth on the *Ann* in 1750. Henry married Jane Elizabeth Allemand in 1757. Henry and Elizabeth had two sons, Henry Jr., born about 1768 and Jacob, born about 1775. Both were baptized at St. Paul's Church. Henry Jr. remained a bachelor. Jacob married Elizabeth Hawthorn in 1801, and they had a large family. Jacob's farm in Cole Harbour was located at the present-day 866 Portland Street, where Maynard and Edith Tulloch and their son Robert later lived before it became part of Dartmouth. The Kuhns moved to McNabs Island from Halifax in 1780. Henry's sister married Peter McNab, who owned the entire island. Jacob and Elizabeth left McNabs Island in 1810, when they purchased 275 acres of land on the Cole Harbour Road.

Jacob's son Alexander, born in 1809, lived in Cole Harbour before buying large tracts of land in the Woodlawn area. Alexander married Jane Bissett, the daughter of James Frederick Bissett and Ann Turner. They had 10 children. When Jane Bissett died in 1865, Alexander sold his Woodlawn property to his children, remarried, and moved to Dartmouth.

The Gammons, also early settlers to the Cole Harbour and Lawrencetown area, arrived after the European Protestants and the United Empire Loyalists. The Gammons descended from James Gammon, who was born in England but lived in Dartmouth in the late 1700s. He had at least four sons – John (born in 1756), William, Richard, and James – and a daughter Ann. There is an indication there was a fifth son, George, who also acquired land in the area. The Gammons married into the Bissett and Beck families. Richard Gammon bought 1,000 acres in 1806 in the Lawrencetown Township. He married Mary Wiswell in 1800 in St. Matthew's Presbyterian Church. They had at least nine children. Richard's older brother John purchased a large lot in the same township in 1808 from James Robertson. John Gammon married Mary Ann Bissett in 1791 at St. Paul's Church in Halifax. They had 14 children. In 1817, George Gammon of Halifax acquired 614 acres, also in Lawrencetown. George Gammon and Catherine Ann Beck, both of Cole Harbour, were married in 1826 by a Methodist minister on the Halifax circuit.

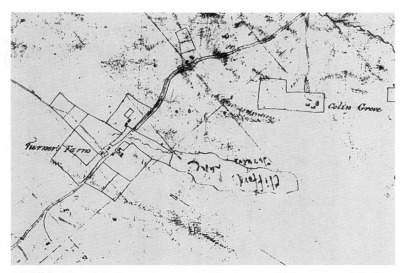

Map 4 – Turner's Farm circa 1808. The farm, which once straddled the road, is now the site of the Colby Village Mall on the south side and the Cole Harbour Heritage Farm Museum on the north. Top of map is southeast. Clifford Lake is now Bell Lake. (NSARM)

The first of the Turners to settle in the Cole Harbour area was William Turner. He and his wife Margaret (Kemp) purchased a lot in 1799. On May 1, 1801, he bought 500 acres in Cole Harbour from Lawrence Hartshorne. The Turners had immigrated to Nova Scotia from Banffshire, Scotland, in the early 1790s. Their sons, Robert and William, were both baptized in Scotland in 1784 and 1787, respectively. Their daughter Ann was baptized in St. Matthew's Presbyterian Church, Halifax, in 1791. Robert Turner married Amelia Marie Cornwall, the daughter of a Halifax physician. They had nine children. His sister Ann married James Frederick Bissett on December 6, 1810. William Turner Jr. lived in Eastern Passage and married Eleanor Himmelman.

The Settle family came to Cole Harbour when John Settle bought 242 acres along the Cole Harbour Road from William Turner in 1840. Settle, who came from Cartmel, Lancashire, England, was born in 1776. He married Hannah Rippon in 1802. They had five children: Mary (1805), James (1808), Robert (1810), John (1812), and Hannah

Mary Seatle (now Settle) made the sampler in 1817 in Cartmel, England before the family moved to Cole Harbour in 1840. Most young girls of this period were taught to sew and embroider at an early age. To demonstrate their achievement, they worked their stitches onto a small piece of fabric. The finished product was their showpiece and was usually treasured and preserved as Mary's was. Samplers often included a proverb or religious verse. (RE/courtesy of Melvin Harris)

(1815). When the family immigrated to Nova Scotia they settled first in Preston on a farm owned by John's Uncle Thomas Settle. The mortgage for Settle's 1840 land purchase refers to John Settle of South East Passage, suggesting that he moved from Preston to Eastern Passage. Since his wife Hannah's name does not appear on the mortgage documents, she may have died before the 1840 transaction. The eldest daughter, Mary, wed George Bell of Dartmouth in 1826. Ten years later the youngest daughter, Hannah, married George Bell's son, George Jr.

Robert Settle married Lerosa Ward in 1833. They had five children: John Daniel, James, Sophia, Robert Jr., and Judson. After Robert Sr.'s first wife died, he married Susannah Kiser (Keizer), daughter of John Kiser of Lunenburg, in 1857. They had five children: Alexander, Mary Ann, Andrew, Melvina, and Susannah Emma. Melvina married James Grant, a farmer from Musquodoboit, at the Grace Methodist Church in Dartmouth. All the children except Melvina are buried in the Woodlawn Methodist/United Church cemetery.

Before his death in 1864, John Settle deeded the eastern half of the family farm (120 acres) to his son Robert in 1862. In 1866 Robert purchased two more acres from his father's estate, to bring his western property line to the shoreline of Turner's Lake, now called Settle Lake. He also acquired considerable acreage to the north of his land, which extended from the Cole Harbour Road to the Old Preston Road, now Mount Edward Road.

The western portion of John Settle's original farm was left to his daughter Hannah. She later sold it to her son George Bell III in 1882.

The Becks are believed descended from Martin Beck, a European Protestant from Durlach, who came to Lunenburg with his brother Michael in 1753. Martin Beck appears to have moved to Missaguash River, the river that is the boundary between Nova Scotia and New Brunswick. He may have gone to the area with Lt.-Col. Charles Lawrence, who built a fort there in 1750. In 1755, Lawrence captured Fort Beauséjour and renamed it Fort Cumberland. In her book *Planters and Pioneers*, Ester Clark Wright lists an entry for Michael Beck in Lunenburg and one for Martin Beck at Fort Cumberland. Martin's profession was listed as baker. His wife's name was Johanna. Their children were Mary, Sophia, Jacob, James, and Martin Jr.

On November 8, 1812, farmer Martin Beck (probably Martin Jr.) of Cole Harbour purchased 150 acres of land from James Frederick Bissett also of Cole Harbour.

There are two distinct Morash families in Cole Harbour. One Morash family descended from Johannes Michael Morasch, who came to Cole Harbour from Lunenburg about 1775. His son was Michael, and his grandson was George M. Morash. The other Morash family came to Cole Harbour later.

As the farms and population in communities east of Dartmouth grew, other essential facilities such as schools, churches, and support industries would be added. These early families who settled in Cole Harbour-Lawrencetown-Woodlawn areas – the Conrads, Gileses, Russells, Kuhns, Gammons, Bissetts, Turners, Settles, Bells, Becks, and Morashes – and their descendants were instrumental in the future growth and development of the area.

9

THE FIRST SCHOOL

Public education for children was not high on the list of priorities in the early years of the settlements at Halifax, Dartmouth, and the adjacent communities of Woodlawn, Cole Harbour, and Lawrencetown. Children born into wealthy families were often tutored privately at home, and there were some church-operated schools, most notably those of the Church of England, but for the majority of children there was little in the way of formal education.

Walter Bromley established the first public school in Halifax in 1813, when he opened the Royal Acadian School. It was non-sectarian and offered inexpensive education to middle-class children, free education to poor children, and a workshop to train the unemployed. One of the students at this early public school was Joseph Howe, a future premier and Lieutenant-Governor of Nova Scotia. Another student was Daniel Cronan, considered one of Halifax's wealthiest citizens at the time of his death in 1892.

Management of the school was given to a voluntary board of trustees, assuring the school of prestigious patronage and continued financial support from both government and private citizens. Branch schools were established in Dartmouth, Woodlawn, and Cole Harbour the year after the first school opened in Halifax. The Dartmouth school began operation in July 1814. Lieutenant-Governor John Sherbrooke wrote to Provincial Treasurer Michael Wallace in February 1815, instructing Wallace to pay a sum of £12 and 10s to trustees Seth Coleman and Robert Hartshorne for the support of the Dartmouth school.

The school was held in the Quaker Meeting House on Queen Street, which had been built when the Nantucket Whalers lived in the community. School trustee Seth Coleman was a Quaker who had remained in Dartmouth when most of the whalers left for Wales. Lawrence Hartshorne and Jonathan Tremain were also trustees.

The first Dartmouth schoolteacher was Thomas Cook, who continued in that capacity until 1816. (It is possible that the Quakers themselves had operated a school in the Meeting House before Bromley's school was established. Seth Coleman's diary records a payment to teacher Abigail Proctor before 1812.)

After the Dartmouth school, another was established in the Woodlawn area in 1814. Edward H. Potts was the first teacher. The school was located by Allen's tannery (near the present-day Woodlawn United Church), probably on the estate known as Brook House.

The first school in the Cole Harbour area opened in July 1814. James Bennett replaced Edward McNamara, the first teacher, just a year later. In July 1817, Bennett moved to the Woodlawn school. School trustees during this period were Joseph Bissett, Jacob Kuhn, and Martin Beck.

James Bennett, who left Cole Harbour for Woodlawn in 1817, eventually moved to New York City. There he founded the *New York Herald*, the newspaper that sent Henry Stanley to Africa to find Dr. David Livingstone, the Scottish explorer and churchman. Bennett died in 1872.

The rapidly appearing public schools were opposed by the Rev. John Inglis of the Church of England, the son of Bishop Charles Inglis of Nova Scotia. The Reverend Inglis was secretary and Ecclesiastical Commissary to his father and would eventually assume his father's role of bishop of the province as well. The Reverend Inglis's main concern was that the church could lose some of the rights and privileges it enjoyed as the only legally recognized church in the province, such as

Cole Harbour's one-room school, long since removed from the landscape, provided education to many of the community's young residents. The students pose with their teacher in 1901. Seated (left to right): Frank Elliott, Percy Bell, Victor Settle, Robert Bissett, Norman Dares, Hilda Morash, Hazel Morash, Stan Morash, Irene Conrod, Bryden Bissett, Sadie Settle, Ethel Bissett, James Bissett, Thomas Bissett, and Arthur Beck (lying down). Back Row (left to right): (standing) Charles Elliot, Edgar Giles, Foster Morash, Daniel Morash, Harold Elliot, Bert Rutherford, Mrs. Simms (teacher), Ella or Blanca Morash, Vella Lawlor, Mary Bell (Mame), Ethel Morash, and Doll Settle. (CHR-SU)

free land for glebe houses and the effective control of education funds. The Reverend Inglis's opposition eventually paid off. The Nova Scotia House of Assembly voted in 1815 not to extend Royal Acadian Schools throughout the province and turned over the administration of the schools to the Church of England and the Reverend Inglis.

When Bromley left the province in 1825, only the Royal Acadian Schools and a few Sunday schools existed in Halifax. The Free School Act of 1826 made it mandatory for each village and town to provide a school and relieved the Church of England of its exclusive role in education. The Cole Harbour school was still operating in 1829, when the Rev. James Morrison, the first minister at St. James Presbyterian Church in Dartmouth, took over administration of the school.

By June 1829, more than 40 students, ranging in age from 4 years to 16 years, were enrolled in the one-room school at Cole Harbour. The school continued to serve the community into the next century.

According to local stories, Cole Harbour's first school was a converted sheep barn donated by Col. John Stuart, and it was located on the south side of the Cole Harbour Road, midway between Bissett Road and Ashgrove Drive.

Colonel Stuart, born in 1753, was serving with the 71st Regiment when Cornwallis surrendered to the American Continental Army at Yorktown in October 1781, ending the American Revolution. The regiment was detained in America until the peace treaty was formally signed in 1783. Most of the regiment returned to Scotland, but Colonel Stuart accompanied a group of Loyalists and soldiers to Nova Scotia. He settled first on the South Shore.

Two years after his arrival in the province, Stuart married Elizabeth Boggs, the daughter of another Loyalist, Dr. James Boggs. Stuart moved from the South Shore to the Guysborough County area, where he was appointed a Justice of the Peace, a coroner for the County of Sydney, a judge of the Probate Court, a member of the House of Assembly, and the Colonel of the Guysborough District Militia.

In 1803, Stuart was appointed a Justice of the Peace for Halifax County, Cole Harbour District. Five years later he took command of a battalion of militia and continued in that capacity throughout the War of 1812. Stuart, who was semi-retired and living in Cole Harbour, was one of the principal sponsors of the Cole Harbour school and was a trustee when it opened in 1814. He subsequently moved to Halifax, where he died on January 15, 1835, at the age of 82. He and his wife had no children. Mary Lawson in her *History of Dartmouth, Preston, and Lawrencetown Townships* records this description of him: "Colonel Stuart was a most cheerful and kindly man, hospitable in the extreme, and a great favorite [sic] with his neighbours."

10

METHODIST CHAPELS

In 1792, Governor John Wentworth established at Preston St. John's Anglican Church, the first permanent house of worship on the eastern side of Halifax Harbour. The church served the United Empire Loyalists who were moving into Dartmouth, Preston, Cole Harbour, and Lawrencetown. Dartmouth at that time had a population of approximately 50 families; Preston had 15 families, Cole Harbour had 12 families, and Lawrencetown had 23 families. Before the start of St. John's parish, the Anglican clergy from St. Paul's Church in Halifax had occasionally held worship services on the Dartmouth side of the harbour. The Church of England was the first church built in Halifax in 1749, but other Christian denominations soon moved into the area to preach the "Word of God" and make converts of the new settlers.

When the Nantucket Whalers established a colony in Dartmouth in 1785, they brought their Quaker faith with them from a tiny Massachusetts island off Cape Cod. They built a meeting house in the centre of the community for business meetings as well as worship services. At the time the Quakers were worshipping in Dartmouth, the Methodist denomination was starting to make inroads in Nova Scotia.

John Wesley, born in 1703, and his younger brother Charles, both ordained Church of England priests, started the Methodist religion. They both attended Oxford University, where they often met with small groups of students to deepen their spiritual lives through prayer and Bible study. The name "Methodist" was given to this group of young theology students of which the elder Wesley brother became leader.

John Wesley served as an Anglican chaplain in the colony of Georgia from 1736 to 1738. During this time, he was strongly influenced by the German Moravian Christians' faith in Christ as they demonstrated it in their lives and words. When he returned to England in 1738, Wesley, his brother, and some of their friends from Oxford became itinerant preachers, travelling the length and breadth of England and often preaching in the open air. They organized small groups called Societies, first in Bristol, then in London, that met for the purpose of religious conversation, singing, and prayer. Other Societies were organized at Kingswood and Bath. Wesley visited these groups to preach the gospel and give spiritual advice. A set of rules drawn up in 1743 for governing the Societies became the rules by which all persons united in the Societies were required to conduct themselves. If they failed to obey the rules they were excluded from the Societies. In time the religious body was termed "the people called Methodist." Wesley's message was that God redeemed humans through the Crucifixion and that each person was responsible for ensuring their own salvation through faith; they should not rely solely on church sacraments.

Wesley's views and practices often brought him into conflict with the Church of England authorities as Methodism took on a life of its own. After Wesley's death in 1791, the last ties with the Church of England were severed. Methodism eventually became the world's largest Protestant denomination.

Methodism came to Nova Scotia with the Yorkshire people who settled in the Cumberland County area between 1772 and 1775. They met together in prayer and fellowship without ordained clergy until one came from the families – the Rev. William Black. He attended the first General Conference of the Methodist Episcopal Church in the United States, where he pleaded for ministers to come to Nova Scotia. James Oliver Cromwell and Freeborn Garrettson both responded. These preachers left New York in February 1785 to work in the province. Garrettson preached several times in Dartmouth and the Cole Harbour area during 1785 and 1786.

The formation of Lawrencetown's first Methodist congregation began with a formal petition dated March 19, 1822, to Sir James Kempt, Governor of Nova Scotia, for financial assistance for a meeting house.

> We the undersigned, on behalf of ourselves and a number of the white and coloured inhabitants of Preston, Cole Harbour, and Lawrencetown beg leave to represent to Your Excellency, that we are almost entirely shut out by

our situation from any of the advantages of moral and religious instruction, and that we have not the means of promoting among ourselves, and our children, the knowledge and public worship of God, having no place in which we can unitedly assemble for this purpose.

We have occasionally on the Sabbath assembled in a private house but have found it exceedingly inconvenient, and have therefore concluded to erect a small building, upon a piece of ground kindly furnished us for the purpose, upon the road leading to Lawrencetown.

The situation is very centrical [sic] and convenient, being acceptable to about 14 families of coloured people, consisting of upwards of 50 persons residing in the southern part of Preston, and also to the individuals of a considerable number (perhaps 50) of families of the white population of Cole Harbour and Lawrence Town [sic].

We have, assisted by the donations of a few individuals in Halifax, already procured some material for its erection, and as little else than labour can be furnished by individuals residing in its vicinity, we beg leave humbly to submit this statement of our case to the favourable consideration of Your Excellency, and should Your Excellency be able to assist us in any way in our undertaking, we as in duty bound shall ever pray.

Joseph Wiswell and John Gammon, who made his mark, signed the petition.

The petition was strongly opposed by the Church of England. On April 29, 1822, the Rev. John Inglis, the Anglican bishop of Halifax, wrote to Sir James Kempt expressing his concerns with the petition "for assistance to erect a building for the public worship of God." His letter with supporting documentation is 10 pages long and includes information supplied by the Rev. Charles Ingles, his rector at Christ Church in Dartmouth.

The bishop pointed out that during the 20 years when there was no clergy stationed on the Dartmouth side of the harbour no effort was made to erect a meeting house. "But now when a[n Anglican] clergyman is placed there who devotes a portion of his time to all the settlements in the neighbourhood, there is a call for contributions towards a Methodist and at a time of peculiar embarrassment distress [sic]."

The rector at Christ Church also wrote disputing some of the numbers likely to attend the Methodist meeting house. He pointed out that along the road from the head of Cole Harbour to Mrs. Green's, a distance of 7.5 miles, they certainly couldn't reckon 10 families. He doubted that there would be a Black family within four miles of it. "Not many Blacks would worship at this building as they are irreclaimably Baptist and Gammon's object being the establishment of a Methodist Society."

The Church of England itself had petitioned for government aid to erect Christ Church in Dartmouth on June 10, 1816. The Anglicans at the time had a meeting location in Cole Harbour because the Reverend Ingles also wrote to his bishop "that Gammon is not more than six miles from our place of worship at Cole Harbour."

When the Methodists went ahead and built their meeting house on the Lawrencetown Road, the Anglicans in Preston decided to build a new church on the Lawrencetown Road to serve the people of Preston, Cole Harbour, and Lawrencetown. A new Anglican church opened in 1828.

The Lawrencetown Methodist chapel got its start when Lawrencetown farmer John Gammon and his wife, Mary Ann Bissett, sold a piece of their land near Cole Harbour on September 7, 1822, for five shillings to John McNeil, George Stirling, John Gammon, Joseph Wiswell, Richard Smothers, Richard Gammon, and Charles Stewart of Halifax, Preston, and Cole Harbour. Witnesses to the sale were: the Rev. William Black, John A. Barry, and John Starr.

According to the deed, the land was on "the road leading from Cole Harbour to Lawrence Town [sic] and was located on the eastern corner of John Gammon's property where it abutted James Robinson's land. It was 115.5 feet along the side of the road and was 198 feet deep." It was on the north side of the road, directly across from the present-day entrance to Sonia Drive.

The names on the deed were some of the most prominent members of the Methodist Society in Halifax at that time. Bishop William Black was considered the founder of Methodism in the Maritimes. John A. Barry was his son-in-law and secretary of the Missionary Society. John McNeil, a merchant, was involved in the selection and later the purchase of a site for a second Methodist Chapel on Brunswick Street in Halifax. Joseph Wiswell, a Halifax carpenter, probably supervised the construction of the Lawrencetown chapel. His daughter Mary was married to Richard Gammon.

The September 7, 1822, deed mentions "a chapel to be built," indicating that the structure was not yet there. The deed also covered the appointment of a steward or treasurer, who shall "receive all the seat rents to which money so received shall be applied towards the interest of all monies due upon the premises or for building or repairing said chapel and towards reducing the principal till the whole be paid."

The chapel, erected within the month, was mentioned in a letter by the Rev. L. Lusher dated October 15, 1822, to his sponsor, the Wesleyan Missionary Society in London: "At Cole Harbour nine miles from Halifax we have a small chapel and a Society of 20 members, which is supplied with preaching every Lord's Day." Lusher had just arrived on the Halifax circuit.

On October 18, 1824, the Rev. William Temple wrote to his superiors in London, "On September 19, preached at Cole Harbour, nine miles on the east side of Chebucto Bay, to a large and attentive congregation. Here I also administer the sacraments."

The following year, a letter from the Reverend Temple states: "At Cole Harbour, 11 miles to eastward of Halifax, the people are by no means so much alive to their best interest as we could wish – an unhappy spirit has crept in between two families – the father of one of them I have been obliged to reprove and suspend. The people are scattered far and wide, some engage in fishing and others in supplying the daily market in town. I visit this settlement once a quarter to meet the class, administer the sacraments, etc. But endeavor [sic] to supply them with the labour of a local preacher once a fortnight."

At the annual meeting of the Wesleyan Methodist Missions of Nova Scotia in May 1826, the Halifax District reported that at Cole

Harbour there was "one chapel 20 by 16 feet, no pews, a small debt provided by subscriptions."

Another Methodist Society was starting up in the Cole Harbour settlement. The Rev. James Hennigar, in a letter to the London Methodists dated July 10, 1827, wrote, "We have been earnestly solicited to extend the regular preaching to another settlement called Cole Harbour, 12 miles east from Halifax. In this settlement we have a chapel and 26 members in Society and the prospects for doing good are promising. So the request of this people we shall attend and give them regular preaching every third Sabbath."

No documents have been found that pinpoint the exact year the Methodist Meeting House was built in Cole Harbour. Records and deeds suggest the building was started in 1830 and completed the following year. Special anniversary celebrations held in the circuit in 1891 also suggest 1831 as the year the Meeting House opened.

John and Abigail Scott sold their property in Musquodoboit in June 1827 and bought 400 acres in Cole Harbour from John and Elizabeth Stuart of Halifax for £1,000. The deed and mortgage describe the property as "Beginning at Smelt Brook at the head of Cole Harbour running thence north westerly by the highway to the eastern boundary of Lawrence Hartshorne land." The property was once part of a 500-acre lot purchased by the Jamaican government to resettle the Maroons. The Commissionary Gen. Col. William Dawes Quarrell, a member of the Jamaican Assembly, acquired this land in Cole Harbour on May 14, 1797. When the Maroons left for Sierra Leone on August 7, 1800, the land purchased for them in Westphal and Cole Harbour was sold at public auction. Michael Wallace, a Halifax merchant and politician, bought the Cole Harbour land in 1801 and sold it the same year to John and Elizabeth Stuart, who in turn sold it to John and Abigail Scott in 1827.

The Scotts sold a quarter of an acre on top of Long Hill for five shillings to the society of people called Methodists at Cole Harbour on March 19, 1830. According to the deed, registered on August 2, 1831, the land was "to erect, build, complete and finish a chapel or meeting house." The trustees were listed as George Bissett, John Scott, Benjamin Bissett, farmers; George Gammon, chair-maker; Gasper

Roast, shopkeeper; Edmund Stevens – all of Cole Harbour and Cow Bay – and the Rev. William Croscombe, who was the senior or superintendent minister on the Halifax circuit of the Methodist Society. He was also head of the Nova Scotia District, which included most of Nova Scotia and all of Prince Edward Island.

The Rev. William Croscombe was born in Tiverton, County Devon, in February 1787. Soon after he was born, his parents moved to their hometown of Bideford, Devon, where he spent the next 20 years. In 1805, a regiment of militia from Cornwall came to Bideford

Helen Horne, former organist at the Cole Harbour Meeting House, chats with Robie Strum, a long-time member of the congregation. Mrs. Horne often played the organ at special church services organized by the Cole Harbour Rural Heritage Society. Mr. Strum redesigned the church's altar based on his recollection of the altar when he was a child. (RE 1970s)

for drill. Among them were a few Methodists. Croscombe attended the prayer meetings held by these men and the few Methodist residents of Bideford. He joined the Wesleyan Methodist Society when he was 18. He became a local preacher on the Methodist circuit and was soon recommended for ministry. In 1811, he offered for the foreign field and expressed a preference for Nova Scotia. He was appointed to what was then called the Nova Scotia, New Brunswick, Newfoundland District, of which William Black was chair.

After spending some time in Newfoundland, the Rev. Croscombe came to Halifax on April 29, 1812. He worked in Nova Scotia until 1819, when poor health forced him to go back to England. He returned to Nova Scotia in 1828 and was stationed on the Halifax circuit. His first recorded visit to the Cole Harbour area was November 30, 1828, when he came to Lawrencetown to marry the daughter of John Gammon and Mary Ann (Bissett) Gammon. The following January he baptized a granddaughter of John Gammon at the Zoar Chapel in Halifax. On February 23, 1829, he travelled to Cole Harbour and Cow

Syd Gosley, a former president of the Cole Harbour Rural Heritage Society, often acted as the master of ceremonies for the special church services conducted in the Meeting House. (RE 1990s)

Bay to baptize a daughter of Benjamin Bishop, a farmer, and a son of Edmund Stevens, a carpenter. From 1829 until 1831, he conducted well over a dozen baptisms in the Cole Harbour area, more than half of which were for descendants of the founding families – the Gammons and the Bissetts.

The Reverend Croscombe left the Halifax circuit in 1833 but continued in active ministry throughout Nova Scotia until he retired in 1855. He lived for a time in Halifax and was associated with the Brunswick Street Church. He moved to Windsor, where he died on August 26, 1859.

Abigail Scott sold her property on January 28, 1836, after her husband died, to Walter Robb of Halifax. The description of the land in this deed is the same as that used in the 1827 deed, except for two exclusions. One exclusion reads, "a certain parcel of land upon which the meeting house used by the sect called Methodists now stands." Deed records clearly indicate that the Meeting House was built sometime between 1830 and 1835.

Shortly after the Meeting House on Long Hill opened, the decision was made to close the Lawrencetown Meeting House that opened in 1822.

The Reverend Croscombe, writing to London in 1829, stated that the Halifax church was small and the country parts of the circuit were not prospering. "Their great distance from town and the badness of roads prevents our local brethren from any assistance. They are poor can do little [sic] towards our support, but that little they do cheerfully." He assessed the situation in the Cole Harbour area and decided to build a new larger chapel closer to Dartmouth.

No records have been found giving a more exact reason for relocating the congregation at Lawrencetown to Cole Harbour, but church reports on other chapels suggests that Lawrencetown's was too small. Methodists' minutes between 1827 and 1832 report on the size of more than 30 chapels in the Nova Scotia District, and the one at Lawrencetown, measuring 20 feet by 16 feet, was by far the smallest. Most chapels were 32 feet by 24 feet or larger.

The location of the old chapel on the Lawrencetown Road was no longer convenient to the growing population on the Cole Harbour

Road, which was by then expanding in the other direction towards the Woodlawn area. In order to attend Sunday services some people would have had to travel over Breakheart Hill and Long Hill in order to reach the 1822 chapel. The ministers coming from Halifax would have had to do the same. The location of the Cole Harbour Meeting House on top of Long Hill was selected as a compromise so people coming from either direction would only have one steep hill to climb. Conference minutes suggest that both the Cole Harbour and Lawrencetown buildings were used until the 1840s, when a lack of ministers finally forced the closure of the Lawrencetown Meeting House.

The early Methodist Society, first in Lawrencetown then Cole Harbour, helped spread the Methodist movement to Dartmouth and later to the Woodlawn area. One of the early leaders in the Cole Harbour church was Nathaniel Russell (1809–87), who was married to Agnes Davidson Bissett, a granddaughter of Jean George Bissett. When Russell and his family moved to Dartmouth, he helped lead in the establishment of Grace Methodist Church. He was a circuit steward, a Sunday school superintendent, a class leader, a lay preacher, a public-spirited citizen, and a friend to the poor. Others active in the Cole Harbour Methodist movement were the Kuhns, the Gammons, and the Bissetts. The Methodist Church remained a strong and influential part of Cole Harbour rural life into the next century.

11

THE CENSUS OF 1827

Cole Harbour was a growing community. According to the 1827 census, the total population was 218 men, women, children, and male and female servants, to use the categories of the census. In total there were 37 families. Lieutenant-Governor Sir James Kempt had suggested the census. He sent a letter to the Nova Scotia House of Assembly in April 1827 requesting funds to conduct a province-wide head count. The legislature approved his request and appointed each county's sheriff as the census-taker. The census was conducted in the fall of the year at a cost of £1,400. In addition to genealogical information, the census included agricultural statistics on the number of bushels of wheat, grain, and potatoes, and the number of tons of hay harvested. It also listed the numbers of cattle, sheep, and swine of each family.

Of the 37 families living in the area, 20 were members of the Presbyterian Church and 17 were members of the Church of England. Only four denominations were listed in the census: Presbyterian, Church of England, Baptist, and Roman Catholic. There was no designation for the Methodist Church. Thirty-six families indicated that they were farm families; one was listed as a manufacturer. There were 26 male servants listed for Cole Harbour (farmhands) and 13 female servants (domestics). Up to September 30, 1827, the community had registered 7 births, 3 female marriages and one death for the year.

During the census year, Cole Harbour farmers produced 18 bushels of wheat, 29 bushels of grain, and 36 bushels of potatoes. Farmers produced on average 12.2 tons of hay.

The population in the Lawrencetown area was slightly smaller than Cole Harbour's, totalling 160 men, women, children, and male and female servants. There were 22 families, of which 10 were members of the Church of England, 11 belonged to the Presbyterian Church, and one belonged to the Roman Catholic Church. Nineteen were listed as farm families and one was listed without an occupation.

This early census gives us an idea today of what Cole Harbour and surrounding area looked like and how the communities evolved.

> Cole Harbour Families
> Martin Beck
> Benjamin Bissett
> Charles Bissett
> George Bissett
> James Bissett
> Joseph Bissett
> Samuel Bissett
> Thomas Cauldwell
> John Cogill

Stephen Collins
Alexander Cummings
John Cummings
John Daley
John Elliott
Jonathan Elliott
John Evans
Daniel Fraser
William Fraser
Joseph Giles
Joseph Hawkins
Jacob Kuhn
Daniel Lawlor
John McKenzie
Keneth [sic] McKenzie
Eusten Morash
Leonard Morash
Michael Morash
William Osborn
Christopher Roast
Leonard Roast
Nathaniel Russell
John Scott
Robert Turner
William Turner
William Turner Jr.
James Welsham
William Yorke

Lawrencetown Families
  William Bathic
  Daniel Bremner
  Thomas Conrod
  William Crooks
  Ebenezer Crowell
  John Gammon

Richard Gammon
Samuel Gammon
John Gates
Henry Green
Joseph Green
William Lloyd
Alexander Mason
Daniel Monavan
Thomas Moor
George Pense
James Robinson
John Shaw
William Stowell
George Sullers
John Wiseman
Harry Wood

12

DIARY OF A FARMER'S DAUGHTER

Rural life in the early nineteenth century entailed hard work with a lengthy daily routine of farming and household chores. Livestock and poultry had to be fed and tended, crops had to be planted and weeded, buildings and equipment had to be maintained. Wood for fuel had to be chopped and stockpiled for the winter. There was the weekly ride over dusty, rutted, and by times muddy or snow-covered roads to the markets in Halifax and Dartmouth. Domestic chores included making butter, spinning yarn, cooking, sewing, and cleaning. Farm families lived and worked in isolated units. Yet, in spite of distance between farms and continual work, there were frequent visits back and forth for afternoon tea and other social activities.

Louisa Collins grew up on a farm on the Cole Harbour Road. Her diary offers a glimpse into early nineteenth-century rural life. Edith

Elliot, the great-granddaughter of Louisa's younger sister Charlotte, gave a portion of Louisa's diary from August 1815 to January 1816 to the Nova Scotia Archives and Records Management in 1953. The Cole Harbour Rural Heritage Society published the diary in 1989.

Louisa Sarah Collins was the second daughter of Stephen Collins, a native of Halifax, and Phebe (Coffin) a native of Nantucket Island, Massachusetts. Her father was the son of Robert Collins, who came to Halifax in 1767 and prospered as a stone mason. Her mother had come to Dartmouth with the Quaker families who established a whaling industry in Dartmouth in 1785.

In 1784, Robert Collins bought a 300-acre farm east of Dartmouth on the Cole Harbour Road, situated on the western slope of one of the highest hills in the area, Breakheart Hill (see the map on page 67). Collins named his farm Colin Grove. The suburban street named Collins Grove, off Spring Avenue in Dartmouth, is in the vicinity of the former farm.

By the summer of 1815, when Louisa's diary begins, her father, Stephen, who inherited the farm when his father died in 1811, farmed Colin Grove. Stephen purchased the other half of the land from his two younger sisters in 1813. In 1815, Louisa was 18 years old; her older sister Betsy was 20. Her younger sisters were Charlotte, 16; Mary Ann, 14; Phebe, 11; Jane, 7; Georgina, 3; and Joanna, 7 months.

Following are some excerpts from Louisa Collins's diary that illuminate daily life. The punctuation throughout has been modernized, but Louisa's wording is preserved.

> Tuesday, August 15, 1815 – The dairy as usual takes up most of my morning on Tuesday, and after finishing there I picked a basket of black currants for Miss Beamish. In the afternoon I sewed a little while and then went out and raked hay. Aunt Clifford's girl and her sister have been over all day picking currants. Mama is now tying up her radishes and turnips for market tomorrow morning. *[Wednesdays and Saturdays were market days in Halifax.]* As that don't belong to my part of the work, I left her to herself. We have had a fine day today.

The official launch of Louisa's Diary, *published jointly by the Nova Scotia Museum and the Cole Harbour Rural Heritage Society, was held at the Cole Harbour Library. Tamara Gross is in costume and posing as Louisa Collins; the Elliot sisters of Dartmouth, descendants of the Collins family, surround her (left to right): Gertrude Elliot, Dorothy Covert Zinck, Lois Richards, and Joyce Earle.* (RE 1989)

Saturday, August 26, 1815 – I have been carding and spinning this morning and in the afternoon I went with the girls to pick some bayberries. Papa has been to town today but has brought no news. I stopped by my little bower this afternoon but it looked so dull I could not stay long, and the weather being very dull hurried me from the spot where I have spent many happy moments.

Sunday, August 27, 1815 – My morning was nearly taken up in the kitchen getting dinner. Betsy and Jane went to Dartmouth in the morning. After dinner Phebe went to Mrs. Prescott's and Charlotte to Mrs. Allen's. I was quite alone until Mr. Beamish came. We went to the orchard to pick some currants and then we took a walk to Mr. Russell's lake. When we returned tea was ready. The fog came in very thick and Mr. Beamish stayed all night.

Monday, August 28, 1815 – I have been picking currants from nine this morning till four this afternoon. We have got a large washing-tub full for wine. I have been raking hay till nearly night. Mr. Beamish and George have left here very early this morning. I did not see them. While I was picking currants my thoughts were employed with where I should be and what I should be doing this day 12 months.

Wednesday, August 30, 1815 – As it was quite late last night when I came home I had not time to write down yesterday's work. I was very busy making wine near all day – and butter. In the afternoon I picked some berries then went to Mrs. Allen's for tea.

Today I have been making hay till I was very tired. After dinner Aunt Elizabeth came up and Mr. Beamish. Mama and Aunt were picking currants all the afternoon and Mr. B. and me took care of Joanna. Mr. Beamish brought me a note from Harriet and I wrote a short one to her. I hope my friend Thomas is near his journey's end for the night looks very dark. How often do I wish there was a bridge across the harbour and that I might see my friends without any danger. *[The harbour ferry was only a small boat powered by oars or a sail.]* I now hear the ferry horn blowing and the night is very dark, which makes it sound quite melancholy. Heaven grant that my friend may get over safe.

Friday, September 1, 1815 – This has been a very rainy day and I have been sewing all day till about five o'clock when it left off raining and Mama and me went and picked some beans and peas. It has rained very hard today and I fear much of our hay is spoilt. I sincerely hope tomorrow may be fine. It has been so cold this evening that I have been sitting by the fire. Winter approaches fast and we have very little warm weather.

Monday, September 4, 1815 – I have not done much of anything today. In the morning I made hay a little while. Charlotte came home from Dartmouth this morning. Mrs. Macy and her daughters have come from Nantucket. There is news of Bonaparte's being taken. I hope it is true. There is no punishment too great for such a wretch. How many lives have been sacrificed for his ambition. *[News of Napoleon Bonaparte's surrender to the English on July 15 reached Halifax on September 3 by a British naval ship.]*

Tuesday, September 5, 1815 – After I finished making butter today I went to spinning. In the afternoon, Mama and the girls went to pick berries and I was left alone except little Joanna who was asleep. Last night the frost was so great as to kill all the cucumbers, and it has been very cold all day.

Tuesday, September 12, 1815 – I was carding and spinning all morning by myself. In the afternoon Mama and the girls came up to the spinning room with me. Eliza and Charlotte sewed and Mama helped me spin. After our work was over we went to the barn and had a swing and a romp in the hay. There was to be some fireworks performed tonight but the rain I suppose will put a stop to it. *[The fireworks were probably in celebration of Napoleon's defeat.]*

Thursday, September 14, 1815 – In the afternoon Mr. Beamish came up and brought his horse. He spent the afternoon mending his gun and making me wait on him with tools. Poor Phebe has met with a sad misfortune. A crow has taken away one of her chickens and it was one of her favorites [*sic*]. Mr. Beamish rode after it with his gun but could not get it. The weather has been very disagreeable all day.

Friday, September 22, 1815 – I had a tedious time making butter this morning – the weather is so cold. *[On cold days it took much longer for the cream to turn to butter.]* After dinner Mama and me walked to Dartmouth. Mama went to town to spend a day or two. In the evening Papa came down on horseback and I rode home behind him. It was late when we arrived.

Sunday, October 8, 1815 – As soon as we done breakfast, Harriet and me walked out to old Colly's to get up a horse to make up a riding party to go to Mrs. Stuart's at Cole Harbour. *[Col. John Stuart owned a large farm on a hill overlooking Cole Harbour about 2½ miles or 2 kilometres away.]* But we soon returned, disappointed in our expectations of riding single-horse. Mr. Beamish came up and dined with us. After dinner we got the chaise and went to Cole Harbour. Harriet and Betsy rode, and Mr. Beamish and me walked. The lady of the mansion was from home but we stopped and had tea with the gentlemen. We returned home early as the evening was disagreeable. Mr. Beamish has not gone home tonight.

Friday, October 13, 1815 – My first employment of the morning was taken up making butter, and secondly ironing. And thirdly spent the evening at Mrs. Allen's at Mount Edward. Sally A., Charlotte and myself formed the party. William came home with us and Sally. It is a beautiful evening. I should like to walk two or three miles with an agreeable companion. The moon is in her full splendour and shed her beams on all around. How delightful to walk now *[that]* we can view from Nature up to Nature's God.

Monday, October 16, 1815 – After dinner Mr. Beamish came up. He had his gun and we went up to the lake. All was still save the gentle breeze that curled the lake. Not a bird was heard through all the wood. How fast the hours fly when in the society of those we esteem. The sun ha*[d]* sunk behind the hills ere we thought of home. Papa has been to the militia the day. *[Most men of military age belonged to militia companies established to protect Nova Scotia from invasion.]* Mr. B. left after tea; he will have a beautiful evening to cross.

Tuesday, November 14, 1815 – I spun till three o'clock then dressed to go out. Charlotte and myself spent the evening at Mrs. Eben Allen's with Mrs. Brinley and Sally, Miss Macy, Miss Coleman, and Miss Foster, and Miss E. Allen, and all the young gentlemen. We spent a very pleasant evening dancing and singing and playing "Blindman's Bluff."

Thursday, November 16, 1815 – This morning I have been washing. Mr. Beamish came up. He helped Papa kill the cow. *[Some of the livestock would be killed at this time of the year to reduce the need for winter feeding. The meat would be preserved by salting or smoking.]* After they finished, Mr. B. and me went to Mrs. Allen's and spent the evening. Betsy and Charlotte came over after tea. Sally and me played backgammon while the rest of the party amused themselves by talking politics. We had to come home in the rain. Mr. B. has taken my bed tonight.

Sunday, November 19, 1815 – Papa went to church this morning – Mr. Ingles preached in Dartmouth. *[This is the first mention of any member of Louisa's family attending church services. Mr. Ingles was later appointed rector of Christ Church in Dartmouth.]* Mr. Beamish came up and dined with us.

Saturday, November 25, 1815 – As this is Saturday my morning was very busy. Papa has been to town today. He bought me *The Pleasures of Memory* to read. There has been a violent gale in Quebec – ships driven on shore and many lives lost. It is very cold this evening.

Thursday, November 30, 1815 – We met with a sad accident last night in the poultry way. A mink killed five turkeys, three ducks, and two hens. The evening is dark and rainy.

Saturday, December 2, 1815 – This morning I have been busy preparing for company. I went to Mrs. Allen's to invite the girls. After dinner Papa came home and brought Harriet and Maria to be godmothers to Georgina and Joanna. Before we got dressed the parson came – Mr. Ingles from Chester performed the ceremony. Mr. Beamish did not arrive until the ceremony was over. Papa stood proxy for him to Georgina. The evening was spent in dancing.

Sunday, December 3, 1815 – Harriet, Mr. Beamish, and myself walked down to church this morning and returned to dinner. Mr. B. left here very early.

Monday, December 25, 1815 – Eliza Coleman came up this morning and spent Christmas with us. John and James stopped to breakfast with us. Charlotte spent the day at Mrs. Allen's and the night. *[Christmas was celebrated with as many festivities as later in the 1800s or today.]*

Wednesday, December 27, 1815 – We spent a very pleasant evening with plenty of dancing. We kept it up until four o'clock this morning. Mama and Mrs. Allen came up to see us in the evening. Our dancing affected us so little that Eliza and me and Mr. Beamish have been on our lake sliding all morning and now Eliza and myself. And Mr. Beamish is going to walk down to Aunt's.

Monday, January 1, 1816 – Mama, Papa, Aunt, and Uncle Brown ha[ve] gone to dine with Mr. Allen. In the afternoon, William Coleman, George and James came up and spent the evening with us. I have beg[u]n the year making corsets.

Tuesday, January 2, 1816 – Uncle and Aunt went home this morning. I have been knitting all day. Mrs. Brinley and Sally came over to tea. Edward came in the evening and wore his frightful mask and the mitre of Patrick from Ireland. *[Edward Allen may have been "mumming," visiting his neighbours in disguise as part of the New Year's festivities.]*

Friday, January 19, 1816 – This is a very stormy day. It has snowed all day, so that Mr. B. has not been able to get home. We have had hard work to keep ourselves warm. Saturday – Mr. Beamish went home this morning before breakfast. Mrs. Brinley has gone to town to spend some time. Sally spent the evening here. Mama and Papa were at Mr. Allen's.

[Here this fragment of Louisa's diary ends.]

Louisa Collins married her "friend," Thomas Beamish, on September 21, 1816, and they moved to Halifax. The family faced difficult times after Louisa's mother died in 1824. Their home burned to the ground on a Sunday in 1827 while they attended church. The family then moved down the hill to Brook House, where the father died in 1831, leaving debts behind. His nephew Hood Clifford bought the farm. Colin Grove was sold in 1885 – the north half to John Kuhn and the south half to Robert Settle Jr. of Cole Harbour.

13

SUPPORT INDUSTRIES

By the middle of the nineteenth century most of the land east of Dartmouth – Woodlawn, Preston, Lawrencetown, and Cole Harbour – was devoted to farming. The farms yielded a variety of crops, dairy products including eggs, and meat. Farther east in the Chezzetcooks the residents made their livelihood by combined farming and fishing. Many crafted and manufactured items continued to be made elsewhere, but a range of support industries and services grew up within the community.

Most of the farmers owned horses for plowing the fields and transporting harvested crops to market; horseshoes and leather harnesses, metal plows, wheels, and wagons were needed. Some farmers produced grain for livestock feed but others used grain for domestic purposes and required gristmills to turn the wheat into flour and cereal. Fishermen along the shore at Chezzetcook and Jeddore needed people to build boats and make sails. Support industries began to appear and flourish. In many cases, farmers served in dual capacities as farmer and industrialist.

One of the earliest industries in the area was a tannery in Woodlawn, owned and operated by Ebenezer Allen, who also farmed. Allen, like many of the early settlers, had come to the area following the American Revolution. He purchased land in 1786 in the general vicinity of the present-day United Church, where he farmed and set up his tannery, turning animal hides into leather. He also provided some of his land for a burial ground for residents of the area. He called it Woodlawn.

Mrs. Eva (Morash) Kuhn sits on one of George Gammon's rocking chairs. These were popular pieces of furniture in many of the Cole Harbour homes in the past. There are still a few Gammon chairs in use in the area after almost 150 years. (RE 1970S)

Another early industry to operate in the area was the gristmill. One of the earliest millers was Allen McDonald, a Dartmouth resident who owned a tobacco and cigar-making business in Halifax. In 1830, McDonald purchased 50 acres from John Elliott on the Cole Harbour Road near Russell Lake. He bought an additional 8 acres from Nathaniel Russell, and before 1835 he operated a flour and snuff mill (snuff being tobacco ground to a powder).

McDonald's milling operation brought him into conflict with another mill operator, Andrew Shields. Shields, a blacksmith by trade, came to Dartmouth from Scotland in 1818. He moved to Woodlawn, where he operated a blacksmith shop, a carding mill, and a tavern. (He was also a poet and wrote under the pseudonym Albyn.) McDonald built a dam to divert water from Russell Lake to power machinery at the gristmill. The dam backed up the stream, causing Shields's nearby land at Ellenvale to flood. Shields brought an action for damages against McDonald and won his case. McDonald paid the damages as well as the court costs, but he never removed the dam.

James Frederick Bissett built a gristmill further out the Cole Harbour Road in 1835, where the Colby Village Shopping Mall is in 2003.

Charles Day (seated on the backhoe) and George Geldart, who grew up on the property, unearthed the millstones from James Frederick Bissett's 1835 gristmill. The millstones are now displayed on the lawn of the old Meeting House on the Cole Harbour Road. (RE mid-1970s)

George Gammon operated a small workshop in Cole Harbour, producing wooden furniture and chairs, which were sold to other farmers in the general area, as well as to markets farther afield. He later moved to Halifax, where he continued making chairs.

The 1839 census for Lawrencetown lists a stonemason, two brickmakers, and a shoemaker. By 1864, Lawrencetown had John and William Crook as both farmers and millwrights. Peter and John McKenna were both farmers and boat-builders. Andrew Robinson was a farmer, and he operated a blacksmith shop. The 1871 census shows William Gammon of Lawrencetown continuing in the family chair-making business. Other business operations in the community at the time included shoemakers, blacksmiths, and millwrights. The latter were a second layer of industry serving the milling industry.

Ron Osborne demonstrates use of a Beck's plow, which is now part of the Heritage Farm Museum's collection of farm implements. (Connie Holland 1993)

In the Cole Harbour area, James Settle operated a blacksmith shop. James Beck, William Sawler, and George Sawler were wheelwrights.

The plow that best suited the area's needs was designed and made by James Beck, who had designed, made, and repaired farm equipment since the mid-1800s. It is believed one of his plows won a third-place award at the Halifax Exhibition in the 1860s. Beck was thought to have patented his plow design, although there are no records available to substantiate that claim. In the nineteenth century, the provincial government offered financial incentives for continuous improvements to plows and other farm equipment. The Cole Harbour Farm Museum was given a Beck's plow in the 1980s by the Thompson family of Petpeswick, who were related to the Becks by marriage.

There were also masons, carpenters, and painters working in the area. Several women in the community added to the family income as dressmakers, mat-makers, seamstresses, weavers, and laundresses.

Most of the small-industry outlets, considered by many as cottage industries, continued to serve the communities of Woodlawn, Preston, Lawrencetown, and Cole Harbour into the twentieth century with some additional businesses springing up, such as broom-makers, barrel-makers, and ladder-makers.

IV

YEARS OF GROWTH
MIDDLE AND LATE 1800S

14
TO MARKET, TO MARKET

15
SPREADING THE WORD

16
A TEMPERATE ANCHOR

17
DYKING THE HARBOUR

18
COUNTY POOR FARM

19
GOODBYE NINETEENTH CENTURY

14

TO MARKET, TO MARKET

The family farms of Cole Harbour, Woodlawn, Preston, and Lawrencetown were a major source of food for residents living in nearby Halifax and Dartmouth. The bounty of these farms supplied vegetables, fruit, berries, meat, poultry, eggs, and butter, plus a variety of non-edible goods.

The Halifax Market, which changed its location several times with the passing years, was the major outlet for the local farm products. It opened twice a week year-round for the farmers and their customers. Each market day a procession of horse-drawn wagons (or sleighs in winter) lumbered along the Cole Harbour and Lawrencetown-Preston Roads to the Dartmouth ferry terminal hours before dawn cracked the eastern horizon. Travel over these roads was often complicated by the weather. During the spring months, melting snow and rain often turned the roads into a muddy quagmire, the summer months made them dry and dusty, and the snow and ice of winter created the need for smooth-running sleighs instead of wagons.

The Halifax Farmer's Market opened in June 1750, a year after the founding of the settlement. Governor Cornwallis and his council designated a market site east of the present-day Bank of Montreal building on George Street. For 50 years, "this flesh, meat or cattle market," as it was known according to *Halifax Farmers Market*, sold produce and livestock from Acadian farms in the Annapolis Valley and from local farms in the immediate area.

By 1799, the first market facilities began to deteriorate, creating a need for a new building. The preamble to the Market House Act of 1799 states, "[I]t would greatly tend to benefit both town and country if a separate market house was erected in Halifax for the sole use of persons bringing from the country, meat, poultry, butter, and other victuals and in which they might expose such articles for sale." [6]

Halifax's open-air Farmer's Market on Cheapside near the ferry terminal in the late 1800s, where farmers sold their produce and other goods from the back of their wagons or set up their wares along the sidewalk. The Green Market, as it was sometimes called, became well known even in the United States and a "must see" for all visitors to the city. (RE/courtesy of Joyce Saulnier LaPierre)

A new market was erected in 1800, but a convenient place to sell vegetables was not provided, forcing the farmers to sell their produce in the streets and the square in front of the market until the middle of the nineteenth century. When Halifax was incorporated as a city in 1848, the city charter conveyed the country market property to the city "for the public and common benefit and use of the City of Halifax according to the true interest and meaning of the original grant."

After considerable debate and despite the strong objections of local merchants, a new market was built in 1854, but the country vendors refused to participate. Years later, in 1918, the *Acadian Recorder* recalled the 1854 events. "All the best stalls being let to the Halifax butchers, the country people from the first refused to use the market as a place for the disposal of their produce and in spite of the fines and threats gathered their teams and wares around the post office block and with the coloured people and the Mic Macs [*sic*] established the picturesque street market, which became a feature of Halifax."

The Green Market, as it was sometimes called, was open Wednesdays and Saturdays. It became well known even in the United States and a "must see" for all visitors to the city.

The city fathers, according to Phyllis Blakeley's *Glimpses of Halifax from 1867 to 1900*, "were untouched by the picturesque scene in the market square because they were besieged by complaints from the merchants of the streets surrounding the post office. The crowds and carts on the sidewalks and roadways interrupted their business." The controversy lasted until another new market was built in the twentieth century.

In addition to vegetables, berries, and fruit, flowers were popular with the city shoppers. In the fall, the women supplied jams, pickles, chow and other preserves along with cakes, pies, and baked bread. Fruitcakes and decorated wreaths were available during the Christmas season. The farmers also sold smelts, rabbits, and sauerkraut. Entrepreneurs known as "hucksters" travelled to the local villages, buying goods from farmers who didn't go to the market.

The market vendors gathered their produce from the fields and loaded it and other goods on their wagons the day before market day. Some left home at 2:00 A.M. on market day, others left earlier, depending on their distance from Halifax, to begin the long trek to Dartmouth and arrive on time to catch the first ferry at 6:00 A.M. If a farmer missed the first boat he might not get across to Halifax until 10:00 or 11:00 A.M.

There were regulations governing the loading of horses and wagons on the ferry. According to an 1884 account in the *Dartmouth Times*:

> [T]he regulation relating to the passing of the teams on the ferry are: Two lines of teams are formed, one on the right the other on the left side of the ferry gate, and a team is taken alternately from each side. Many of the more enterprising of the market farmers come down on Friday evening and have their wagons at the ferry all night ready for the first trip on Saturday morning.

Milk carts and other horse-drawn wagons line up and prepare to board the Dartmouth ferry that will take them to Halifax. Farmers from Cole Harbour and area left their farms before dawn on market day in order to get on the first ferry to Halifax. This practice continued until the Angus L. Macdonald Bridge opened in 1955. (NSARM CA. 1900)

A new regulation has been put in force by the Ferry Company to the effect that milkmen's teams have the preference on the 6:30 A.M. On Saturday morning, any milkman missing the regular boat will have to take his turn on the following trips with the others.

In 1977 the *Dartmouth Free Press* printed comments from a number of farmers who had regularly attended the Halifax Market. According to one farmer, "the drive was long and cold. One had to bundle up well with heavy coats and boots. To help keep warm for a while they heated bricks to put beside their feet. Some people put potatoes made hot in the oven in their heavy boots."

The *Halifax Farmers Market* recounted this story, taken from the *Dartmouth Free Press*:

Fred Giles, the last of the Giles family to occupy the Giles House, was a regular vendor at the Halifax Farmer's Market. (RE 1975)

A man living in Chezzetcook, Dennis (Denny) Bellefontaine, dug clams, shelled them, and on a few occasions hauled them by wheelbarrow to Halifax to sell. Mr. Bellefontaine said he had a flour barrel sawed in two and would haul about 200 quarts of shelled clams. Early in the day he would start off pushing his wheelbarrow, travel to Porters Lake, up Fairbanks Road, walking as far as Bill Mannette's roadhouse at Preston. Here he took lodging for the night. The next morning he started for town.

Oxen were so well trained that they could travel along almost as fast as horses, but sometimes they could be contrary and stubborn, holding up traffic. Included in the vendors' load they had kindling wood, which they sold for 10¢ a bundle, handmade witherod brooms to sell to farmers to be used in the barns.

Farmers used the weekly trip to the market to purchase supplies also, such as flour, sugar, feed, and other items not readily available to them. The trek to the Halifax Market continued to be a weekly pilgrimage for the Cole Harbour and area farmers well into the twentieth century. And it still is for a few.

15

SPREADING THE WORD

By the middle of the nineteenth century, the Cole Harbour Methodist Meeting House was a haven for spiritual growth for many residents of the farming community. Its location at the top of Long Hill, overlooking the harbour, was also shown on navigational charts as a beacon for passing mariners. According to Gary Gibson's history notes, "The spiritual light that emanated from the tiny chapel came from the men and women in the congregation, who, touched by the teachings of the numerous ministers and local lay preachers, carried their faith to nearby settlements. Their outreach led to the construction of four other churches."

The Cole Harbour Methodist Meeting House, which was often used by other denominations in the area for Sunday services, was initially part of the Halifax Methodist circuit, and ministers came regularly from the city to conduct services at Cole Harbour. After 1865, Cole Harbour joined the Dartmouth circuit and ministers were supplied from Grace Methodist Church in Dartmouth.

In the early years, the Methodist movement relied heavily on lay preachers due to the shortage of ordained ministers. Each local society was divided into classes of 12 people, each with its own leader. These classes were often responsible for organizing the Sunday services, particularly in the rural areas where a minister might only visit once a month. One local lay preacher was Nathaniel Russell Jr., a native of Cole Harbour, who moved to Dartmouth and was one of the leaders in the formation of Grace Methodist Church. Another active lay preacher was Hugh Bell of Halifax, a former teacher who owned a brewery as well as soap and candle factories. He served as mayor of Halifax, was elected to the Nova Scotia legislature, and was one of the principal founders of the Nova Scotia Hospital in Dartmouth.

Farm families trying to support the Methodist Chapel's visiting ministers felt the financial burden. During lean years, ministers were sometimes paid in produce rather than in cash. One minister remarked that a certain year "had been a terrible year for turnips." [7] There was little else in the collection. In the first quarter of 1867, offerings at the Cole Harbour chapel amounted to one dollar. Fundraising events such as church picnics and strawberry festivals helped provide the additional funding that was often lacking from the Sunday collections.

The *Provincial Wesleyan* on February 27, 1880, reported that

> The ladies of Cole Harbour Methodist Church gave a very enjoyable entertainment in the Anchor Lodge on Thursday evening. A large number from the city (Halifax) and Dartmouth went out in sleighs and the audience completely filled the hall. Mr. E. Foster presided and the opening address was delivered by [the] Rev. John Weir on Intemperance. Readings and music followed and Mrs. Joudrey's Wax-Works admirably managed by Miss A. Foster closed a very pleasant evening.

On September 24, 1880, the same newspaper reported that "the sum of $70 recently raised at a picnic will provide quite a sufficient amount to make the proposed repairs at the church in Cole Harbour."

December 9, 1881, the *Provincial Wesleyan* reported the "Rev. S. F. Heustis spent part of last Sunday at Cole Harbour, Halifax County, where the young pastor Mr. Weir is doing good work. Two persons were baptized and six were received into membership. Two others who had passed their term of probation were absent through illness. Most of those received were heads of families – one man was more than three score and ten."

A popular fundraising endeavour was the Christmas tree festival. One such event held on December 19 was glowingly reported in local newspapers:

> For many years it had been the custom with the ladies of the Methodist Church at Cole Harbour to hold an entertainment at Christmas time with the object of raising money for circuit purposes. The entertainment was held in the Temperance Hall on the evening of the 19th. After paying all expenses it was found that the sum of $32.50 had been cleared. The principal attraction of the evening was the large tree tastefully decorated with the various fancy articles for sale. At an extensive table erected for the purpose, a substantial supper was served, and from time to time the young people surrounded the organ and sang some familiar hymns.

The little chapel was saved from near disaster one winter evening when sparks from the wood stove fell into the kindling and set fire to the building. John Settle, who was returning from a courting visit, noticed the fire. He rushed in and extinguished the blaze.

Between 1865 and 1877, the Cole Harbour Methodist Chapel was part of the Dartmouth circuit, and ministers were supplied from the Dartmouth Church. In 1877, the Lawrencetown circuit was established, which included Cole Harbour, Lawrencetown, and mission churches at Woodlawn and Waverley. The first minister of this circuit was the Rev. Robert Williams. The Dartmouth circuit shifted in 1891 to Woodlawn, and the Woodlawn church opened a parsonage on Portland Street in 1895.

The Cole Harbour Meeting House is surrounded by the graves of the early settlers to the area with as many as 30, and possibly more, there. Very few stones remain. Some family stones for Bissett and Turner are missing. Among those buried in the cemetery are John Gammon and his wife, Mary Ann (Bissett), who donated the land for the very first Methodist Meeting House in Upper Lawrencetown in 1822.

The Cole Harbour Anglican community regularly held Sunday services in the Methodist Meeting House before they had their own building. The Anglicans, like the Methodists, had difficulty raising sufficient funds for the support of the minister and his family. A committee of George Morash, James Bissett Jr., and W. Lawlor was

Above, the Cole Harbour Meeting House, October 1979. The grave marker in the foreground, one of the few headstones to be found in the cemetery, is that of James Beck who was influential in getting the chapel built in the 1830s. (CHR-SU)

Young choir members with Marjorie Morash at the organ lead the hymn singing during a morning worship service at the Cole Harbour United Church, formerly the old Methodist Meeting House on the Cole Harbour Road. Built in the 1830s, the structure is now a Provincial Heritage Building, owned and operated by the Cole Harbour Rural Heritage Society. (RE ca. 1950/CHR-SU)

appointed in 1835 to raise money to help support the minister in the parish. The amount they raised is unknown.

The Anglican church had actually been the first to set down roots in the area with the construction of St. John's Church in Preston in 1791. The first minister, the Rev. Joshua Wingate Weeks, also held regular Sunday services for the 12 families living in Cole Harbour as early as 1794. By 1824, the Cole Harbour mission had established Sunday school for the children. The first recorded Anglican baptism at Cole Harbour was Robert Rippon Settle's on April 8, 1867.

For 31 years the Cole Harbour congregation was a mission of the Preston parish, but in 1826 it became a mission of Christ Church parish in Dartmouth, established in 1817. Shifting the mission to the Dartmouth parish meant a greater distance for the minister to travel for Sunday services and to administer the sacraments. When the Rev. M. B. Desbrisay was the rector of Christ Church in 1831, he travelled 20 miles on horseback each Sunday, first to Eastern Passage then to Cole Harbour for evening services before returning home to Dartmouth. The young minister died as a result of a fall from his horse while visiting a sick parishioner.

The parishioners of Eastern Passage, Cow Bay, and Cole Harbour concurred that they were an impractical distance from Christ Church in Dartmouth and that a separate parish should be established as soon as a clergyman became available. The suggestion for a separate parish was further advanced at an Easter meeting in 1869: "Eastern Passage, Cow Bay, and Cole Harbour, [should] be separated from Christ Church and become the Parish of Eastern Passage." [8]

A committee consisting of Peter Himmelman, George Bowes Jr., and John Bissett was appointed to guide the affairs of the new parish. The committee arranged for $800 from Christ Church to build a rectory and an additional $200 towards the construction of a church. The bishop gave his approval and the new parish became a reality with the Rev. Charles Burns as the new rector.

The parishioners immediately set about erecting their own church building for Sunday services and other activities on the Cole Harbour Road near Bissett Road. The building was ready for occupancy in November 1871. The following year Bishop Binney formally consecrated the new church, which was named St. Andrew's. Some of the Cole Harbour families involved in the life and work of St. Andrew's were Morash, Giles, Elliott, Bissett, Lawlor, Wentzell, Settle, and Bell.

Improvements and furnishings were added as money became available. An organ was purchased in 1887, but the collection appears to have dropped off because the next capital expenditure didn't occur until 1923, when new carpeting was installed.

In the early days of St. Andrew's parish a wood stove in the centre of the floor was the sole heat source. The temperature in the church depended entirely on the person appointed to light and maintain the fire for the service. If he was enthusiastic, the heat was often stifling. If he was late arriving, parishioners sat through a chilly morning service during which they could see their breath. The parishioners usually donated the firewood. The wood-burning era didn't end at St. Andrew's until the 1940s, when a coal-burning furnace replaced the wood stove.

When gold was discovered near Mineville in 1862, it brought an influx of people to the Lawrencetown area. Gold mining activity peaked in 1868 and 1869, but there was still some mining activity in 1877. The influx of people created the need for a Methodist church closer than the Cole Harbour chapel, which had served as the centre for the Methodist community since the 1840s.

In 1875, William Crook, Edwin A. Lockhart, James T. Sellers, William A. Gammon, John Crook, and Henry Sellers, trustees for the Lawrencetown Methodist Society, nominally purchased for one dollar a half-acre of land for a Methodist Church. The land, donated by William and Elizabeth Sellers, was located on the Lawrencetown Road near the Mineville Road. No attempt was made to reuse the site of the first Methodist Chapel in the area; a house had since been built on the land.

The new Lawrencetown chapel, its second, was the same size as the Cole Harbour chapel (24 feet by 32 feet). It opened for worship in 1876. The building continued in use until church union in 1925, when the Methodists moved to the Presbyterian Church. Records indicate that at least 13 people were buried in the nearby cemetery when the church was abandoned in 1925.

The original St. Andrew's Anglican Church was built in 1871 and served the community until 1987, when a new building was erected on Circassion Drive. The original church was decommissioned and sold to a developer; it now forms part of an apartment building. The original pulpit and some pews can be seen in the Cole Harbour Meeting House. (early 20th century/Maurice Strum collection)

The Presbyterian Church on MacDonald's Hill on the Lawrencetown Road had been part of the community since 1840. Originally the Church of Scotland, it joined with other congregations in 1860 to form the Presbyterian Church of Nova Scotia. Later it became Calvin United. The building burned in 1965, and its replacement serves its congregation on the Lawrencetown Road west of the former location.

Woodlawn area Methodists were served by preachers from the Grace Methodist Church from 1856, until a church building was erected in

1884 on land donated by the children of Alexander Kuhn. By 1895, the Woodlawn church had 18 members plus 9 more on a trial basis. By the turn of the century, the membership had increased to 39.

In the Woodlawn Cemetery adjacent to the church rest Jane Elizabeth and Margaret, daughters of Mr. and Mrs. John Meagher of Lake Loon, whose tragic deaths at the ages of six and four, respectively, created one of the saddest chapters in the history of the area. In 1842, the girls were the subject of a week-long, wide-scale search in the nearby woods before their tiny, frail bodies were finally located near Lake Major.

Known locally as the "Babes in the Woods," their story has been the subject of numerous newspaper and magazine articles, pamphlets, poems, and songs over the years.

The two girls wandered into the woods near their father's farm on the warm sunny morning of April 11. Their father at the time was sick in bed with the measles, their mother was confined to her room with a newborn, and their older sister was busy with household chores. No one saw them enter the woods. When the children failed to return home by late in the afternoon, the family's hired hand immediately conducted a search deep into the woods at the end of the field but returned without finding them. John Meagher left his sickbed, and with the aid of his neighbours carrying flaming torches to light their way after nightfall, they tramped even farther into the forest, calling out the names of the two girls. Their search also ended in failure.

The next day hundreds of volunteers from Halifax and Dartmouth who heard the news of the lost children joined the search. Hope for finding the girls brightened when they found footprints in the snow and learned from a young man who lived on the opposite side of the lake that he thought he had heard children crying on the previous night. In the days following, the search party grew and the hunt intensified with neighbours, nearby farmers, soldiers and sailors, merchants, and professionals all joining in. However, the weather began to turn cold and hope of finding the children alive began to dwindle.

Halifax newspapers published appeals asking for every available man to gather in Dartmouth on Sunday April 17 to join the search.

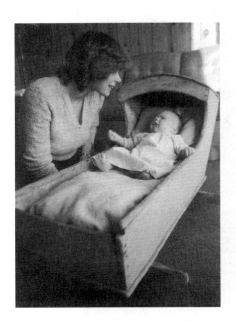

Sandra Glazebrook watches over her son Jamie resting in a cradle once used by the Babes in the Woods. Harry Elliot, who said its connection to the Meagher family was a story handed down in his family, donated the cradle to the Cole Harbour Heritage Farm Museum in 1980. (RE 1981/courtesy of the Glazebrook family)

Nearly 3,000 people turned out. At noon that day, the bodies of the two girls, locked in each other's arms, were found on a hill near the head of Lake Major. Margaret's face was pressed against the face of her older sister, Jane Elizabeth. Margaret's expression appeared calm, while Elizabeth's showed traces of fear and conveyed suffering from days of cold and hunger. Their arms were scratched, their dresses in tatters. The girls had wandered about six miles from their home.

The hero of the search was Rover, a shepherd dog. He sniffed the trail of the girls then ran up the side of the hill to the sheltered side of a boulder, where his barking alerted the searchers to his find. Searchers left the children undisturbed until their father was brought to the site to identify them. Members of the search party later took their bodies to the Meaghers' home.

The small bodies were placed in one coffin and buried in Woodlawn Cemetery. The five-pound reward, paid to Peter Currie, the owner of the dog, was returned to start a fund to buy a grave marker for the family. For months after the event, newspapers throughout North America reprinted Halifax newspapers' accounts of the tragedy.

16

A TEMPERATE ANCHOR

Cole Harbour, like most rural communities across Nova Scotia, was served by an active temperance society throughout most of the nineteenth century. Its success in fighting the "evil of drinking" rose and fell like the ocean's tides.

The temperance movement was born in puritan New England in 1813 as the Massachusetts Society for the Suppression of Intemperance. Two decades later the movement had a million members in 6,000 societies, and by 1827 it had spilled into Canada, eventually making its way to Nova Scotia. Historians generally agree that the movement was created to curb the excessive drinking of alcohol. Some historians insist that churches, particularly those with an evangelical bent, were the major influence behind the temperance movement. Others contend that it was the rising middle class, which deemed its future prospects might be threatened by widespread drunkenness. Still others suggest that the temperance movement was principally a social phenomenon that attracted young single men and women to meetings that often featured lectures, book discussions, poetry readings, and music.

It is easy to understand the need for temperance in the larger centres, particularly port cities, but in rural communities where farming was the principal occupation, the idea of a temperance movement seems almost paradoxical. Farmers were hard-working individuals, who generally rose at dawn to begin their daily chores, and they often didn't cease until early evening. Then it was to bed to rest for the next day. Even on Sunday, the daily regimen was only altered by attendance at a local church service with the family. Why then did the temperance movement take root in rural Nova Scotia in the early nineteenth century and continue into the twentieth century?

There are several answers. Rural communities were generally isolated, and boredom, sickness, and sometimes poverty were conditions some believed could be alleviated by liquor. Since there were few social functions and little entertainment, some residents turned to drink. Liquor was sometimes used as medicine either to cure or to prevent illness. In a province where there was often a shortage of cash, liquor was frequently used as payment for goods and services. Barn raisings and election campaigns were events commonly accompanied by drink.

One of the early preachers of the temperance gospel in the 1830s was Father Dennis Geary, pastor of St. Peter's Roman Catholic Church in Dartmouth. In a community where drinking establishments outnumbered any other single business and were open on Sundays, alcohol abuse was a serious problem for many members of his flock. Father Geary formed the St. Peter's Total Abstinence Society as one way to overcome this problem. Other groups in Dartmouth organized similar societies.

The various religious backgrounds and lifestyle of the Cole Harbour residents made them susceptible to the lure of temperance. Regular visits to the Halifax Market provided additional encouragement towards temperance.

Halifax in the 1800s was both a garrison town and a busy seaport, where off-duty soldiers stationed at the Citadel and visiting sailors and merchantmen found their chief source of entertainment in the bars and brothels. The city was notorious for the drinking that went on there. News of barroom brawls and public drunkenness often made its way to Cole Harbour.

The temperance movement in Cole Harbour began in the 1830s, although the exact date of the first temperance society is uncertain. Records indicate that in 1835 the Cole Harbour society was involved in a petition to the government for legislative changes concerning drinking. They were not demanding the prohibition of alcohol but stricter limitations on its licensing and sale. The petition requested that tavern-keepers be forced to charge higher prices for their drinks. It was felt that higher prices for alcohol might put it beyond the financial reach of many.

Andrew Shields, who owned and operated a carding mill and tavern in the Woodlawn area, was president of the society in 1835. In the early days of temperance societies, one could take a drink or own a tavern and still belong to a temperance society. It was only when local societies joined with the international temperance lodges that temperance came to mean total abstinence rather than moderation.

By 1854, the Cole Harbour women, in conjunction with the women of the nearby Dartmouth society, had joined forces to petition the provincial government to "prohibit forever the sale of intoxicating liquors." [9]

Early temperance societies in Canada and the United States were independent, organized by concerned individuals in the community and not allied with any larger group dedicated to the promotion of temperance. However, as the movement spread across the land, centralized "parent" organizations gradually developed. Grand Lodges such as the Independent Order of Good Templars (IOGT) and the Sons of Temperance were created, which changed the local temperance societies into highly structured and unified organizations.

The Sons of Temperance provided the main competition to the IOGT. Both arrived in Nova Scotia in 1847 and both were American in origin. The Sons of Temperance was by far the larger and more aggressive organization and was subdivided into other groups such as the Women's Christian Temperance Union and the Band of Hope for Children. Cole Harbour's independent temperance society joined with the IOGT and became Anchor Lodge No. 215. There are no records to indicate why Cole Harbour joined the IOGT and not the Sons of Temperance.

Although the IOGT were non-denominational, religion was an integral part of the order and consequently of the Anchor Lodge. The inherent religious overtones of the IOGT were identified in its general rule: "No person can be admitted to membership in the order unless he believes in Almighty God." [10] The organization considered itself a missionary society dedicated to spreading the temperance message. They advertised in newspapers, developed new temperance lodges, organized choirs, held public meetings, published various forms of temperance literature, hired lecturers, and pursued other avenues to increase membership.

Anchor Lodge members paid regular dues and were required to take a pledge to abstain from liquor and avoid contact with "the evil drug." The pledge simply stated: "No member shall make, buy, sell, use, furnish or cause to be furnished to others as a beverage any spirituous malt liquors, wine, or cider: and every member shall discountenance the manufacture, sale, and use thereof in all proper ways." The pledge meant that members must not drink at weddings, funerals, or other social occasions or use liquor or brandy in cooking.

At some point in the Anchor Lodge's history the members decided to build a lodge hall for weekly meetings and other social events. It's uncertain just when and how the hall was built. Shauna Whyte, in her honours thesis titled "The Anchor Lodge Temperance Society and Cole Harbour Community," states that "the lodge hall was used by the Anchor Lodge between 1882 and 1888. The building was centrally located in the community on Lodge Road (now Caldwell Road) and was probably erected over a period of time by the members themselves. Since most members were farmers many would have past experience and expertise in erecting barns and other buildings."

The lodge hall featured a large meeting room plus two anterooms. In addition to its use by the members, the hall was occasionally rented out to other organizations such as the Methodist Church and the Salvation Army. Money raised through renting went towards the hall's maintenance and upkeep.

The lodge met weekly, usually Tuesday evenings, except around the Christmas season when attendance tended to drop off. Between 1882 and 1888, Anchor Lodge met 192 times.

Membership in the IOGT was open to men and women of all races and each one was eligible for any office in the lodge. According to the 1881 census, all Anchor Lodge members were farmers, and all the women except one dressmaker had no declared trade or occupation. Two women were daughters of a brass founder, one was the daughter of a ship's captain, but almost all were daughters of farmers. Although Cole Harbour had a small Black population and nearby Preston had one of the largest Black populations in the province, there does not appear from past records or minute books to have been any Black members in the Anchor Lodge. The absence of Black members may have been due in part to the distance that Preston residents lived from the lodge hall.

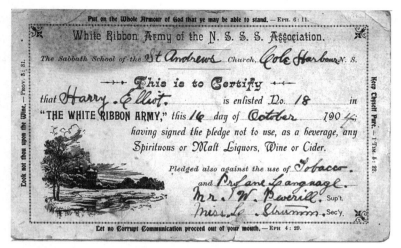

Pledge card for Harry Elliot for the White Ribbon Army of the Nova Scotia Sabbath School Association in 1904 attests that he promised not to use spirituous or malt liquors, wine, or cider. (Harry Elliot collection)

The average age of the Anchor Lodge members was 26. The majority of members were younger than 26, but a few members over age 65 raised the average level.

Women were by far the most vocal group in the lodge because they had more to lose through alcohol abuse than men. Inebriated husbands were more likely to beat their wives and children than sober ones. Excessive drinking by husbands often left women and children without sufficient money for clothing, food, and shelter. Drink frequently took men away from their work and their families. In the Anchor Lodge women represented only 30 per cent of the total membership. The lower membership was due to the fact that most lodge members were in their twenties, and most women that age were married with young children at home. Possibly their husbands attended meetings while the wives were left to look after the children.

Women were never elected to the highest executive positions within the lodge, such as the Worthy Chief Templar, the highest, or the Worthy Secretary. The highest post that women achieved was that of the Worthy Vice-Templar.

The Anchor Lodge, headquarters for the Temperance Society, sits atop the hill in the distance. In addition to the regular temperance meetings, the building was used for many years as a community centre for other meetings and social events, all of which alleviated the long, snowy winters. This photo was taken from the present site of the Cole Harbour Heritage Farm Museum, looking southeast. (ca. 1900/Melvin Harris album)

The latter part of the nineteenth century was a time of tremendous change, particularly regarding women's roles in society. In spite of women's lesser involvement relative to men in Cole Harbour, many scholars and historians believe that the larger temperance movement was the catalyst for the women's movement in the twentieth century.

Religious beliefs may have been the initial reason that many young men and women of Cole Harbour joined the temperance movement, but it did not inspire them to press for a change of alcohol consumption beyond the walls of the lodge hall. The Anchor Lodge became primarily a social organization. Cole Harbour lodge members were not rabid missionaries preaching the temperance gospel to the wider community. They were generally passive in their outlook and relied on other temperance societies around them to actively promote temperance in the broader community. They never initiated their own petitions but readily endorsed those circulated by other groups. Entertainment, including readings, songs, recitations, and discussion groups, was the main feature of the Anchor Lodge meetings.

Temperance societies across Canada were the driving force in bringing about the Temperance Act in 1878, which gave the cities and counties jurisdiction over the sale or prohibition of alcohol. A petition signed by 25 per cent of the electorate could bring about a plebiscite, and if the majority voted against the sale of liquor, the municipality became dry.

By the mid 1880s, attendance, membership, and general interest in the temperance movement had begun to wane in Cole Harbour. The movement had been around for half a century, and people were tiring of reading temperance newspapers, hearing lectures on temperance as well as Sunday church sermons on how people had destroyed themselves and others through excessive alcohol use. The Cole Harbour lodge became a social club that held three picnics during the summer and sleigh rides in the winter. Topics for speeches and discussions at weekly meetings were frequently on themes unrelated to temperance.

Although the Anchor Lodge's prime function was to bind its members to their personal pledge of total abstinence, the lodge was sometimes a source of friction and discord within the community. Antagonism often developed within the organization because members were required to report other members who violated their pledge by drinking. Tension also existed between those who drank at one time and those who never drank.

During a six-year period between 1882 and 1888, Cole Harbour temperance society had a membership of 114, which represented a considerable percentage of the population. Attendance peaked in 1884 then began to decline. After 1884, resignations, suspensions, and expulsions began to increase. By 1887, meetings were sporadic.

Between 1882 and 1888, 52 members left the lodge: 29 men and 11 women were suspended for non-payment of dues; 8 men and 3 women resigned; and 1 man was expelled for violating his pledge. Members who left the organization constituted a "who's who" of Cole Harbour families: Bell, Beck, Bissett, Morash, Kuhn, Settle, Turner, Eisener, and Farquharson. Members devoted to the society like secretaries Justus Morash and Andrew Turner admitted to having broken their pledges.

Although the lodge drastically declined in 1887, it did not die out. The next year it bounced back with a new lodge number, new members, and a new executive.

There are documents suggesting that the temperance society continued until 1895 and beyond. The late Ira Settle, who was born in the first decade of the twentieth century, remembered attending meetings at the lodge with his father in his early years.

The Anchor Lodge successfully provided some members with tools useful in other endeavours, teaching them parliamentary procedure and organizational skills. Members of Anchor Lodge were active in establishing other societies and institutions in the community.

Several members of the lodge were active in building churches and organizing Sunday schools in Cole Harbour. Andrew Turner became the first superintendent of the Methodist Church in 1884. Justus Morash, another active lodge member, was the first superintendent of St. Andrew's Anglican Church in the 1880s. Other members – Joseph Giles, George Bell, and George Morash – became officers and board members in various church societies. Some of the female lodge members were influential in establishing the Women's Missionary Society in 1890.

Several lodge members were involved in the formation of the Dartmouth Agricultural Society on June 28, 1880, and they served on its executive committee. The Agricultural Society, which was not open to women, was formed for the improvement of horticulture, agriculture, stock, farm management, and rural economy in the district. This organization, unlike the temperance society, did not have its own meeting hall but met in schools, members' houses, and other meeting halls, including the Anchor Lodge. The Agricultural Society continued as an active community group until the early twentieth century. The society had 66 members in 1881. Membership peaked at 118 by 1884 and then declined to a low of 40 from 1895 to 1905.

The temperance society in the Cole Harbour community kept the demon rum from the doors of most homes. It not only curbed alcohol abuse among its members, but it changed the overall attitude towards drink, making it socially unacceptable. Temperance societies remained active in the early twentieth century and were largely responsible for bringing in prohibition during World War One and having it continue until the close of the 1920s. When Prohibition ended, interest in the temperance movement generally declined both provincially and nationally.

17

DYKING THE HARBOUR

Reclaiming land from the sea by building dykes was a centuries old practice. The Low Countries of Europe employed dykes to successfully reclaim large tracts of irrigable land from the sea. The Acadians in the Annapolis Valley reclaimed large areas of land by dyking sections of the Minas Basin as well as other areas of the province.

To the farmers challenged by the rugged landscape around the Cole Harbour, the nearby marshes proffered a tempting invitation. The marsh hay, although inferior, was suitable as winter fodder for the cattle.

The first Bissett in the area, Jean George Bissett, had strongly opposed the idea of reclaiming the land. He was the first to cut hay on the marshes near his home, and upon hearing talk of dyking the harbour he had petitioned the government in 1826 to grant him permanent use of the marsh product for 30 years. His petition wasn't granted as others in the area also received small grants of several acres each.

Reclaiming land by building a dyke across the harbour's mouth had been an idea among several farmers for years before it blossomed into a plan. In 1842, Jean George Bissett's great-grandson John George chaired the first meeting to plan the dyking of the harbour.

On Wednesday, September 21, 32 farmers in the area gathered at Mrs. Lawlor's home at the bottom of Long Hill to form a company and raise whatever capital was necessary to develop a suitable plan for dyking the mouth of the harbour. Margaret Kuhn Campbell in her book *A Tale of Two Dykes* writes, "[T]hirty-two at the meeting would tax Mrs. Lawlor's accommodations to the utmost and the grassy slopes between the house and the road would be filled with horse-drawn vehicles. Doubtless many walked. It was a well-espoused cause with signatories from Lawrencetown to the centre of Cole Harbour." (Margaret Kuhn Campbell's father, Peter McNab Kuhn, was a later owner of the dyke property.) At the first meeting, George Bissett was elected chair and surveyor John Chamberlain was elected clerk. The company was called Cole Harbour Dyke Company, and the members agreed to raise £5,000 divided into 400 shares, which could be paid in cash, guaranteed labour, or a combination of both.

John Chamberlain, the leading investor, developed a set of company bylaws and he agreed to buy the balance of any shares not sold. The meeting approved the bylaws unanimously and the decision was made to build a dyke across the mouth of the harbour. Those attending the meeting were George Bissett Sr., John Robertson, Thomas Conrad Sr., John Bissett Sr., Henry Sellers, William Lawlor, John Gammon Sr., Charles Bissett, Alex Bissett, William Gammon, Robert Turner Sr., J. F. Bissett, James Lawlor, Henry Lawlor, William Turner, Daniel Turner, Robert Turner Jr., J. G. Beck, Robert Settle, Phillip Morash, George Morash, William Bissett, Samuel Bissett, Hector Elliott, Thomas Conrad Jr., James Robertson, Francis Bissett, John Knock, Joseph Giles, Joseph Bissett Jr., John Settle, and George Gammon.

The next three years were spent developing the plans. Finally, on March 28, 1845, the Nova Scotia legislature passed, "an Act to Incorporate the Cole Harbour Dyke Company" [11] with 15 men named in the act to represent all the shareholders. The company had to wait another year for the act to be ratified by Queen Victoria in London before the work could proceed. Additional construction time was lost as the initial plans were changed to include a bridge across the top of the dyke.

The bridge was considered a necessity for West Lawrencetown residents who would save time and mileage travelling to Dartmouth by avoiding the 12- to 13-mile trip around the head of the harbour. With a bridge at the harbour mouth connecting to Bissett Road, Lawrencetown residents could travel through Cole Harbour to Dartmouth. Previously a ferry had transported Lawrencetown residents across the harbour to Bissett Road, but the service had long since ceased.

This dyke with a bridge for pedestrians and horse-drawn wagons was never completed. Kuhn Campbell wrote in *A Tale of Two Dykes*,

Lawlor House was the site of the original meeting to plan the construction of a dyke across the mouth of Cole Harbour in 1842. It was believed that the Maroons built Lawlor House, at the bottom of Long Hill, during their sojourn in the area, 1796–1800. L. B. Jensen, artist who drew Lawlor House and other Cole Harbour historic scenes, is the person in the photo. (RE 1976)

"The hopes, dreams, and plans of five years, along with the investment of labour and capital collapsed into the sea." Regrettably no records exist to indicate exactly what happened, only that the first attempt to dyke the harbour ended in failure.

According to Mary Lawson's *History of the Townships of Dartmouth, Preston, and Lawrencetown*, "a great deal of money has been expended at Cole Harbour in an endeavor [*sic*] to dyke a portion of the low harbour. Several unsuccessful attempts having been made, the work was at last thought to be perfect, but the sea rushed in and the whole undertaking ruined."

Three decades elapsed before a new generation of men far removed from the farmlands of Cole Harbour decided to dyke the mouth of the harbour. The three men were James Van Buskirk, a land surveyor from Dartmouth; John Watson, a civil engineer based in London, England; and Thomas Watson, a mining engineer in Whitby, Yorkshire, England. These men were given a grant of what seemed to be the whole of Cole Harbour. This time there was no delay pending the approval of the Queen. The Provincial Secretary on behalf of the Queen and her representative in Nova Scotia signed the grant on July 14, 1870. The deed simply reads, "five thousand acres of land and land under water."

According to Margaret Kuhn Campbell's account of the dyke story, "the people around the shore all signed away their rights. The written agreement must have been an act of cooperation [sic] on the part of the landowners to ensure them a share of the outcome, as terms were set in the deed to secure them this right." The deed gave owners of the land abutting the shore one acre of reclaimed land for every 10 acres of their own; this at the price of $30 an acre not to exceed 10 acres to any one individual.

Other conditions of the grant stated that work on the dyke must start within two years and be completed within five, and it must include a road across the top of the dyke. The roadway added to the earlier plan was also incorporated in the new plan, only now the route to Dartmouth lay through Cow Bay and Eastern Passage not Bissett Road and Cole Harbour.

Within a month and six days after the necessary paperwork was completed, the three partners sold the entire land grant and all the conditions attached to Henry Ramsay Taylor for £500. Three months later, Taylor, in turn, sold the entire land package to John Watson, one of the three earlier partners. Ten days later, Watson moved to Cole Harbour and transferred the deed to a joint company named the Cole Harbour Land Company.

Work on the dyke began in the spring of 1877 with a sizeable outlay of capital and manpower. The mouth of the harbour where the tide rolled in was closed to a more bridgeable opening by a causeway from the Cole Harbour shore. The heavy fill needed for the causeway was carried and dumped in place using a small gauge railway.

The dyke consisted of four sets of sluice gates to control the tides, each separated by three central bridge-supporting piers. These piers were timbered to an elevation well above the high-water mark and topped with log cribs filled with rocks. The gates, which swung out at the falling tide and closed when the tide rose, measured 8½ feet wide and 6 inches thick. The piers featured ice deflectors on both the upstream and downstream sides. These blunt-ended triangles were pointed towards the stream to deflect the ice floes and facilitate water flow. The roadway across the top of dyke was 12 feet wide.

The impossible had finally been achieved – the western entrance to the harbour had been dyked and the smaller eastern opening was closed with a dirt and rock dam strengthened with trees and branches. However, in the course of construction several workers had been sucked out to sea and drowned in the struggle to control the powerful current.

During two years of construction, the Cole Harbour Land Company had also built a colony of farm buildings at the tip of Flying Point, the main peninsula jutting into the harbour, and constructed a 1½-mile road over the point to allow work horses, oxen, and grazing animals access to the marshes.

The dyke and its roadway were completed within the two-year period, but the financial solvency of the company was in ruin. Before

Looking east across Cole Harbour salt marsh. The dyke was located at the mouth of the harbour, at the far right of this photo. (RE 1980s)

the dyke could be put to use the Land Company went bankrupt. John Watson, who remained in Cole Harbour for a time after the company went bankrupt, had proved more zealous than prudent by overspending on the project. He had provided well for his workers and had built the dyke with quality material and workmanship.

The Supreme Court of Nova Scotia awarded two creditors Mather B. Almon and James C. MacIntosh, both of Halifax, claims that with court costs amounted to $10,469. Since the company was unable to pay the debt, the entire property was put up for sale.

The High Sheriff of Halifax County sold the property on April 25, 1879, to Alexander Ramsay for $16,300. *[text resumes page 132]*

Squire John George Bissett managed the Cole Harbour dyke lands for Eliza Inez Crawley of London, England, from 1879 until 1891. He was first president of the Dartmouth Agricultural Society and represented the Cole Harbour area on County Council from 1882 to 1898. (RE/prob. 1890s, courtesy of Mrs. Lutz)

Peter McNab Kuhn was the owner and operator of the Cole Harbour dyke from 1891 until its demise in the spring of 1917. (RE/ca. 1880, Margaret Kuhn Campbell album)

MIDDLE AND LATE 1800S

Kuhn's cattle graze on the dyked land of Cole Harbour in the early 1900s. (RE/Wilfred Bissett album)

Jack Settle mows hay on the dyked land in the early twentieth century. (RE/Roy Settle album)

Map 5, early 20th century

This chart shows Cole Harbour before the railway was constructed in 1916. The dyke is in place and faces the full force of twice-daily tides and ocean storms. The barrier beach on the eastern side of the harbour entrance is continuous with Strawberry Island in the middle. Today, the Dartmouth Trap & Skeet Club is located on the northern end of this island.

The road from West Lawrencetown runs over part of the marsh, the beach and the dyke to connect with Cow Bay and thence, by either Eastern Passage or Cole Harbour to Dartmouth. Maintenance of the dyke would include the upkeep of the barrier beach that protected the marsh behind it.

The western side of the harbour entrance has been extended by a causeway to narrow the gap to a reasonable length for a dyke. This area, known today as Cole Harbour Dyke, is the site of several permanent homes. Traces of the road that linked the two sides of the harbour mouth are still visible at Rainbow Haven Beach.

The road along the western side of Flying Point (top centre) came from Upper Lawrencetown and was used to reach the dyked marshland. At high tide parts of this road were often under water.

This chart shows buildings at the tip of Flying Point. These were the houses and farm buildings built by the Cole Harbour Land Company before the property was taken over by Peter McNab Kuhn. For years the company employed a farm manager, Henry Jacob Conrad, who maintained the dyke and worked the dykeland. Henry married Margaret Bissett while living on Flying Point, and four children were born there. Already abandoned by the time this chart was made, these buildings have almost totally disappeared today – only a few scant remains of foundations and a large, stone-lined well are distinguishable amongst the undergrowth.

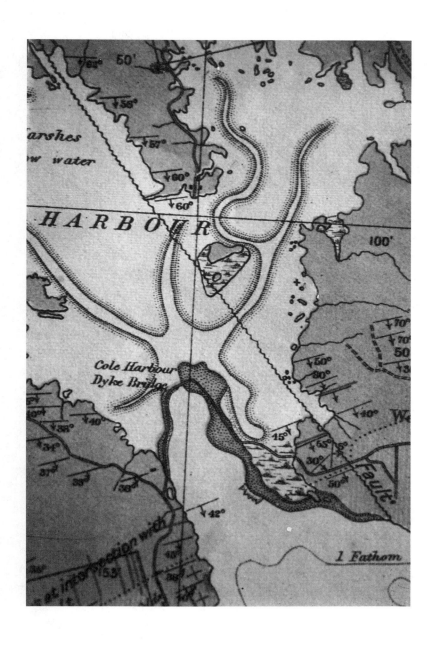

Four days later Ramsay transferred the title and all the original conditions to George Baden Crawley of London, England. Crawley died within two years and left the property to his wife Eliza Inez, who operated the dyke for 12 years under the local management of Squire John George Bissett, a great-grandson of the first George Bissett to occupy the family lands on the western shore. His title of squire was due to his membership on the first County Council, the seats of which went to those with the largest land holdings. Bissett operated out of his home on the western shore and hired as head farmer and practical manager, Henry Jacob Conrad.

One resident recalled that root crops were grown on the reclaimed land in the early years of the dyke. Others dispute this, saying that drainage of the harbour from the gate system was less than satisfactory, and five or six inches of salt water always seeped into the harbour inside the dyke. The salt water precluded the growing of tender vegetables.

Eliza Inez Crawley married a British naval officer, John Elliott Pringle, on September 21, 1891. She sold the dyke property and deed copied from the original land grant to Peter McNab Kuhn. Peter McNab Kuhn's great-grandfather Henry Kuhn is believed to have come from the Canton of Zurich, Switzerland. His mother was a Bissett.

Kuhn sold the family farm in Woodlawn and purchased from the Pringles the Robertson homestead at the head of the eastern arm of Cole Harbour, where he moved his family. The property included about 500 acres of woodland on Flying Point, a few cleared fields, a farmhouse, and a barn. The accessory to the Robertson place was the additional 5,000 acres that included all of Cole Harbour. The harbour and its marshes extended for more than two miles from the house to the dyke gates. The nearest neighbour was a mile away; there were no shops or schools nearby. Kuhn remained there for the next 31 years. According to her book, *A Tale of Two Dykes,* Margaret Kuhn Campbell is uncertain how much her father paid for the two properties. For one or the other or both he paid $8,000.

Several years before she sold her property, Elizabeth Inez Pringle had started the transfer provided for in the original deed to those with land abutting the marshes, who were entitled to up to 10 acres each of the reclaimed land. She sold three 10-acre lots of marsh to

John Bissett in 1887. Other sales were 5 acres to Enos Conrad in two pieces and 5 acres to John Morash. Each of the purchasers paid Mrs. Pringle the designated price of $30 per acre.

For the next 26 years, Peter McNab Kuhn raised beef cattle on the marshes. The various species of grass supplied feed to help them grow. Seventy-five tons of hay and 80 head of cattle are mentioned for one summer's production. Cranberries were another crop harvested from the reclaimed marshland. Farmers from as far away as Chezzetcook came regularly to the marsh to buy fodder for their livestock. They bought the hay standing, and cut and stacked it in the summer. When the harbour froze over in the winter, they returned over the ice to haul it home on sleds. Horse-drawn mowers often cut the hay, but the farmers who came from far away brought only their scythes.

18

COUNTY POOR FARM

In the early 1880s, the Municipal Council of Halifax County was faced with escalating welfare costs. By 1886, the County Council decided that the creation of a Poor Farm somewhere in the county would reduce expense and improve efficiency in providing shelter and proper care for the mentally challenged, the aged and the homeless poor of the county.

Council appointed a special Committee on the Poor to consider the feasibility of creating such an institution. Members of the Poor Committee were County Councillors Donald McLaren as chair, Dennis Deloughry, Alex W. Smith, George J. Longard, and John Hayes. The Committee on Public Property was asked to examine suitable locations for such a facility and make the necessary recommendation. The Committee on the Poor, reporting at the annual meeting of the council in 1886, stated, "If such an institution was procured for the county and properly managed it would in a great measure relieve the taxpayers of much of the present expenses and would also be the means of cheering up the spirits of the very often depressed and suffering poor."

The residents were called collectively "the poor" and thus, the new institution, "the Poor's Farm,"; but it soon became better known as the Poor Farm. Before the creation of the Poor Farm in Cole Harbour, Halifax County had sent its "paupers" and the "harmless insane" to the Mount Hope Asylum in Dartmouth, for which the county paid three dollars a week for each patient. There were frequent disputes with the asylum's administration as to whether or not certain inmates were a proper charge to the taxpayers of the county.

The committee recommended that the council ask the Nova Scotia legislature to pass an act authorizing the county to borrow money to purchase a poor farm and erect the necessary buildings to contain the poor of each district. County Clerk W. H. Wiswell prepared a bill for the Nova Scotia legislature to purchase, equip, and manage a poor farm. The bill also asked for authority to borrow $6,000, which would be repaid in yearly instalments over the next eight years.

After examining several properties, the Committee on Public Property reported that a tract on Bedford Basin, later occupied by the Bedford Ammunition Depot, was considered the most desirable. However, the conditions of the title were so complicated that it was ruled out. The next best property was in Cole Harbour, a little more than six miles from Dartmouth, in District 31.

Harriet Roche owned the land, 300 acres in total. She was the widow of Michael Roche, a master mariner and farmer from Canso, Guysborough County. Michael Roche and his wife had purchased the land in 1846 from Joseph and Catherine Bissett of Cole Harbour. The county subsequently purchased the land for $1,730 on July 31, 1886. Several acres of land were already cultivated and the remainder was heavily wooded with "fine hardwood suitable for fuel." Hay on the land, which was cut and stored in the existing barn and other areas of the property was estimated at 8 to 10 tons.

Plans to establish the Poor Farm in Cole Harbour met strong opposition within both the council and the community. County Council sessions saw considerable discussion, and often heated debate, concerning the location, operating cost, and the proposed buildings for the farm. The three Cole Harbour districts - 28, 29, and 31 – sent petitions opposing the creation of a Poor Farm to council meetings.

When the Committee on Public Property report concerning the purchase of the land for the Poor Farm was finally put to a vote, it passed by the slim margin of 14 to 12. The council also voted to make the Committee on Public Property responsible for the operation and management of the institution.

County Clerk Wiswell advertised in the local newspapers on December 21, 1886, calling for tenders to build a "Poor's Asylum" in Cole Harbour to close on Saturday morning, January 8, 1887, at ten o'clock. Six contractors replied:

> M. E. Keefe Contractor, Quinpool, Halifax - $4,363
> P. Fahey, Gottingen Street, Halifax - $4,488
> Johnston and Caldwell - $4,950
> Eli Evans - $4,320
> John Wilson, Upper Water Street, Halifax - $4,250
> John Myrer, Dartmouth - $5,800

John Wilson's bid, which was the lowest, was accepted.

The Poor Farm initially consisted of three two-storey buildings each 80 feet by 33 feet, each with a finished basement. The basement contained the kitchen, dining areas, baths, and storage facilities for vegetables. The chimneys were brick and the buildings were heated by wood. The first floor contained the reception area, day rooms, keeper's office, and sleeping area. The top floor contained mostly bedrooms. All three buildings were connected by covered walkways.

Construction began almost immediately with completion and occupancy scheduled for not later than September 15, 1887. As the work progressed, the Committee on Public Property members discovered that the cost of the buildings, grounds, and incidental expenses absorbed the full amount of the $6,000 raised through the debenture. When it was time to formally take over the buildings, the committee was without funds to furnish and equip the institution.

The committee hired James Turner of Cole Harbour as the Farmkeeper (a title that was later changed to Superintendent) and his wife

The County Poor Farm opened on the shore of Cole Harbour to care for the mentally challenged and the homeless poor of Halifax County. The farm initially consisted of three residences. As the population at the farm grew, it was expanded to five buildings, which were all connected with walkways. (date unknown/Album 994.01)

as the Matron at the annual total salary of $300. James Turner was a descendant of one of the early Cole Harbour families. He took partial charge of the facility on September 15 and full charge on October 6, when he received the keys. When he took over the buildings he discovered that the kitchen and dining areas were without closets and sideboards. He built two dining tables 15 feet by 3½ feet as well as a pantry closet with the necessary shelving.

In 1887, the Poor Farm's first year of operation, two males were admitted. The following year the population increased to 22 inmates, 11 men and 11 women. Most of the arrivals had been transferred from the Mount Hope Asylum. The committee enclosed an open space on the property with a high fence to allow patients to enjoy the outdoors without the risk of their escaping or straying off the property. An old house on the site doubled as a wash house and shed for tools and other equipment.

In 1889, the farm population almost doubled to a total of 38 patients, 20 men and 18 women. The visiting physician's report to council in the same year called attention to the crowded conditions at the farm and the necessity for increased accommodations.

Architect H. B. Fellon was hired to provide an estimate for the construction of two additional buildings. His estimate for two buildings, including heating facilities, was $3,000.

Speaking during the semi-annual meeting of the County Council on April 15, 1890, the warden said, "[T]he legislation to increase the accommodation at the Poor Farm has been granted and I trust that the committee in charge of that institution will lose no time in doing everything necessary to make it equal to the requirements of the county." [12]

The Committee on Public Property report later that year stated:

> [T]he new wings authorized by the council in 1890 have been completed and are ready for occupancy. We may also state that the two new buildings have been constructed with special reference to occupancy by the insane, which are not only better adapted to their needs than the other buildings were, but will separate and relieve the sane poor from the annoyances [to which] they have been subjected in the past. Owing to the present number of inmates and the anticipated increase it was found that the ovens and kitchen room were not equal to the demand on them and it was deemed advisable to enlarge them before additional inmates arrive from the asylum. [13]

A building to be used as a stable and shed for wagons and tools had been built. The Farm population increased marginally in 1890 from 38 to 41, but in 1891 the population jumped to 58. County officials estimated that in 1891, when the new buildings were occupied, $1,000 to $1,200 was saved annually over the cost of keeping the insane at Mount Hope Asylum.

During 1891, Superintendent Turner informed the council of more construction: a storehouse measuring 14 feet by 8 feet for provisions and a dead house 10 feet by 6 feet. The latter was used to hold deceased patients until families claimed them or until buried on the farm property. Some bodies were held throughout the winter, when burial was impossible due to the snow and frost. Turner also mentioned at this time that the old barn needed thorough repair or replacement.

In his report for the year ending in 1892, Turner stated, "[T]he past year had been a success in respect to crops and farm labour. The hay crop had been in advance of the previous year. The potato crop had been exceedingly good both in quality and quantity. Turnips, cabbage, peas and beans give no reason for complaint. The farm has been very much improved by breaking 1 and 3/4 acres of very stony ground also digging 30 rods of drain four feet deep, three feet wide at the top and two feet in the bottom."

The staff at the farm consisted of two men and three women: Hugh Morash was

Eunice and James Turner, the first matron and superintendent of the Poor Farm. (photographers and dates unknown/courtesy of Shirley Turner)

paid $15 per month; Andrew McDonald, keeper of the insane, $15 per month; Florence Turner as seamstress, $7 per month; Clara Turner in charge of the kitchen, $6 a month; and Ann Booth, kitchen help, $3 per month. Many of the male inmates who were able worked as farmhands. Female patients were often assigned domestic chores.

The stock on hand consisted of a horse, four cows, two pigs, and one steer for beef. The farm also produced 300 bushels of potatoes, 110 bushels of turnips, 5 bushels of beets, 8 bushels of carrots, peas, beans, onions, cucumbers, and cabbage plus about 8 tons of good upland hay.

In 1894, the farm population totalled 69 patients, of which 49 were men and 20 were women. The interiors of the buildings were repainted and the hallways were wall papered. The amount of cultivated ground was extended that year.

According to the superintendent's report for 1895, the population at the farm increased to 71, consisting of 32 adult males, 31 adult females, and 8 children – 4 boys and 4 girls. The children's ages were not mentioned. Turner's report boasted a substantial increase in the produce harvest over the previous year.

Most of the produce and food produced by the farm was consumed by the patients. Any surplus was sold to markets in Halifax and Dartmouth, and the revenue went back into the operation of the farm.

The farm doctor, N. F. Cunningham, reported in 1895 that there was less sickness than the previous year. He did state that an epidemic of measles had visited the Poor Farm during the autumn months, but the cases were mild and there were no ill results. He reported that the wards and sleeping apartments were always clean, warm, and well ventilated. He concluded his report by stating that a visit to the institution would convince anyone that the poor of Halifax County were well clothed, well fed, and well cared for generally.

Most of the residents living at the County Poor Farm had been transferred from the Mount Hope Asylum (later renamed the Nova Scotia Hospital). Family and relatives committed others. Still others were taken to the facility when found wandering the streets, as in the case of an elderly East Dover woman found in Dartmouth. She was cared for until relatives were located and came to get her.

The Municipality of Halifax County was divided into districts, and when a district sent one a residents to the Poor Farm there was a charge back to the taxpayers of that district toward that patient's upkeep.

The *Atlantic Weekly* newspaper published an account of the Christmas celebration at the Poor Farm in 1896.

> Through the kindness of friends, the superintendent, and matron, the inmates of this institution were able to celebrate this festival season in a true homelike way. Christmas day was Christmas indeed. The managing committee of the County Council placed funds at the disposal of Keeper Turner to provide goose, roast beef, plum pudding and all other requisites for a big old fashion *[sic]* Christmas dinner.
>
> To this the inmates composed of the poor who are practically helpless, harmless insane, and a few others did ample justice.
>
> On Wednesday evening, the Christmas tree, which had been provided by the generosity of friends was duly picked and the contents distributed. Captain Graham extended an invitation to a representative of the *Atlantic Weekly* to drive down with him, which was gladly accepted. Everything around the institution is in first-class order. The inmates or such as were capable came to the assembly room to take part in the event. The tree, gigantic in its proportions, had several things for everyone in the Farm: fruit, confectionary, nuts, and some useful articles were passed out.
>
> Councillor Bissett presided. Quite a number of persons interested were present. John Settle was present and took an active part in helping. Many a joyful face was seen as the tree was stripped. It is impossible not to think of the wonderful change, which has taken place in recent years. Now the poor and helpless of all classes are cared for and cared for well. In former days they were left to die or farmed out to the lowest bidder.

> Mr. Turner, the popular manager, and his capable wife deserve the good will of all who are interested in this very necessary institution. They are most valuable persons doing everything possible to make happy the lives of these poor unfortunates. They desire to thank the various donors especially the King's Daughters who sent 70 parcels of Christmas treats, one to each. To J. W. Allison, C. H. Harvey, John Black, Captain Graham for boxes for the tree. Captain Graham, in addition had seven dollars handed over to him by various parties for the same purpose. The evening closed by all present singing "God Save the Queen."

Reporting in 1897 for the previous year, the superintendent stated there were 68 patients, of which 7 were children. A total of 41 were admitted during the year, 14 were discharged, and there were 7 deaths. An acre of uncultivated land was put under crop; a root house was built with an ice house connected to help preserve meat and milk during the summer. The produce harvested on the farm that year did not compare favourably with other years due to bad weather.

In 1899 the Committee on Public Property suggested that Superintendent Turner hand in his resignation due to his advanced age and partial incapacity through sickness. The resignation was to take effect May 1 and applications were immediately accepted for his replacement.

Before James Turner's resignation could take effect, his death was reported in the *Atlantic Weekly* on April 22.

> James Turner, the well-known keeper of the Cole Harbour Poor Farm, and one of the most highly respected residents of East Halifax, died at Cole Harbour at an early hour Tuesday morning. The deceased was appointed keeper of the farm when it was first opened and during the time it was under his care the institution was well conducted. Unfounded charges were made against Mr. Turner on several occasions, but after an investigation they were unsupported by any evidence.

Finally Mr. Turner's resignation was called for on some slight pretext and he was to have left his position May 1. Mr. Turner had been ill for some time previous to his death but his disposition was not viewed in a serious light. The many friends of the deceased will learn with regret of the demise of one who was always so courteous and obliging to those who came in contact with him. Funeral took place on Thursday and was very largely attended.

Although the advertisement for Turner's replacement drew a large response, about two-thirds of the applicants were either unqualified or unfit for the position. The committee eventually hired J. M. Henneberry as the new superintendent of the Poor Farm.

In the year Henneberry was hired, the council also adopted a new set of bylaws and rules to guide the management of the County Poor Farm into the new century. In spite of early opposition, the farm complex of buildings that now overlooked the harbour would remain part of the community's landscape for the balance of the nineteenth century and all of the next century.

19

GOODBYE NINETEENTH CENTURY

During the nineteenth century, science and technology led to new inventions that brought the world and the people closer together via modes of transportation and communication and made life generally more comfortable. However, the century was marred by continual war and uprisings, resulting in death and destruction in locales around the globe.

Great Britain, ruled by the popular but austere Queen Victoria, expanded her empire through industrial growth and by flexing her military muscle around most of the world. The century opened with Britain and Napoleon at war. The French Emperor was defeated at

Waterloo in 1815 and exiled to the Island of St. Helena. While wars raged with France, Britain also took up arms against the United Sates in 1812. The Americans themselves engaged in a bloody and costly civil war from 1861 to 1865 as well as wars with Mexico and Spain. Before the century ended, Britain was involved in wars in Afghanistan, the Sudan, the Crimea, and South Africa.

In spite of the wars, numerous advancements in science brought vast changes in transportation, communication, agriculture, medicine, as well as in everyday life. James Watt's improvements to the steam engine in the eighteenth century were being employed to propel ships throughout inland waterways as well as across oceans. Although sailing vessels were still in use, the days of sail were numbered. Steamships were making ocean travel faster and considerably more comfortable than the ships that brought the early settlers to Nova Scotia. Steam engines were adapted to locomotives, and railways suddenly made land travel faster, safer, and more comfortable than it had been by horse and wagon.

Thomas Edison's invention, the incandescent light bulb, was lighting the homes and streets of North America, making them brighter and safer and ending the use, for the most part, of smoky, smelly kerosene lamps and candles. Alexander Graham Bell's new telephone had a significant impact on communications within communities, while Guglielmo Marconi's wireless signals, across first the English Channel and later the Atlantic Ocean, seemed to narrow the distance between nations. Advances in medical science led to cures for diseases, improved hospital care and surgical techniques. Anaesthetics revolutionized surgery. New machinery to assist farmers in planting and harvesting were developed along with such household items as pasteurized milk, canned foods, and sewing machines. The industrial age was spawning new foundries and factories, generating more employment opportunities. Population growth in towns and cities brought with it a host of new social and environmental problems.

In 1867, Confederation united Nova Scotia, Ontario, Quebec, and New Brunswick as a new independent country-Canada-within the British Empire. The confederation issue tore the province of Nova Scotia apart for several years with heated and bitter exchanges on both sides of the debate before it was finally resolved. Before the century ended, new provinces joined the confederation-British Columbia, Manitoba, and Prince Edward Island-and the young nation began to take shape.

Halifax and Dartmouth, the largest population centres in Nova Scotia, were starting to be serviced by many of the new inventions of the century. By the 1890s, electricity was lighting streets and homes. The railway joined both communities to the rest of the nation. Halifax Harbour was regularly visited by transatlantic steamships bringing passengers and cargo from all parts of the world and taking locally produced goods to European and American destinations. Homes and businesses in Halifax and Dartmouth were connecting to water and sewer systems. Pavement was appearing on city and town streets, eliminating mud and dust.

But for the farm families living in Cole Harbour and the surrounding area, life in the closing decades of the nineteenth century hadn't changed much from life at the start of the century. The population had grown; new farms appeared in the area through marriage and new arrivals. The prevalent family names were pretty much the same: Giles, Settle, Bissett, Bell, Kuhn, Morash, Conrad, Gammon, and Turner. Many of the technological advances and inventions that were being used in nearby Dartmouth had yet to appear in the rural area, where families still hauled their drinking and wash water in a bucket from the well and used outdoor privies. Kerosene lamps and candles were still the principal source of light when the sun went down. There were no telephones or telegraphs, and the railway was still almost three decades away. Horse or ox teams carried out the spring plowing and transported the produce to market.

However, as the century unfolded and the population grew, institutions and infrastructures were added to the area – churches, schools, improved roads, the dyking of Cole Harbour. Churches nourished the spiritual and much of the social life of the community, along with a very active temperance lodge.

Rather than automobiles travelling the roads, runaway horses and carriages seemed to have been a fairly common hazard in the area, according to reports in the local newspapers. In August 1884, the *At-*

lantic Weekly reported that "a gentleman and two ladies were driving on the Cole Harbour Road recently [and] went into a house for refreshments. While within, the horse took flight and ran away and was not captured until after a long and exciting chase by the three persons who found him entangled in the bushes somewhat injured and the wagon completely wrecked."

In November 1899, the *Dartmouth Times* reported a similar occurrence. "While Mr. Arthur Giles and some friends were driving near M. Worral's Sunday evening, the horse took flight and jumped over a low stone fence beside the road. The horse was soon caught, but the buggy was badly damaged."

Local Dartmouth newspapers devoted considerable space to the activities and life in communities beyond the town boundaries. The *Dartmouth Times* on November 3, 1883, presented this somewhat florid account of life in Cole Harbour.

> One of the earliest efforts of settlement outside Dartmouth was on the shores of this pleasant basin and beyond near the extensive salt marshes of Lawrencetown. The Germans with an eye to the practical and valuable nestled in these nooks and corners of nature and their descendants are today enjoying the advantages of a quiet prosperity. The names and speech of Morehash [*sic*], Mosher, Conrod, and Hiltz speak well for the place and its stability. Cole Harbour is a large, landlocked, shallow basin.
>
> At its mouth so near do the Cow Bay and Lawrencetown sand beaches approach each other that the feasibility of bridging the narrow part was apparent, and a few years ago an English Company was formed to build a dyke and reclaim the cultivated land enclosed in the basin. Upland was purchased, farmhouses erected, plows and utensils sent out from England and a small beginning made of farming on a large scale. After the expenditure of nearly a hundred thousand dollars the dyke was completed but proved ineffectual in draining

the basin. The water in the harbour does not now rise and fall with the tide and it cannot be reduced to low tide level, which would leave most of the bottom bare. As it is, scarcely an acre has been rescued from the sea and made fit to produce anything but the coarsest grass. A further effort is necessary to reduce the water to lowest level and then the experiment can be tried in earnest of making Cole Harbour an assemblage of flourishing farms.

The dyke has proved a benefit by being utilized for a roadway to and from Lawrencetown and the drives to Cole Harbour. Lawrencetown is one of the most pleasant of the many delightful jaunts near the capital. The trout fishing at Cole Harbour has been much improved and city sports patronize this locality with a success that is frequently heralded in the City Press.

The farms around the harbour are extensive; market farming is extensively followed and most of the residents look to Dartmouth and Halifax as the places of sale, though considerable of the farm product has in the last few years found a ready market in Newfoundland.

Little Salmon River flows into the harbour, the fishing in which up to its source in the Lake delights the followers of old Isaac [sic] Walton. The old road to Cole Harbour passes from Dartmouth over a succession of hills steep enough to gratify the most fastidious. The difficulties of teaming over these hills caused a new road to be cut almost level branching from the Preston Road about four miles from Dartmouth.

The many more things that could be said of forest, streams, hills, and valleys, ocean surf and sandy beach at Cole Harbour and vicinity we leave our readers to enjoy by actual visit: Enough to say that Cole Harbour is one of the most important suburbs of the "sister city" as some Halifax papers facetiously term the municipality of Dartmouth.

On November 24, 1883, the *Dartmouth Times* carried an equally pastoral piece on Lawrencetown.

> Upper and Lower Lawrencetown with the stretches of sandy beaches, extensive marshes, fertile upland, good fishing by sea, and lake, and stream, the gold mines, and the sand dunes and ocean surf afford a panorama within the limits of an hour's drive from Dartmouth that is unsurpassed in any part of the world. In winter or summer the natural scenery is enduring and beautiful; of course, the summer season is more varied and inviting.
>
> Facing a northwest wind across the marshes on a cold February morning is certainly invigorating but not fascinating. In summer the contrast is complete: the verdure, cool breezes, green ocean and white breakers with their continuous booming on the shore cause one to realize that nature is lavish to some places with her choicest varieties. The old road to Lawrencetown wound around Cole Harbour and afforded little variety till we arrive at the settlement; but the dyke across the mouth of Cole Harbour now enables us to proceed from Cow Bay across the embankment along the road running on the beach between the sea and the marsh and then over Conrod's Hill to the settlement – a way that is shorter and much more picturesque.
>
> Methodist and Presbyterian Churches and three schoolhouses comprise the public buildings. The farms are quite fertile and extensive, each one comprising more or less of the marshes. Sea manure is abundant so that with the good markets of Dartmouth and Halifax and the export trade to Newfoundland the farmers and market gardeners of this region are highly favored [*sic*]. Poverty is unknown among the people. Truly they are very pleasantly circumstanced in the midst of peace and prosperity.
>
> At Salmon Hole at the head of the marshes where

This foursome cool off by wading through the chilly water at Cole Harbour Beach (later called Rainbow Haven Beach) in 1928. The women are in swimwear of the period. The men's custom of retaining shirt and tie, merely rolling up the trousers to wade, continued a few more decades. (RE/CHR-SU)

the Salmon River flows into still water are the gold mines that some 15 years ago made a great stir in Halifax.

Mismanagement perhaps caused the works to be abandoned for a time but no doubt gold is there and any day a rich vein at Lawrencetown may be discovered. Here also is very fine salmon and trout fishing.

The marshes produce great quantities of hay, which is put up in large stacks near where cut and hauled away to the farms to market in winter. Of the rural scenery there, none in our estimation is equal to the ocean surf and sand hills of Lower Lawrencetown. The Presbyterian Church is built upon a hill and just to the eastward of the church the sand dunes extend a half a mile or more. The heavy ocean billows rear up their green crests from the bosom of the mighty Atlantic and with curving sweep and never ceasing reverberation crash themselves into foam upon the smooth sand. At the time of a southerly storm these

Lawrencetown Beach in recent years has become a popular spot for surfing enthusiasts. Nova Scotia's award-winning author Leslie Choyce, a resident of Lawrencetown, takes to the surf. (2003 photo courtesy of Leslie Choyce)

billows assume gigantic proportions and their power is such that the solid [s]and quakes and for miles away the roar is heard as of continuous artillery.

In the calmest of days the breakers are very fine in appearance with the sunshine sparkling upon the lines of white surf or glinting through the green tips of the curling waves. A person could spend hours upon the brow of this hill or on the top of one of dunes watching the ceaseless attack of old ocean.

Just above the tide with the highest waves are the dunes, sand hills 20 and 30 feet high rising abruptly on the ocean side and falling away abruptly on the land side: frail looking hills even if of rock yet only sand covered in part with coarse grass but in reality defying storm, and frost, and rain and ocean and saying to the sea, "Thus far shall thou come and to the land and farms beyond you need not fear, we will protect you."

On February 2 of the following year, the same Dartmouth newspaper printed a delightfully vivid account of the Acadian settlement at West Chezzetcook.

> The home of the Acadian French [sic] as far as this country is concerned is 20 miles east of the city and topographically is a large landlocked basin mostly of shallow water and marshes cut in various directions by channels and surrounded by rising land of greater or less pretensions to altitude and fertility. Some of the hills consist of red alluvial clay; others are of the darker mold [sic] and the balance rock. The harbour extends some six miles up from the ocean head and lands with a width of two miles or less and has a continuous settlement along its three sides. The eastern and western side of the harbour nearest the ocean are settled by the Dutch and their descendants.
>
> Lower West Chezzetcook is now known as Seaforth. Then comes West Chezzetcook where are the Roman Catholic Church and glebe and the fine large schoolhouse. These are centrally located upon fine high rolling ground commanding a charming view of hills and dales, ocean, harbour, islands and marsh with the bright settlement of East Chezzetcook right across the harbour and forming the distant foreground with its more distant background of dark spruce-covered hills. North and south of the chapel the settlement is dense enough to warrant a more pretentious appellation than village, but the inhabitants are not ambitious for high-sounding titles and therefore [are] contented and happy with their simple Acadian home and name. Some 200 Acadian French families now have their homes within the sound of the vesper bell of Chezzetcook. These are descendants of a few of the exiles who returning 120 years ago to Acadia settled on these then bleak shores and have lived and loved as their forefathers did on the shores of the basin of Minas [sic]. The

Bellefontaines, Lapierres, Romeaus, Pettipas, and Bonans are the most frequent names in the place: no doubt the lineal descendants of old Basil the blacksmith now reside there only waiting for some member of the Historical Society to resurrect the manuscript proofs either from the archives of the Province Building or from the work basket or cupboard of some ancient Acadian dame.

Their speech manners and customs have scarcely changed during the past century, and we presume also their appearance. Many of the women and children cannot talk English and their French is the Maritime Patois of Normandy of 200 years ago. They are a sober, industrious, frugal, and moral people. The men are fishermen, brick-makers, carpenters, or laborers [sic]. Many of them come to the city and get employment part of each year. As servants, gardeners, etc., they are highly valued for carefulness and fidelity. But for industry the men are eclipsed by the women – work never ceases for them. Farm work and marketing, berry picking and knitting, with all the household duties make up the busy round of a Chezzetcook woman's life. They knit interminably, when sitting in the house or visiting a neighbour, when walking to and from the city or into the bush for berries or for straying cows, the needles are kept afly and thus thousands of pairs of stockings, mittens, and garments are prepared for the Halifax Market.

In addition they supply the market with eggs, poultry, berries, and fish (smelts and clams). Market gardening is not much practiced by them such as brings gain to the people of Eastern Passage and Lawrencetown. But it is only a matter of time and enterprise. Most of those who understand gardening find employment in the city gardens at the expense of their own. This will no doubt soon be remedied.

Along the head of the harbour the settlement is not dense; it seems the fringe edge of Chezzetcook proper.

But it is Chezzetcook pure and simple in its people, its houses, its enclosures.

The Mi'kmaq, who had been forced to leave their Cole Harbour summer encampment after the European settlers took over the land, returned in the latter years of the nineteenth century to take up a more permanent occupancy. For them, a reserve of approximately 45 acres was established near the end of Morris Lake in 1880. This new reserve was part of the Truro band and was administered from the Millbrook band office. Although the population fluctuated over the years, as many as 27 families lived on the reserve at the same time.

The Native people living there made hockey sticks, ash axe handles, splint baskets, and quillwork, which they sold at the city market in Halifax or door to door. Some of the Mi'kmaq men worked as hired hands on nearby farms, and occasionally they joined the local farmers hunting or chopping wood.

The Cole Harbour reserve had a chapel for Sunday services as well as a school. Kate Giles, the wife of William Giles, a Cole Harbour farmer, taught at the reserve school around 1900.

The *Atlantic Weekly* reported on November 30, 1895, that "a part of the Cole Harbour bridge gave away last week behind a team of horses driven by Charles Conrod, the driver and horses had a hairbreadth escape. Since then some repairs have made it sufficiently strong for the passage of teams."

Mrs. Margaret Ann Phillips, shown at her home in 1972, was at one time the sole resident of the Mi'kmaq reserve on the Caldwell Road when many of the families had moved to other areas of the province. Several Native families have since moved back to the reserve. (RE 1972)

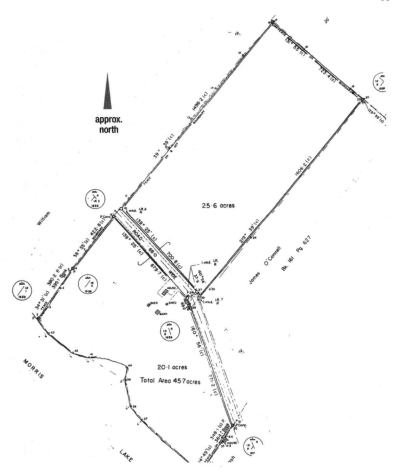

Map 6 – Plan of the Cole Harbour Mi'kmaq reserve. It extends back from Morris Lake to Astral Drive. Caldwell Road runs through it. (RIMS/retraced by Dawn Reiss)

The same edition reported that on Monday of the week about 2,000 loads of seaweed had landed on Cole Harbour bar. Many eager farmers from the surrounding district gathered to collect it as free fertilizer. Among them was Jacob Conrad, one of Cole Harbour's older and respected citizens. He reportedly was as active as a boy in his 87th year.

In March 1896, the *Atlantic Weekly* reported on the success of a 10-day mission held in the Anglican Church of Eastern Passage and Cole Harbour. "Great interest was manifested and churches were crowded to their utmost capacity. Many people having to sit on hassocks and chancel steps. Over 100 men and women professed to have received blessings and expressed an earnest desire to live a Christian life. This is very encouraging to the rector, the Rev. E. Roy. Mr. I. A. Winfield, the lay evangelist of St. Paul's Halifax, was the missionary."

In January 1897, the farmers of Cole Harbour met to protest the dumping of "inferior American farm products" in the Maritime provinces. According to the *Atlantic Weekly*:

> [A] large meeting of the farmers of District 31 was held in the Temperance Hall in Cole Harbour on January 4.
>
> The question at issue [is] the necessity of some steps being taken by the Dominion Government in their revision of the tariff that will stop to a certain extent the Maritime provinces being made a dumping ground for inferior American farm products. The following were

Part of an 1865 document citing the custom of harvesting sea manure. (NSARM)

appointed delegates to place the matter before the Tariff Commission when it meets in Halifax: Judson Baker, S. W. Lydiard, John G. Bissett, Peter Kuhn, and George Tullock.

On January 23, 1897, the five men appeared before the Tariff Commission demanding protection against the refuse of Boston markets on the grounds that most of the goods shipped were not fresh and were sold at low prices in order to clear, and also on the grounds that very much of it came in clear of duty owing to the juggery [sic] of the importers. They claimed that they were heavily enough handicapped by nature, the season being in favour of their American neighbours. They felt that if protection was to be given to other industries they should have a share when they were so seriously affected by adverse conditions. "When considering the disadvantages of climate under which we labour the discrepancy, if any, should be in our favour." The Cole Harbour farmers stressed in their brief to the Tariff Commission that the earlier season enjoyed by their southern neighbours enabled them to monopolize the local market for two or three months of the year.

United States market gardeners enjoyed what may be called the "cream" of the market, while local farmers had to be content with what was left. Further, the Americans not only enjoyed a monopoly on the local market but also had successfully excluded competition in their own. It was a known fact, the brief added, that many of the vegetables imported into Halifax were sometimes duty free. "This is one of the evils of which our farmers justly complain." The brief reminded the commissioners that the United States Government imposed duty on farm produce imported into their country.

The Cole Harbour brief concluded by stating, "All things being equal we are firm supporters of the policy of the present government. But we think it should also be extended towards those who adopt a similar policy towards us. We believe in the policy of free trade but we also believe in the policy of fair trade. We are not advocates of retaliation but of self-preservation."

On February 6, 1897, the *Atlantic Weekly* reported:

> [T]he young people of Cole Harbour have organized a literary society having for its object the introduction of literature and discussion of subjects relative to agriculture.
>
> Subscribing for agriculture literature in clubs to be distributed among the members will be one feature of the organization. Another, the collection of a library of standing works on agriculture, to be managed on the circulating library system.
>
> We have nothing but words of commendation for such associations. One of the best evidence of industrial progress is the eagerness with which men turn to standard works to [acquaint] themselves with the latest development on the subjects which particularly interest them.

A major fire in the Cole Harbour area was reported in the *Atlantic Weekly* of September 23, 1899.

> Quite a serious loss occurred at Tullock homestead on the Cole Harbour Road yesterday morning.
>
> The alarm of fire was rung in about ten o'clock; the firemen responded readily and reached the place in quick time. On arrival it was found that the large barn on the property was well in the grip of the ravenous fiend, fire. All possible efforts to stop progress of the fire [were] resorted to but it had gained too much headway and the building and its effects were completely destroyed.
>
> About 30 tons of hay, the property of Mr. C. Lydiard, was stored in the barn, all of which was consumed. This is a heavy loss for Mr. Lydiard as he had no insurance. The barn also was not insured. How the fire started is not definitely known, but it is supposed to have been the result of a spark lodging on the roof.

In July 1900, the Cole Harbour Methodist community said farewell to their minister, the Rev. D. K. Smith, at a social gathering held at the parsonage. They presented to the departing cleric a writing desk with all the essentials for writing. A spokesperson for the congregation expressed regrets that the Methodist Conference had decided not to return Mr. Smith to the community for another year.

> Our loss will be another community's gain and we hope his labours for the gospel will be abundantly blessed.
>
> During his five years among us he has been universally loved and respected. Always kind and considerate, a powerful speaker and one who carried his religion into his daily life, he was a great power for good among the people of this circuit and the mention of his name will always be an impulse for good.

Two weeks later, the congregation welcomed their new minister, the Reverend Davis, who came to Cole Harbour from New Germany. In the afternoon he held services at the Woodlawn church, and in the evening he preached at Lawrencetown.

The Poor Farm erected on the shore of Cole Harbour in the mid-1880s continued to expand its cultivated acreage and improve its facilities, providing a much-needed home for the mentally challenged and homeless.

For farm families living in Cole Harbour and the surrounding area, their lives in the nineteenth century revolved around the farm, the market, and their respected churches. On the morning of January 1, 1901, they wakened to a new day, new year, and new century that would bring momentous changes to the peaceful rural community.

V

HELLO TWENTIETH CENTURY

20
DAWN OF A NEW CENTURY

21
WAR IN EUROPE

22
THE DECADE THAT ROARED

23
THE DIRTY THIRTIES

24
THE HOME CHILDREN

25
WORLD WAR TWO

26
FARMING A COLE HARBOUR TRADITION

20

DAWN OF A NEW CENTURY

The twentieth century began at midnight December 31, 1900, with little or no fanfare in the Cole Harbour area. If there were celebrations, they were quiet and private, unlike observances in nearby Halifax and Dartmouth, where late-night church services brought throngs of people into the streets at midnight to wish each other happy New Year and to welcome the new century. Some celebrated the dawn of the new era in a prayerful manner; others toasted its arrival at public and private parties. Various New Year's Day levees were held in the city, but those farmers who attended also did their daily farm work of milking cows, feeding livestock and poultry, among other chores. However, before the end of the century, the area would undergo momentous changes, both to the land and the way of life.

The twentieth century opened in much the same way as the previous one, with Great Britain entangled in war, this time with the Boers, South African farmers of Dutch descent. The war had started in 1899 and continued until the Boers' eventual defeat in 1902. As part of the British Empire, Canada also went to war, making it the first time Canadian troops fought on foreign soil. It would not be the last. Approximately 100 young men from the Dartmouth area volunteered for service and adventure in South Africa. Many never returned home.

The start of the twentieth century coincided with the end of the Victorian Age and start of the Edwardian era. Queen Victoria died in January 1901, ending a reign of almost 64 years, the longest of any British monarch. Her reign had brought rapid expansion of the Empire, industrial growth, and prosperity particularly for the middle classes. Queen Victoria was succeeded by her eldest son Edward, the Prince of Wales, who became King Edward VII. He was 60 years old when he ascended the throne, and his reign lasted only nine years.

In Cole Harbour, the Poor Farm began the new century with a new man in charge of operations, as Superintendent J. M. Henneberry succeeded James Turner. During 1901, the farm sheltered about 60 residents; there were 19 new admissions, 10 were discharges, and 7 deaths. The farm had 6 employees: 3 men including the night watchman, a new position, and 3 women. In 1901 the farm harvested 230 bushels of potatoes, 250 bushels of turnips, 25 bushels of carrots, 21 bushels of parsnips, 13 bushels of beets, plus cabbage, peas, beans, and 10 dozen cucumbers. There were also three barrels of sauerkraut. The farm produced 14 tons of hay and 2 tons of fodder. The institution maintained four milking cows, a heifer, two horses, and two pigs.

Completion of a new addition to the buildings enabled Dr. N. F. Cunningham, the farm's physician, to isolate patients stricken with contagious and infectious diseases, to prevent epidemics.

By September the following year, the farm's population had increased to 72 patients, but before the year ended the number dropped to 66 as a result of discharges and deaths. Production at the farm showed a slight increase over the previous year.

In his report for 1906, J. M. Henneberry recommended that a telephone communication be established between the Poor Farm and the Town of Dartmouth. Two of the six miles from the town to the farm were already lined with poles and wires, leaving four miles to be completed. He proposed that the farm could install poles and wire for one mile, leaving three for the county to complete. The County Council adopted the superintendent's report, but the suggestion for a telephone system was deleted. It was Henneberry's last annual report to council.

A new superintendent, James W. Conrod, presented the Poor Farm's annual report the following year. The County Council's report does not say why Henneberry left.

In his 1909 report, Superintendent Conrod pointed out that the Nova Scotia Telephone Company had a line passing by the door of the Poor Farm and for a very reasonable cost the farm could have a telephone installed. In spite of all the discussion and negotiations with the telephone company, the Poor Farm continued to operate without a telephone. The 1910 annual report changed the name of the

Mrs. Rebecca MacDonald (left), her son, and Mrs. Isobel (Glazebrook) Giles at the Poor Farm. These Poor Farm buildings were destroyed by fire in 1929. (photographer unknown ca. 1920s/ source unknown)

institution from the County Poor Farm to the County Home. By 1912, the home's population rose to 87 residents, a slight increase over the previous year's figure of 82. The County Home and the telephone company were still negotiating for telephone service.

During the winter of 1902–1903, severe storms with high winds and waves had opened a new channel through the beach between Cole Harbour and the ocean. If the erosion had been allowed to continue, the dyke's dam would have been by-passed and the harbour's marshlands flooded with salt water. Peter Kuhn and his two sons, 15-year-old Max and 10-year-old Wilfred, spent long hard days in bitter cold to repair the dam with little more than their hands, horses, and a few small tools. They left home about 4:00 A.M., and drove to the dyke along the West Lawrencetown Road, a distance of about six miles. For several days they worked in the rain, wind, and ocean spray, hauling rocks and logs and cutting small trees to block the opening created by nature. The father and sons often worked at the dyke long after sundown before travelling two hours back to their home, exhausted, soaked, and chilled to the bone, ready for a hot meal and a warm bed.

They eventually won out over the sea and filled the gap by placing small spruce trees in the opening with their stumps pointing towards the ocean allowing the branches to restrain the sand so they could gradually build up the dam to withstand the tides.

The Kuhns' battle to protect the dyke and keep out the salt water was one of many against the damage of winter storms and spring thaw ice floes. Shortly after taking over the dyke and the marshland, Kuhn discovered that the gates on the dyke were not working efficiently, so he redesigned and rebuilt them in order to improve their function.

Initially, he planned to raise beef cattle on the drained marshland. He quickly discovered that the soil was poor and it was an ongoing challenge to keep the marshland well drained. It turned out that the only crops the family could produce from the marshes was marsh hay, far inferior to the cultivated upland hay, and cranberries, which grew wild. The marsh hay was cut and stacked during the summer and hauled home during the winter for cattle feed. The family picked the cranberries for use at home and any surplus was sold for $10 a barrel.

Kuhn and his sons expended a great deal of time and effort maintaining the dyke gates and working the marshes. Owning the dyke and marshlands was not the great business opportunity that Kuhn had anticipated. On the contrary, owning the dyke often brought him into conflict with his neighbours. Some resented his ownership of the marshes; they preferred to have them open for free public use. Hunters from the area and from Halifax and Dartmouth regularly spooked his horses during the haying season by firing their guns, and Kuhn had to chase them away.

In January 1909, Kuhn brought a lawsuit in the Supreme Court of Nova Scotia against James Conrod, superintendent of the County Home, for hunting on the marshes. Conrod obviously didn't recognize Kuhn's ownership of the marshes, claiming that they were navigable public waters and he had a right to hunt there as he had done before 1867. Kuhn claimed damages of $100.

Unknown persons dynamited the dyke gates on Saturday, April 23, 1910, causing considerable damage. Kuhn managed to put them back in operation. The culprits were never caught. Only months later, in July Kuhn won a judgement in court against a Mr. LaPierre for trespassing on his harbour property. In spite of the difficulties with nature and his legal entanglements, Kuhn continued to maintain the dyke and farm the marshland for another seven years.

While community arguments were occasionally waged at court, churches catered not only to the spiritual life of residents in the various communities, but to the social life as well. Church suppers and tea parties, held in church or community halls, were important for both fundraising and social gatherings. Strawberry teas, bean suppers, harvest festivals, Christmas socials, and Sunday school picnics during the summer were always popular events that brought young and old together.

The Methodist Church held weekday evening meetings of the Epworth League for young adults. Although these meetings were primarily for religious education, they also created an opportunity for young people from Cole Harbour, Lawrencetown, and Woodlawn to socialize.

The Woodlawn Mission circuit, organized in 1891, consisted of the Methodist churches from Cole Harbour, Lawrencetown, Woodlawn, Three Fathom Harbour, Mineville, and Montague. When the Rev. J. B. Heal became the minister in 1912, he requested a vote at the Quarterly Board Meeting concerning a possible union with the Presbyterian and Congregationalist Churches. Eight of the Board members voted in favour of the idea; two were opposed. On May 27, 1912, a special meeting of circuit organizations was called for a general vote on church union, and again the vote favoured union. Although the Woodlawn Methodist circuit voted in favour of church union as early as 1912, other Methodist and Presbyterian Churches were not as eager to embrace the idea. More time and discussion would be needed before the idea would be widely accepted.

The second decade of the twentieth century had barely started when the world witnessed one of the greatest marine disasters of all time, the sinking of the *Titanic* in April 1912. The luxury passenger liner, believed by many to be the unsinkable apex of marine technology, struck an iceberg off Newfoundland and went down, taking 1,513 passengers and crew members with her. Many of the bodies were brought to Halifax for burial.

A little more than two years later, the world witnessed an even greater loss of life when most of Europe, the British Empire, and the United States were plunged into a devastating war that lasted four years.

21

WAR IN EUROPE

The summer of 1914 had an ordinary beginning in Cole Harbour and surrounding area. Church groups were busy planning strawberry festivals, Sunday school picnics, and other popular social and fundraising events. County Home had several roofs reshingled that summer – and it finally had a telephone installed after years of discussions with the telephone company and pleading with the County Council. This was the first telephone installation in Cole Harbour. This new communication link, although shunned initially, would shortly find its way into the farmers' homes.

A report in the *Dartmouth Patriot* on July 4, 1914, stated, "the fine weather of the past two weeks has made a great change in the appearance of the crops in Cole Harbour. Planting is over and farmers are anticipating a fair crop." Farmers continued their weekly trek to the market to sell their produce and other wares. Some farmers were also selling their vegetables, fruit, and berries door to door in both Halifax and Dartmouth.

Work was finally underway to extend the rail line from Dartmouth to communities along the Eastern Shore and into the Musquodoboit Valley. After the railway bridge across Halifax Harbour collapsed in 1893, Dartmouth was without a rail link, until a new spur line was built from Windsor Junction into the town in 1895. The line was later extended to service the Acadia Sugar Refinery in Woodside, just outside

The railway from Dartmouth through Cole Harbour to the Musquodoboit Valley was started in 1916 to transport both passengers and freight. Most of the railway workers who helped build the line were Italian immigrants. Here some of the workers take a break from the strenuous labour. (ca. 1916/ Wilfred Bissett album)

the town boundaries, but that was where rail service ended. Extending the railway through Cole Harbour, Lawrencetown, the Chezzetcooks, and Musquodoboit Harbour would be a boon to farmers and fishermen living in those areas.

While life in Cole Harbour unfolded as usual, ominous events were occurring in Europe that would deeply affect Nova Scotia and the rest of Canada. When the heir to the Austrian throne, Archduke Francis Ferdinand, and his wife Sophie were gunned down in the streets of Sarajevo on June 28, 1914, by Serbian anarchists, the Austro-Hungarian Empire issued an ultimatum to Serbia on July 23, which was followed by a declaration of war five days later. Russia, an ally of Serbia, declared war on Austria. Germany, allied to Austria, retaliated with a declaration of war on Russia. France, an ally of Russia, declared war on Germany. Germany's Kaiser Wilhelm II, a cousin of England's King George V, expected the British would stay out of the continental

David Settle, left, was one of several young men from the Cole Harbour area to enlist in the army during World War One. He is shown with a comrade during his training on a military base at Rippon in northern England. (ca. 1915/Roy Settle album)

conflict; however, his hopes were dashed when the German army violated Belgium's neutrality and invaded the tiny nation in order to open a road into France. Germany's action against Belgium was promptly answered with a declaration of war from England on August 4.

Great Britain's entry into the European conflict also meant Canada's involvement as a member of the British Empire. Almost immediately, recruiting stations opened up across the nation to sign up eager young volunteers willing to trade their civilian clothes for an army uniform.

The Rev. D. Edwards held Harvest Festival services at St. Andrew's Anglican Church. On October 13, a tea in aid of Belgian Relief was held at the Temperance Hall. The following month a pie social was held to aid the people of wartorn Belgium.

At least two young men from the Cole Harbour area, Frank Kuhn and David Settle, enlisted early for service overseas. By mid-August, a train carrying the first contingent of Maritime troops left Halifax for basic training in Valcartier, Quebec. On October 10, 1914, the Canadian Expeditionary Force left for England and arrived in Plymouth Harbour a week later. From there they were marched to their encampment on the Salisbury Plain. Later, in December 1915, a recruiting meeting was held in the Anchor Lodge Hall.

The call to arms was heard and also promptly answered in the nearby Black communities of Preston and Cherry Brook. Their enthusiasm to fight for King and Country was quickly chilled after they visited the recruiting offices. Black volunteers for the Canadian Expeditionary Force were turned away and told, "This is a white man's war." The first enemy these Black men had to confront was not soldiers on a foreign battlefield but racism at home. Black leaders across the country, with some support from the white population, made the rejection of Black volunteers a national issue, which was eventually debated on the floor of the House of Commons. Some Black soldiers did manage to find acceptance in combat units and fought and died alongside their white comrades at Vimy Ridge, Ypres, the Somme, and Passchendaele.

After almost two years of debate, a decision was finally made on April 16, 1916, at a meeting of the Militia Council to organize a Black Labour Battalion. On July 5, 1916, the No. 2 Construction Battalion – the first and only Black Battalion in Canadian military history – was authorized. Lt.-Col. Daniel H. Sutherland, a railway contractor from River John, Pictou County, commanded the new unit. Capt. Roderick Livingston from Dartmouth was also an officer in the unit. The battalion's chaplain, Capt. William Andrew White, a Baptist minister serving in Truro, was reported to be the only Black commissioned officer in the British Forces during World War One.

Following basic training in Pictou and Truro, the battalion at a strength of 19 officers and 605 other ranks sailed from Pier 2 in Halifax on March 28, 1917, aboard the ss *Southland*, and after a 10-day sea voyage arrived in Liverpool, England. Members of the Black Battalion from the local area were Pte. Henry Bundy and Pte. William H. Bundy, Cherry Brook; Pte. Charles Drummond and Pte. John Williams, Preston Road. Early in May the battalion was reduced to a company status, assigned to the Canadian Forestry Corps, and they sailed for France. Members of the company dug trenches, built bridges, defused land mines, and faced mustard gas as well as enemy fire.

Many people believed the war, which began in August, would be over by Christmas and the troops would return home. By the time the Black Battalion sailed for overseas, the opposing sides were locked in a fearsome struggle of trench warfare throughout Belgium and France. In addition to regular enemy bombardment, the troops endured living in wet, muddy, rat-infested dugouts, where dysentery and other diseases were regular companions.

At home, ships gathered in Halifax Harbour to cross the Atlantic in convoys, and army units poured into the local area awaiting transportation overseas. Suddenly, new markets were opened for local food supplies. In 1916, a new market building better suited to the needs of the local farmers opened on Market Street. By 1921, the Green Market, the informal produce market, had disappeared. The new building served the farmers extremely well for the next 50 years, until it was torn down to make way for a housing and commercial complex – Scotia Square.

In the midst of wartime, the much dreamed-of and talked-about railway from Dartmouth down to the Eastern Shore and through the Musquodoboit Valley became a reality for Cole Harbour residents by 1916. Older residents of the area remember the construction phase, when the rail line was built across the middle of the harbour using four bridges over the main channels. Most of the workers laying the tracks were Italian labourers according to Wilfred Bissett. Harvey Patterson recalls the days he worked in the blacksmith shop at the Lawrencetown lumber mill, where they sawed the wood for the sleepers. The wood used for the railway ties was mostly spruce and hemlock, which came down from Porters Lake to Lawrencetown in a boom. Patterson said it took two years for the railway workers to complete the line across the harbour.

Passengers wait at the Cole Station for the train to take them into Dartmouth. The wooden building was 9 feet by 12 feet and had a bench inside to seat 10 people. (RE/ ca. 1930?/ Wilfred Bissett album)

The line continued to the Musquodoboit Valley. It transported lumber, gravel, lime, and wood chips. Farmers and fishermen living farther down the Eastern Shore used the rail service to bring their produce to market. Most Cole Harbour farmers continued to rely on their horses and wagons to get to the weekly market.

The tiny train station on the western side of Cole Harbour and was known simply as Cole Station. For some reason the word "harbour" was omitted. A pot-bellied stove heated the wooden building, 9 feet by 12 feet, in the winter. The one room held a bench that seated about 10 people. Passengers purchased tickets after boarding the train, which came through Dartmouth-bound from Musquodoboit in mornings and stopped again on the return trip later in the day. The fare from Cole Harbour to the Dartmouth train station near the ferry terminal was 25¢ at the start of the service, but gradually increased to more than $2.

Two locomotives were often used to pull the 3 to 5 passenger coaches and as many as 40 boxcars for freight. Coal was the principal source of fuel. During the hot dry summers, the sparks coming out of the train stacks created brush fires in the area and sometimes set fire to houses and barns near the tracks.   *[text resumes page 174]*

Map 7, Cole Harbour ca. 1960

The railway line dominates the middle of the harbour, and the locations of the four bridges may be seen. "Cole Harbour" marks the station, more often simply marked "Cole." The buildings on the end of Flying Point are gone but the Halifax County Home buildings and the road in to it are still shown. These, like the Ware House, the building marked on the County Home road just east of Bissett Road, were actually long gone by this time.

Due to the restricted size of the opening, the tidal flow under the bridge that replaced the dyke gates was notoriously dangerous and had claimed several lives up to the mid-1960s. However, the western (left) channel, once wide and deep and the main entrance into the harbour, was becoming increasingly filled with sand, while the eastern channel was growing. By the 1970s, the western channel had completely filled with sand and the eastern channel had become the sole connection between the harbour and the ocean. It remains so today.

Behind the sand barrier in the former the western entrance is a slow-moving lagoon that fills and empties twice daily with water from the main harbour. The lagoon is gradually reverting to salt marsh. This is the reverse of the earlier situation when a salt marsh grew behind the barrier beach which closed the western side. (Compare with Map 5, page 131.) Coastlines are dynamic places, always changing, and undoubtedly there will be more changes where land and sea meet at Cole Harbour beach.

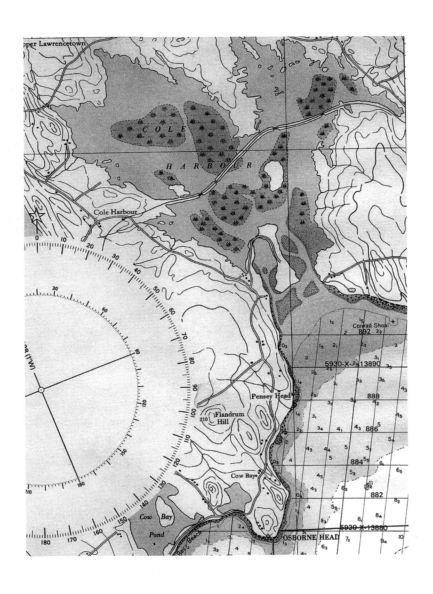

By March 1917, the Dartmouth Patriot reported the names of several Preston Road area men serving overseas in France: Sgt. Gerald Flinn, Cpl. Donald Turner, Pte. Gerald Montague, Pte. Leo LaPierre, Pte. Alex McDow and Pte. Russell Tobin in the 219th Battalion; Ralph Turner, 63rd Rifles; Grant Eisener, Royal Canadian Engineers; and Sapper Percy Turner, 239 Railway Construction Battalion.

Serving in the home guard at the time were E. Ernst, Arthur Ernst, John McDonald, Walter McDonald, and James Emino.

Pte. Frank Kuhn went overseas with Dartmouth Platoon of the Highland Brigade. In April Mrs. Martha Kuhn of Cole Harbour Road received a letter from Lt.-Col. E. H. Phinney stating that her son, Pte. Frank Kuhn, had died on the field of battle, "somewhere in France." The letter stated:

> I wish you to know that you have my most sincere sympathy on your sad bereavement. Your son died doing his full duty. The recent battle has taken its toll of brave men and we have lost many true comrades but the results they have accomplished are wonderful. It is a sad time for all of us but we must, both here and at home, muster our strength to see that German power is finally crushed. The whole Battalion mourns with you for we have lost a true comrade and friend.

Violence was not so far from home, either, although no one was injured. The Cole Harbour dyke, which for years had withstood the ravages of nature as well as a previous dynamite explosion, was dynamited again on May 11, 1917. Sometime before dawn one or more persons blew the dyke gates apart, allowing ocean water to rush in and cover the parts of the harbour that had been drained for farming. Peter Kuhn, the dyke owner, had made the dyke operable again after the 1910 dynamiting, but this time the damage was too great. It was the end of the dyke and of farming on the harbour. As in the earlier dynamiting incident, whoever was responsible escaped prosecution.

With the dyke finished, Kuhn turned to lumbering full-time. His son Max who tended the crops and took them to market carried on the market gardening operation of his farm. Kuhn had started lumbering in the early 1900s. He bought standing trees on various properties east of Dartmouth, cut them down, and hauled the logs to his mill site. He owned two steam-powered portable sawmills, which he moved from site to site to saw the logs into lumber. He usually marketed them by contract. He logged and sawed near Lake Echo, various parts of Porters Lake, and Musquodoboit. He also owned a steam-powered boat, *Lady of the Lake*, which he used to tow floating booms of logs down the lake to his mill near the highway.

In addition to lumbering and farming, Kuhn owned a grocery store in Dartmouth after his dyke was destroyed. He operated the store for only a few years during World War One, but he continued lumbering until his death in 1922.

News of local boys overseas continued to occupy everyone's minds. On July 21, 1917, the *Dartmouth Patriot* reported that Pte. Percy Giles of the Highland Regiment was at the 2nd Northern Hospital in Leeds, England, suffering from trench fever. Private Giles was also suffering from shell shock, the result of a shell bursting close to where he stood in the trenches.

Mrs. Lawrence Bellefontaine of Cole Harbour Road was notified that her son, Pte. Michael Bellefontaine, had been wounded in the leg on August 8 but remained on duty. Before enlisting in the army, young Bellefontaine was employed at the Starr Manufacturing Company in Dartmouth.

By the end of 1917, the war in Europe that was supposed to have ended by Christmas of 1914 was still going strong with heavy losses on both sides. The battlefield was a scarred landscape with the opposing sides dug into trenches that zigzagged from the North Sea across Europe almost to the Swiss border. Many of the towns and cities of Belgium and France were reduced to rubble by the heavy artillery bombardment, bringing severe hardships upon the residents. Canadian cities and towns had been spared the devastation that was inflicted on Europe, but all that changed for the residents of Halifax and Dartmouth on the morning of December 6, 1917.

It was a cool, sunny morning as residents of the two communities left their homes for work or school and housewives prepared for their daily round of chores. Some were already at their jobs in factories and other places. For certain the farmers of the area were tending to their daily chores. While people went about their morning routines, two vessels were moving from opposite ends of Halifax Harbour. The *Mont Blanc*, loaded with high explosives, was steaming towards Bedford Basin to join a convoy that would provide safe passage to France. At the other end of the harbour the Belgian Relief ship *Imo* was leaving the basin and slowly heading for the ocean, destination New York City to pick up a cargo of grain and clothes for wartorn Belgium.

The ships collided in the Narrows at 8:30 A.M. When the two vessels finally pulled apart by reversing their engines, the *Mont Blanc* caught fire and drifted towards the Halifax side; the *Imo* drifted towards Dartmouth's shore. At approximately 9:05 A.M., the *Mont Blanc*, by then a fiery bomb, exploded into thousands of pieces. The aftermath was death and destruction on both sides of the harbour.

Harvey Patterson, who grew up in Lawrencetown, recalled the day of the explosion years later in an oral history interview for the Cole Harbour Rural Heritage Society.

> I was living in Woodlawn at the time, where I operated a workshop for building and repairing wagons and carriages. I was at my bench when the explosion occurred, and all the rims that were hanging from the ceiling came crashing down all around me.
>
> My wife's sisters Margaret, Mollie, and Jane Kuhn were boarding at a house in north Dartmouth while attending schools in Halifax and Dartmouth. I harnessed my horse and wagon and headed for town to check on their safety and well-being. When I arrived at their boarding house the girls had left and their landlady was dead on the floor.

Mr. Patterson said he spent the remainder of the day transporting injured people in his wagon from Dartmouth to the Nova Scotia Hospital for treatment. "The streets around the downtown post office were lined with doctors and nurses treating people who were suffering injuries. That night we had a major snowstorm that lasted well into the next day."

Patterson's sisters-in-law Margaret and Mollie were attending a 9:00 A.M. school assembly on the top floor of the Halifax Academy when the explosion occurred. The principal, Sam Martin, was reading the Bible. He promptly left the platform to organize a fire drill to get the students out of the building. Their first thoughts were that the Germans were bombing the city. They remembered seeing a pillar of smoke in the sky in the north end of the city that turned into a mushroom. Neither sister remembered hearing the explosion.

They eventually left the school and walked towards the ferry terminal over glass-littered sidewalks. When they arrived in Dartmouth they went first to their father's grocery store on Water Street (now Alderney Drive). The plate glass window in the front of the store was smashed in, and their father was in the back of the building with bandages on his head and hands.

They later went to their boarding house, where they learned that their landlady, Mrs. Clara Evelyn Rice, had been killed. Their younger sister Jane found the woman's body on the kitchen floor when she returned home from Greenvale School. Mrs. Rice's two children, ages two and six, had survived. The children's father, a lieutenant in the army, was stationed in Sydney at the time. Later in the day, the sisters' brother drove in from Upper Lawrencetown and took them and the Rice children to their parents' home in Lawrencetown. Mr. Rice arrived a few days later and took his children.

The snowstorm that night, which continued into the next day, caused terrible discomfort for everyone and delayed the arrival of the relief trains from outside the area.

When Mrs. Rice's body had been removed from the house, it was wrapped in a cashmere shawl belonging to Mrs. Kuhn. A few days after the explosion, one of the Kuhn girls returned to Dartmouth and went to the undertaker, in hopes of retrieving her mother's shawl. She recalled her shock at discovering the makeshift morgue.

"When I opened the door and saw all the naked dead bodies in the room, I shut the door as fast as I could and gave no further thought to my mother's shawl."

Years later, both Margaret and Mollie Kuhn married men named Campbell who were not related.

Gordon Eisener, a Cole Harbour resident who grew up in Woodlawn, was attending Woodlawn School on the morning of the explosion.

> School had just started and we were singing "O Canada" at the time. Most of the windows were smashed in and a few people got cut but the cuts were not serious.
>
> My father left home for Halifax to see if he could help out in any way. There was a terrible snowstorm that night. Father later told me that he saw women's bodies frozen in the snow and people cutting off their fingers to get their rings.

Murray Ritcey of Cole Harbour remembered entering the school on the morning of the explosion just after the bell had rung. "Suddenly something was falling all over the ground that looked like red hot shot shells, but it was the rivets from the ship that had exploded."

Jessie Joslin (nee Way) came as a child with her family to Dartmouth from England in May 1914. At the time of the explosion the family was living in a house behind the rope factory in north Dartmouth. Jessie Joslin recalled the event during an oral history interview for the Cole Harbour Rural Heritage Society.

> We went to Victoria School on Wyse Road, but on the morning of the explosion we were at home gathering firewood and water for our mother. Around nine o'clock there was a terrible crash and mother said, "My God, the Germans are here. We're in God's hands now."
>
> The roof of our house was blown off and the house was broken in two. The family was in the back of the house at the time and was saved from serious injury. We went outside and black dirty water from the harbour came crashing down on us. The cannon from the ship *Mont Blanc* flew over our home.

Later that day the family went walking along the railroad tracks by the harbour where Mrs. Joslin recalled seeing the body of a woman on one side of the track and her head on the opposite side. She also remembered smelling human flesh burning in the houses across the harbour. The wood and coal stoves used to heat homes had been knocked over by the explosion, setting houses on fire. People trapped inside died before they could be rescued. She remembered her father obtained a roll of tarpaper to patch their roof and other parts of their house, which gave them some protection from the fierce storm that descended on Halifax that night. She added in her recollections that "a few days later trainloads of doctors and nurses arrived in the area from the United States with medical and other supplies from the people."

The following year, the Way family moved from Dartmouth to Cole Harbour, where Jessie's father took up farming.

The explosion caused some damage in Cole Harbour, knocking out windows and smashing in doors, but the damage was minor compared to what Halifax and Dartmouth sustained. Fifty-three of the County Home's window panes were smashed by the explosion along with two window sashes and several doors. The building was drafty and hard to heat until repairs

Rosemary Eaton displays part of one of the original windows from the former Methodist Meeting House that were blown out during the 1917 Halifax Harbour Explosion. The original windows were replaced with windows of a simpler design. (Dale McClare 1987)

could be made. One person died at the County Home as a result of the 1917 Explosion – Catherine McDonald. There is no information in the record as to her age or where she came from. The Methodist Chapel lost most of its windows as well.

On November 11, 1918, an armistice was signed with Germany, bringing an end to the war. Within months, some young men who had left Canada for the war in Europe returned home to their jobs and their farms to pick up their lives again. Some returned blind, others with limbs amputated. Still others never returned and are buried in cemeteries in France and Flanders. People called it "the war to end all wars" and "the war to save democracy"; it was neither.

22

THE DECADE THAT ROARED

When the 1920s began, Halifax and Dartmouth were still rebuilding from the disastrous Halifax Harbour Explosion of 1917. New housing was needed to replace the homes knocked flat in both communities. Churches, schools, and other public buildings on both sides of the harbour needed to be refurbished or replaced. Cole Harbour's damage was put right within months.

The 1920s, later known as the "Roaring Twenties," was a decade of change and challenge. With the war in Europe over, the troops returned home looking ahead to a time of peace and prosperity. Jazz music swept across North America, bringing new dance crazes. Automobiles were replacing the horse and buggy on the streets, and gas stations became an added feature on community landscapes. The Wright Brothers' flying machine evolved from a novelty to an engine of war to crossing the broad Atlantic non-stop. Radios were gradually appearing in homes for entertainment, and Hollywood movies began to talk.

The Roaring Twenties was also the decade of Prohibition, which made buying, selling, and drinking alcoholic beverages illegal and spawned a new and very lucrative industry in Canada and the United States – rum-running and bootlegging. Prohibition went into effect in both countries during the closing years of World War One in order to stop the sale and distribution of hard liquor, beer, and wine. In 1920, the Volstead Act in the United States prohibited the making, selling, and transportation of intoxicating beverages.

In Canada, jurisdiction over the control of alcoholic beverages was split between federal and provincial governments. All provinces except Quebec enacted legislation banning the sale and distribution of liquor as early as 1917. The following year, the federal government passed laws ending the legal importation of liquor into Canada, its manufacture, and transportation to any country where its sale was illegal. The federal government repealed its Prohibition laws in 1919, making it legal to manufacture and distribute liquor, but provincial laws continued to ban its sale and consumption. For the balance of the decade there was a continual battle for the stricter enforcement of Prohibition laws by one group and for the legal sale and consumption of alcoholic beverages by another group.

Nova Scotia had a long and strong temperance tradition going back to the middle of the nineteenth century. Cole Harbour's Anchor Lodge had been an active force promoting temperance through most of the nineteenth century and the early twentieth century. The evils of strong drink continued to be preached from most church pulpits. Temperance adherents regarded the consumption of alcohol as the root of most social evils: poverty, crime, disease, industrial and automobile accidents, spousal abuse, and even the subversion of the country's electoral process; a bottle of liquor was often exchanged for a vote at election time. However, Prohibition never really stopped the sale or consumption of alcohol; it forced it underground, where rum-running and bootlegging made millionaires of some people and criminals of others.

The rum trade began in the West Indies where rum was manufactured and shipped in five-gallon kegs (small barrels) to St. Pierre and Miquelon, islands owned by France situated off the coast of Newfoundland. The Prohibition laws in Canada and the United States affected neither the West Indies nor the French islands. The rum was loaded onto schooners and other vessels that had sailed from Nova Scotian or

During Prohibition rum-running was common in the Cole Harbour/Lawrencetown area. This rum-runner has just off-loaded its cargo at Lawrencetown Beach before heading back out to sea. Capture by police could bring hefty fines or a term in prison. (ca. 1920s/Effie Crowell Neiforth album)

other Maritime ports and brought down the coast of Nova Scotia and the Eastern United States outside the 12-mile limit and away from the RCMP, U.S. Coast Guard, and other law enforcement agencies.

Smaller motor-powered boats made the run out to the larger vessels, off-loaded the rum or other liquor and transported it back into small coves and inlets along the east coast. Cole Harbour and Lawrencetown, like other inlets along the Eastern and South Shores, were prime locations for smuggling liquor ashore and hiding it until it could be sold to local bootleggers or transported to new locations.

Mrs. Effie Nieforth, who grew up in Three Fathom Harbour, recalled several incidents from the area's rum-running days in an interview taped for the Cole Harbour Rural Heritage Society on March 23, 1982. Once the schooner *Frances T.* got the wrong directions and ended up on the East Lawrencetown Beach on a Friday evening in the early 1920s. She was going to church at the time and watched the frantic activity on the beach below. In a mad scramble of people, one group unloaded the kegs and another group tried to hide them before residents in the area got up in the morning.

On another occasion, when Effie Neiforth and her brother were travelling by horse and wagon to the Halifax Market before dawn, she noticed cases of whiskey hidden under the bushes along the road. When they passed by returning home later in the day, the cases were gone.

Mrs. Nieforth said people engaged in the rum-running trade often hid their rum in the Lawrencetown church basement for safekeeping. "No one would ever think that rum would be hidden in the church basement. The owners of the liquor waited until the evening service began and everyone was in full song, then they removed the barrels."

She said that in the summer months, kegs of liquor were sometimes hidden in a Lawrencetown gravel pit. If the kegs were not properly buried, the sun would heat them up and passersby could smell the rum along the road.

"Sometimes the rum-runners dug holes on the local beaches and hid the rum there until it could be moved to safety before the police found it."

Mrs. Nieforth remarked that some small boats took rum into Cole Harbour through the dyke opening but couldn't take it up to Little Salmon River because of the railway bridge across the harbour.

The rum and whiskey that arrived in five-gallons kegs was then diluted. One pint of rum usually made two pints, sometimes three pints. A lot of rum and whiskey were sold locally, but a lot was also shipped to the United States.

In the 1982 interview, Mrs. Nieforth said that during Prohibition, liquor went out of nearby Seaforth on the train by the boxcar load. The rum was packed in boxes marked "smelts" or some other type of fish. Real fish would be put in the boxes to cover the rum. Sometimes the liquor was hidden in a boxcar loaded with gravel. She said she didn't know how they got the liquor across the United States border.

"I don't really think the officials on the train knew they were carrying liquor because they were shipping a lot of fish and gravel to the United States at the time."

During the 1920s and early Depression years, rum-running and bootlegging were great sources of income, provided the bootleggers didn't drink too much of the product themselves.

The Mounties and the police did catch some people. If convicted, they were fined or jailed for three months to a year, sometimes longer. If people were caught at sea, the rum and boat were confiscated. Several times rum-runners were forced to dump their cargo into the ocean to avoid being captured with the goods on board.

Mrs. Joan Langille, who moved to Cole Harbour Dyke in 1951, recalled during a taped interview that her father-in-law from Eastern Passage went rum-running during Prohibition and was nearly caught by the RCMP. He usually sailed on schooners and transported the rum to the Boston market.

Rum-running and bootlegging were part of the way of life for many Nova Scotians throughout most of the 1920s. Towards the end of the decade pressure built from various lobby groups for a repeal of the Nova Scotia Temperance Act. The question of Prohibition came to a head in 1929, when the Nova Scotia Government decided to conduct a province-wide plebiscite on October 31 to determine if the people wanted Prohibition to continue. The results of the vote published on November 1, 1929, showed that over 85,000 people wanted some type of government control over the sale of liquor; of those, 61,226 favoured retention of the Temperance Act; 24,248 favoured rigid control.

Prohibition ended in Nova Scotia in 1930, when the sale of liquor in the province came under provincial government control. Three years later, the Americans repealed their prohibiting laws governing the sale and distribution of liquor.

In the midst of the illicit liquor trade during the 1920s, other significant events also made a direct impact on the Cole Harbour area: the creation of both the Victoria Hall Community Centre and Rainbow Haven, a fresh-air summer camp for children, as well as the union of three major religious denominations in Canada – Presbyterian, Methodist, and Congregationalist – to form the United Church of Canada.

On April 1, 1921, a portion of the property on the Cole Harbour Road of the late Robert K. Turner was sold to the Board of Trustees of the Community Hall of Cole Harbour Road by the heirs of the estate - Andrew Turner, Walter J. Turner, Bessie Turner, Sophia Turner, Robert Turner, and his wife Isabella – for one dollar. The land was sold with the one provision that the building erected on the land

Victoria Hall, on the Cole Harbour Road, was the centre of social life in the farming community for years. The building was used for the credit union, business meetings, tea and sales, church suppers, and dances. It was eventually sold to the credit union. Also see Victoria Hall in photo on page 197. (Verna Osborne album ca. 1933)

would not be used for dancing except at socials, picnics, or tea meetings. The clause was inserted to prevent the use of the hall for a public dance pavilion. The building erected on the property served the people of Cole Harbour as a community hall for many decades.

Rainbow Haven, which was organized and supported in part by the Halifax Herald Limited as well as public donations, opened in 1923 on

Hattie Bissett, later Mrs. Stuart Harris, sits behind the wheel of Harry Elliot's "Hupmobile," one of the earliest cars owned in Cole Harbour. Many years later the car was sold at auction to a New Brunswick antique car collector and left the area. (ca. 1929/Harry Elliot album)

the beach near the entrance to Cole Harbour. The camp's purpose was to provide disadvantaged children in the Halifax-Dartmouth area with a seaside summer vacation away from the city. This summer camp continued to serve the community until the end of the twentieth century.

Church union among Presbyterians, Methodists, and Congregationalists had been considered in the Cole Harbour area as early as 1912, when the Woodlawn circuit Methodists voted overwhelmingly in favour of union. In some areas of the country, Presbyterians and Methodists shared the same building for Sunday services and union of these two groups seemed like a natural move. Other churches were somewhat slower to embrace the idea. By 1923, formal discussions of union were entered into by all three denominations. Arguments for and against the proposal were hotly debated during meetings. The Presbyterians were not as enthusiastic about the idea as the other denominations.

The House of Commons passed federal legislation sanctioning the union of the churches, and the matter was debated in the Senate in 1924. The following year, the union of the Methodists with some Presbyterians and Congregationalists was sealed. All three Methodist Churches in the Woodlawn circuit along with the Presbyterian Church in Lawrencetown immediately became members of the new United Church of Canada.

As the decade moved to a close, a local disaster occurred on February 28, 1929. A fire swept through the new wing of one of the County Home buildings, which contained the living quarters of the sane men, their hospital, and dining room, and the steam heating plant. It rendered 140 residents homeless.

Mrs. Conrod, Matron, assisted by the Home's staff of six, shepherded residents from the blazing building, organized the firefighting, and then called the Dartmouth and Halifax fire departments for assistance. Men from the Dartmouth Engine Company and the Halifax Fire Department rushed to the scene over snow-covered roads. Although hampered by a lack of water and an inability to operate the steam and motorized pumpers, they were able to check the fire's progress and keep it contained in the barracks-like building.

The residents were wrapped in blankets and taken in sleighs to the farm cottage at the entrance to the grounds, and later taken in sleighs and taxis to the City Home in Halifax. Superintendent Conrod was in Halifax at the time, meeting with the Halifax County Council.

Fire Marshal J. A. Rudland gave a report on March 4, 1929:

> Under the evidence available it was not possible to definitely determine the origins of the fire.
>
> It's the opinion of those who gave evidence that burning tobacco from a pipe or a lighted match was dropped through one or both of the holes in the plaster and lath partitions, igniting accumulations of dust, rubbish, etc., [t]hus starting the fire within the partitioned walls.
>
> I have no hesitation in stating that the buildings now standing are especially liable to fire both from the nature of their occupation and also by reason of poor construction. It is therefore strongly recommended that the use of the existing institution be discontinued and

Interior view of the Farmer's Market built in 1916 on Market Street in Halifax. Vendors vied for the best locations in the market just as they did when selling on the street years before. (Ron Osborne 1940s/ courtesy of Ron Obsorne)

that it be replaced at the earliest possible date by a modern building constructed for the purpose of an asylum.

Dr. G. A. MacIntosh, Inspector of Humane and Penal Institutions, in his report of March 13, 1929, concurred with the fire marshal that the present structure should not be repaired or continued in use. Dr. G. A. MacIntosh also suggested that the present buildings be replaced by a new and modern facility. Subsequently, an agreement was entered into with the City of Halifax to board all the County Home's patients for a period of five years at a rate of $3.50 a week per patient.

The fire at the County Home ended that facility's life and a chapter in the history of Cole Harbour. The burnt-out ruins were eventually removed, and the property was cleaned up. However, another decade passed before a new facility was erected to replace the County Home.

Conditions and the general operation of the Halifax City Market also drew criticism, this time from area farmers, who voiced their complaints through the Dartmouth Agricultural Society to Halifax County Council on March 4, 1929. They targeted the unsanitary conditions, the high prices for tables, and the operation of the market in general. Speaking for the Agricultural Society and its members, Everett Harrison complained that the charges for the tables had been increased the previous year without any warning to the vendors. He added they had heard rumours that the prices for tables were to be increased again. Harrison also told the council that the market was inadequately heated. "During the winter it's colder inside the market than outdoors."

He suggested that one of the farm producers be appointed to the Market's management board to serve the interest of the county farmers. As a result, the council appointed a special committee of Councillors Peverill, LaPierre, Maddill, Mosher, and Guilford to meet with representatives of the Dartmouth Agricultural Society to further discuss the conditions and operation at the Halifax City Market.

The Roaring Twenties came to a shocking close in October 1929, when the New York Stock Exchange crashed. A decade of prosperity came to a halt, and a period of worldwide economic depression began. The Great Depression would only end with another war in Europe.

23

THE DIRTY THIRTIES

Collapse of the New York Stock Exchange in October 1929 had far-reaching effects. It precipitated an economic tailspin for Canada, the United States, and most of the industrialized world that lasted for the balance of the decade. Companies went bankrupt, factories closed down, creating mass unemployment, millionaires became paupers overnight, and thousands knew the pangs of hunger; some even starved to death. The prosperity of the previous decade spared few from the pangs of economic disaster.

At first, business leaders, politicians, economists, and stock analysts all believed the effects of the crash were short-term, a mere blip on the economic scale that would quickly correct itself. Some business leaders even predicted 1930 and the new decade would bring unprecedented economic growth.

In the beginning, governments shunned any responsibility to assist those in need. The federal government passed on the responsibility for feeding the hungry to the provincial governments, which in turn declared it a municipal matter. Municipal governments were poorly equipped to deal with what proved to be a monstrous problem. Before the decade ended, governments at all levels had to get involved.

Historians and the people over the years have assigned various names to the decade: the Hungry Thirties, the Dirty Thirties, and the Great Depression. Each was a meaningful label. Western farmers faced harsh times worsened by repeated crop failures due to drought that turned the western provinces into "the dust bowl." Farmers in Nova Scotia were marginally better off than their western counterparts; they didn't have to contend with drought. Although crops were reasonably good throughout the Depression, cash was always in short supply and prices for farm goods were always low.

Nobody in the Cole Harbour area lost their farm during the Depression; farmers managed to keep them going by barely scratching out a living from the soil. The majority of farmers in the area were market gardeners, producing a wide variety of vegetables. There were some dairy and poultry farms and a few piggeries. For the most part, farmers continued their weekly trek to the Halifax Market. Some sold their products to wholesalers; others sold door to door. By the 1930s, many of the area farmers had retired their horses and wagons in favour of trucks. Those who continued to employ the horse and wagon still began their journey to Halifax long before the sun peeped over the horizon.

When Prohibition ended at the start of the 1930s, it sounded the death knell of the temperance movement across the nation. As the temperance movement slowly faded away, so did the use of the Anchor Lodge as an important community centre. The lodge hall was eventually torn down and replaced by a community centre on the Cole Harbour Road, Victoria Hall.

Mrs. Thomas Bissett, who was born in Cumberland County, came to Cole Harbour in 1926. She attended grade 9 in the one-room school, which had an enrolment of about 60 children for all grades. Three years after her arrival she was a married woman. Many years later, she recalled some of the activities held at Victoria Hall and its importance to the community.

"We had regular dances, suppers, meetings and many other activities. It was a two-storey building with the downstairs area used for suppers and the upstairs for concerts and dances. People all took a turn working there. Everything was on a volunteer basis."

Mrs. Vinie Patterson, nee McKay, moved to Cole Harbour from Eastern Passage in 1937. Mrs. Patterson recalled her husband kept six dairy cows and sold the milk and cream in Woodlawn and Dartmouth. Eventually, he sold his milk to Woodlawn Dairy, which came to the farm to collect it. She usually milked the cows between 5:30 and 6:00 A.M., and then fed them. After the milk was separated, she made butter. She also recalled some of the activities at the hall.

"They often held box socials to raise money for any family that was burnt out. The boxed lunch was auctioned off to the highest bidder, and the money raised was given to the people in need. There were also dances in the hall, particularly at Hallowe'en, and suppers which were often organized by the various churches."

Throughout the Depression, churches in the area continued to play a leading role in the spiritual, social, and recreational life of the farm families.

Another important event in the Cole Harbour area that took place during the Depression years was the formation of a credit union. The man responsible for bringing the credit union to the Cole Harbour area was the Rev. George Russell, the son of a Stellarton coal miner. The Reverend Russell, an ordained United Church minister, received his first pastoral assignment in Sherbrooke, Guysborough County, in the early 1930s. While serving in Sherbrooke, he became interested in the Antigonish Movement and credit unions.

The Antigonish Movement, as it was called, was largely the brainchild of Father James J. Tompkins, vice-president of St. Francis Xavier University, who developed a plan to bring education to the community rather than serving only the affluent who could afford to attend university. "Education must go to the people," he said.

In the 1920s, Nova Scotia was one of the most impoverished regions of Canada. Often mortgaged to local merchants, farmers, fishermen, and miners needed a source of manageable credit as well as education in how to use it wisely. Father Tompkins' dream was eventually realized when the university organized an extension department to bring education to the community. Under the direction of Father Moses Coady, Father Tompkins's cousin, the department became a prime mover in the co-operative movement in Nova Scotia. Another clergyman well remembered in Cole Harbour and influential in the credit union movement was the Rev. J. D. N. MacDonald.

In 1931, Angus MacDonald, one of the early supporters of co-operatives in the province, invited Roy F. Bergengren to visit the university and speak on credit unions. The following year the provincial legislature passed the Nova Scotia Credit Union Act, and on December 10, 1932, the first credit union in the province opened for business at Broad Cove.

The Reverend Russell's first attempt to form a credit union in Sherbrooke had ended in failure. His next pastoral charge was Liscombe, a small fishing village also in Guysborough County, where his effort to organize a credit union was crowned with success.

In 1938, he came to the Cole Harbour church, with churches also in Woodlawn and Lawrencetown. Sunday services were held in Lawrencetown in the morning, Woodlawn in the afternoon, and Cole Harbour in the evening. (When World War Two broke out, he held a fourth service at 9:00 A.M. on Sunday for the members of the artillery shore battery stationed in Lawrencetown.) Shortly after his arrival at Cole Harbour, the Reverend Russell set about organizing a credit union for the area. "It was one way for the people to better themselves through self-help," he recalled years later during a taped interview. "The 1930s, or the Dirty Thirties as they were called, were hard times for the farmers; prices were low and they didn't have a lot of spare cash."

The Reverend Russell pointed out that the ordinary person at that time couldn't get a loan at the bank unless he had good strong security. Banks weren't interested in lending out $200 and having it paid back at 50¢ a week. "Our first loans were in the amounts of $50 to $100 and were paid back at the rate of 25¢ a week."

The minister spent a lot of time promoting the credit union to his congregations. "In those days a minister had some influence in the community," he added. "At first we organized a credit union study club in 1938 and held 10 to 15 meetings in the Victoria Hall discussing credit unions, their benefit, and how to go about organizing one. The following year the credit union was officially opened with members representing Cole Harbour, Woodlawn, and Westphal." Some of the early members were Murray Ritcey, Norman Morash, and Gordon Eisener.

The Reverend Russell recalled they held a meeting one night to name the new credit union. Since Woodlawn, Westphal, and Cole Harbour were all represented, they tried to get a name that would represent all three communities. The meeting dragged on and it was getting late. Someone made a motion that it be called the Russell Credit Union. The motion was seconded and passed unanimously.

The Russell Credit Union opened for business every Monday night in the Victoria Hall, where members could come to make a deposit or arrange a loan. On the first night of operation, the credit union took in $22. "It was a start," the reverend remembered.

The Reverend Russell himself took out the first loan – the small amount of $50.

> I did it to set a good example for the others. People at that time were afraid of debt. They felt it meant that you couldn't pay your way. Everything was on a cash basis. The credit union needed to lend out money at a small rate of interest in order to make money.
>
> Farmers sometimes took out small loans in the spring to purchase seed and fertilizer for the planting season. Then in the fall when the crop was harvested they came in and paid off their entire loan.

The Rev. George Russell was the primary promoter and organizer of the credit union during the difficult years of the Depression. It was later called the Russell Credit Union. Shown here are (left to right) Lloyd Eisener, Ross Osborne, Ralph Settle, long-time board members; the Reverend Russell; and Donna Conrad (loans officer, Credit Union Atlantic). Ross Osborne was also the first manager. The occasion is the presentation to the Rural Heritage Society archives of a portrait of the Reverend Russell and a sketch of Victoria Hall. When the credit union took over Victoria Hall, they enclosed the front stairs in a porch. (Joseph Robicheau 1944)

Most of the farmers in the area joined the credit union, but there were some of course who had no need for a credit union and didn't join. There were others who didn't need the organization but put money into it anyway, just to help out.

After the credit union was up and running in Cole Harbour, the Reverend Russell helped organize one for the people living in Lawrencetown. The Reverend Russell remarked that the credit union was beneficial to the area because it compelled three neighbouring communities – Woodlawn, Westphal, and Cole Harbour – to think together as to how they could help one another.

He also helped people in the area get a rural postal route for mail delivery. Before that, farmers had to travel to Dartmouth for their mail. "We organized a petition signed by the majority of the people requesting a rural mail route for the Cole Harbour area." Everyone had to have a mailbox by their front gate, and a mailbox at that time cost seven dollars. A lot of people thought twice about spending seven dollars for a mailbox," he said.

The man who delivered the mail in the Cole Harbour area was also involved with the credit union, and members often left money in their mailbox for him to deposit for them.

After the credit union was formed, efforts were made to organize co-operatives. The farmers banded together to buy feed and fertilizer in order to get a better price. At first the co-op had only a limited degree of success, but eventually it did get off the ground.

At the close of the Dirty Thirties, construction got underway for a new County Home in the area to replace the one that partly burned down a decade ago. The new facility was not located on the harbour shore as the first one, but on Bissett Road, overlooking Bissett Lake. Under changing names, the new facility served the mentally challenged people of Halifax County for the balance of the twentieth century and briefly into the twenty-first century before it was closed down and the residents were moved to new facilities.

By 1938, storm clouds of war were gathering again across Europe, brought on this time by the territorial demands of Adolf Hitler and Germany's governing Nazi Party. The clouds finally broke into a storm on September 1, 1939, when the German army invaded Poland. It was the beginning of a horrific period of barbarism that would continue for the next six years.

Although the war brought an end to the economic hardship of the 1930s, it created devastating hardships and circumstances for the people of Europe, Asia, and North America. Before it was over, hundreds of cities and towns would lie in ruin and millions of people – civilian as well as military – would die.

24

THE HOME CHILDREN

Two well-known Cole Harbour residents, Stuart Harris and Charles Devenport, were among the thousands of children who were sent to Canada from Great Britain during the mid-nineteenth century and early twentieth century to work as free farm labourers in a government-sponsored program. The young workers were known as Home Children, because most of them came from orphans' homes. The program began in the late 1860s and continued into the 1930s. Its purpose was supposedly to give orphans as well as poor and underprivileged children a new start in life.

Several books have been written on the subject as well as a film documentary made, all of which suggest that child welfare was not the prime motivation for the program. Moreover, the new lives in countries foreign to the children were not necessarily an improvement over their lives in Great Britain. Stories of misery and abuse are legend, and there is little doubt that this saga of human history brought unspeakable suffering to many of these children. There were stories of beatings, poor food, and having to live in rat-infested attics.

Not all the children suffered to the same degree, nor did they all experience exploitation and mistreatment. Most of the children in the program survived and established reasonable lives for themselves, in spite of the emotional scars. Many went on to get an education, find employment, marry and raise a family, and generally make good lives for themselves. Most of the boys sent to Canada were placed on farms to be labourers; the girls for the most part did domestic work in homes.

One of the more fortunate of the Home Children was Stuart Harris, an orphan, who arrived at Halifax's Pier 2 in 1910, when he was about five years old. He was one of a group of children from Middlemore Home in England. Nothing is known of Harris' early life in England. He was sent first to Cape Breton, but within a few years he came to Cole Harbour to live with Andrew and Hattie Settle who were childless. He grew up on their farm, attended Cole Harbour School, and learned farming techniques from Andrew Settle. He lived and worked his whole life on the Settle farm and eventually inherited it when they died. Harris married into one of the founding families of the community when he married Hattie Bissett. They had three sons: Melvin, Douglas, and Donald.

The Harrises drop in for a visit with the Settles at Upper Lawrencetown. Left to right: Jack Settle, Stuart Harris, Hattie Harris, and Clara Settle. A Sunday car drive was a popular pastime during the 1920s and 1930s and usually ended with a visit to a friend's house. (RE/Melvin Harris album)

When the Nova Scotia Government expropriated Stuart Harris's farm in the 1970s for the Forest Hills Land Assembly, it was a devastating blow. He died shortly afterwards.

Stuart's son Melvin discovered through research that other Home Children had made their way to Cole Harbour to live and work on farms. In fact there had been another young boy on the Settle farm before Stuart Harris's arrival. Arthur Slade came in 1904 but apparently did not remain for long. Once a child reached age 16, or in some cases age 18, they were allowed to leave and make their own way in the world. Other Cole Harbour area farmers who had Home Children were Robert Settle, M. Kuhn, Thomas Conrad, and Wallace Peverell.

Charles Devenport's journey to Nova Scotia in 1927 is a poignant story and at times reads like a Charles Dickens novel, featuring an unwed mother, a workhouse, an abusive foster home, trouble with the law, relocation to another country, and a life-long search for his mother.

Devenport was born in Wales in 1912, the son of Ellen (Nellie) Devenport. His early life was spent in a workhouse because of bronchitis and intestinal problems caused by malnutrition. The Child Welfare Society took him from his mother who was unable to properly care for him and placed him in a foster home with a Mrs. Hemsley whom he came to dread, for she showed him little or no affection.

When he was 16 years old, Devenport and some of his friends fell into trouble with the law. He recalled the incident in a newspaper interview years later:

> Just outside Nottingham where I was living at the time there were apple orchards [that] were surrounded by iron railings. One evening we jacked the railing apart and went into the orchard to get some apples and got caught by a big chap with two dogs.
>
> Then a bobby came along and I wound up in front of a magistrate and was sentenced to one year probation and had to go to the Nottingham Boys' Brigade two days a week for a year in lieu of going to a reform school.

At the club, 12 boys were asked to volunteer to go to Canada. Forty boys applied; Devenport was among those selected.

> Two weeks later we were told to pack our clothes and go to the railway station. I was sitting on the platform with my suitcase waiting for the train when I saw my mother coming towards me.
>
> She said, "You're leaving me," and I told her I was going to Canada.
>
> She gave me a five-pound note and a box camera and told me to save my money, be a good boy, and to write her. She kissed me then started to cry.
>
> She wrote me one letter and I answered faithfully. I wrote her another letter at the same address; she replied again, and then there were no more letters.

They sailed for Canada and when they arrived in Halifax they were immediately put into a quarantine shed. About the shed,

Charles Devenport is one of thousands of Home Children who came to Nova Scotia between the 1860s and the 1930s. Devenport arrived in 1927 after a minor brush with the law in Britain. He returned to England with the Canadian army during World War Two and came to Cole Harbour in 1952 to work at the Halifax County Hospital. (ca. 1940s/courtesy of Joan Devenport)

Devenport later recalled, "It was full of soot and everything you touched you got black and filthy. They gave us a box lunch but it was cold, hard, and dry, and fit for nothing but pigs." Devenport and his companions stayed in quarantine for 24 hours, then they travelled by train to Windsor. From there they were transported across the bridge to Falmouth to a farm known as the Dakeyne Street Lads Club Farm. The Players Tobacco Company and the Nova Scotia Government jointly owned it.

In a magazine article about some of the Home Children who came to the Maritime provinces, Devenport described his life at the Falmouth farm. "We'd cry at night and I could hear the other boys crying for quite a while. We missed our own native streets, and all the gang. We had been disinherited from our own country." The farm was eventually shut down due to poor treatment of the workers.

Devenport spent only six months on the farm before a kind bachelor farmer hired him as a farmhand in Hillcrest, near Kentville. He worked there and on other farms in the area, married and had a family. When World War Two broke out, he enlisted in the Royal Canadian Artillery. He shipped to England for training before being sent into combat in North Africa and Holland, respectively.

Melvin Harris, son of Stuart Harris, arranged a meeting of Maritimers with British Home Children connections at the Heritage Farm in May 2003. More than 35 former Home Children and relatives – the youngest of whom were his granddaughters Brigid and Brogan Harris, shown here with their grandfather – attended. (Sadie Harris 2003)

While in England, he began a 45-year search to reunite with his mother. His foster mother erroneously informed him that his real mother had died. He spent time looking for a grave without knowing that his mother was still alive. She had become a nurse and was married to a tailor named Michael Walsh.

When Devenport returned to Nova Scotia, he divorced his estranged wife, who had by then become an alcoholic, and took custody of his three children. He later married Joan Coomber, whom he had met in England. He bought a dairy farm in Cumberland County between Pugwash and Oxford, and his life began to turn around.

In 1952, he and his family moved to Cole Harbour, where he got a job at the Halifax County Home and Mental Hospital as a janitor.

After the County Hospital he worked at the Caldwell Road and Colonel John Stuart Schools. He also obtained a government contract to deliver mail in the Cole Harbour area. Most of his children were baptized in the old Meeting House, a United Church, where he was an elder.

As Devenport's circumstances improved, he continued his search for his mother. He made several trips to England and hired a number of genealogists. With the help of local newspapers, the radio station, and a weekly newspaper, several of his mother's friends came forward with helpful information. He found his mother's last known address by 1985, only to discover that she had died of a stroke in 1979 at the age of 89. She was buried in an unmarked grave in Bolsover Cemetery, Derbyshire.

Devenport had a grave marker erected at this grave and organized a memorial service, which was attended by his mother's friends and the people who had helped him in his search.

Devenport lived out his retirement in Cole Harbour, where he died on May 17, 1995, at 83. He was buried in the Dartmouth Memorial Gardens. Charlie Devenport's life and his quest to locate his mother were part of a 90-minute film documentary entitled, *The Lost Children of the Empire*, which won a Golden Globe Award.

In recent years, a few of the original now very elderly Home Children, as well as surviving spouses, children, and grandchildren have been getting together annually to compare stories, retrace connections, and acquire leads to their former lives.

Stuart Harris's son Melvin has been tracing his family history and has become involved with such a group. The Middlemore Home Children's Group has been holding annual reunions in the Maritime provinces for the past 22 years, bringing together Home Children and those with Home Children connections.

The Home Children program in which more than 240,000 boys and girls were shipped out of Britain to colonies and commonwealth countries under the Child Immigration Act to work as free farm labourers is a shameful, if little known, part of Canadian history.

25

WORLD WAR TWO

Nazi Germany's invasion of Poland on September 1, 1939, was quickly answered with a declaration of war from Great Britain and France on September 3. After a week-long debate in Parliament, Canada issued its own declaration of war on Germany. Almost immediately, recruiting stations opened up across Canada, and young men of the day answered the call to arms. They left their jobs, their farms, fishing boats, and schools, and exchanged their civilian clothes for military uniforms. For some young men still out of work from the Depression years, enlisting in one of the services meant three meals a day, a place to live, clothes, and $1.30 daily pay on top.

The war brought rapid changes to Halifax, Dartmouth, and the surrounding area in the form of a building boom and a significant population increase as soldiers, sailors, and airmen poured into the area along with their families. Others flooded in to work in the shipyards and factories that were turning out badly needed products to aid the war effort. Halifax Harbour was choked with ships of all shapes and sizes – warships, troop transports, and merchant ships to carry troops and vital supplies to Britain. Bedford Basin was the staging area for the convoys that left the safety of the harbour and threaded their way through a gauntlet of menacing German U-boats lurking off the Atlantic coast.

In Dartmouth, army bases were built at Faulkner's Field in the north end and at Hazelhurst in the south end. The open field at the foot of Dawson Street that once was the Fairfield Estate was quickly filled in with a group of buildings that became known as the Naval Armament Depot. The air force station at Eastern Passage, which had been enlarged as a make-work project during the Depression, now hummed with airplanes and men patrolling the eastern coast for enemy ships and submarines. Both McNabs and Lawlor Islands at

Airmen stationed at the RCAF Bell Lake Radar Station during World War Two participate in a recreational game of volleyball. The station closed down shortly after the war ended in 1945. (Harvey Patterson album)

the mouth of Halifax Harbour were fortified with coastal artillery to protect the harbour approaches. A submarine gate was installed across the harbour entrance.

Hartlen Point, near Eastern Passage, was transformed into the A-23 Training Unit, which was equipped with searchlights and anti-aircraft artillery guns to protect against possible aerial attack. A coastal artillery base was established at Lawrencetown, and an air force radar station was built near Bell Lake in Cole Harbour to search the sea and skies for enemy intruders.

The war years brought prosperity. Factories busily produced wartime necessities, and local shipyards worked around the clock building and repairing warships. Cole Harbour and area farmers found a ready market for their produce, eggs, milk, butter, chicken, and meat with the greatly increased population. Although the roads in the Cole Harbour area remained unpaved during the war years, there was a significant increase in daily traffic by military vehicles.

According to the Rev. George Russell, who ministered to three churches in the area from 1938 to 1941, World War Two created an entirely different community. After the hard years of the 1930s, the farmers began to prosper and have money. Many farmers saved their extra cash in the credit union. During the war, the Russells had a young air force couple from the Bell Lake radar station living with them, and a number of other families in the area also took in boarders during the war years because of the housing shortage. The Reverend Russell left Cole Harbour in 1941 for new ministerial duties in Glace Bay.

Cole Harbour lost much of its isolation during the war years with added military installations and the daily coming and going of military personnel from all over. By the start of World War Two, most of the farmers had some form of motorized transportation, making trips to Halifax and Dartmouth a lot easier and quicker. An air force corporal stationed at Bell Lake organized a Cub and Boy Scout troop, which he operated from Victoria Hall.

Several young men from Cole Harbour, Lawrencetown, Woodlawn, and Preston contributed to the war effort by enlisting in one of the services for duty overseas. Unlike World War One, the Black men of the area were able to enlist in regular military units. There was no segregated Black Battalion.

One resident who vividly recalled the war years in the Cole Harbour-Woodlawn area was Marion L. Settle, the daughter of Frank and Beatrice Settle. She was born and grew up on Farview Farm on Breakheart Hill.

> During the years of World War Two farm cash did not seem to be quite so tight. After Gram was gone we had a big house for four people plus those who worked with us and boarded at our house. There was an RCAF station at the other side of Bell Lake and lots of servicemen wanted places to bring their wives and/or their families so we rented rooms in Gram's side of the house. This helped Dad and Mother to save a little and buy a few Victory Bonds.
>
> We always had plenty to eat on the farm, but we also had to have ration cards for such items as sugar and butter. Gasoline was also rationed, all for the good of the war effort.

An airman stationed at the Bell Lake Radar Station during World War Two waits at Woodlawn Forks, where Woodlawn Road branched off the Cole Harbour Road. It is now the intersection of Portland Street and Woodlawn Road. (Harvey Patterson album)

We did not suffer as some did in the loss of loved ones, but there were sad times when a few we knew did not come home. The young men from our community who went into the services were sent boxes from time to time, and our Young People's Union helped with this. We also created a newsletter to help them get news from our area.

There was a very frightening time when a ship in Halifax Harbour [the *Trongate*] had to be sunk, and we thought the enemy had entered the harbour. It must have been a danger in some way, though not an enemy ship.

But it was sunk by gunfire. What a relief to get word the danger was over. [Fire had broken out on the *Trongate* anchored near Dartmouth for repairs. Since it had munitions on board, the authorities feared another Halifax Explosion and sank it by firing on it.]

The service people who lived at our house came and went and others came. Most of them were fine people who kept in touch with Mother many years after the war was over.

Victory Bonds and War Saving Stamps were quickly issued and sold by the federal government at the start of the war to raise additional funds to aid the war effort. The bonds were usually sold at rallies and annual campaigns. War Saving Stamps were sold for amounts less than a dollar to schoolchildren or anyone else that wanted to make a contribution. A group of young girls known as the Miss Canada Girls were organized in Dartmouth to sell War Saving Stamps. Clad in their bright red tunics with a red maple leaf, the Miss Canada Girls sold these stamps weekly to farmers from the area travelling to the Halifax Market and to others on the Dartmouth ferry each Saturday morning. The sale of Victory Bonds and War Saving Stamps continued until the end of the war.

Unlike World War One, when the local daily newspapers were the only source of news, a new medium – radio – was making its presence felt as a means of keeping abreast of war news from Great Britain and continental Europe. Most homes in the area had a radio in the living room as a source of news and family entertainment.

In the early years of the war, the news was grim with reports of the retreat from Dunkirk, the setbacks in the African desert, the Blitz on Britain, the constant U-boat attacks on merchant ships in the North Atlantic, and Canada's failed raid on Dieppe.

At home, there was some good news. Long after the fire at the former home in 1929, its replacement opened in the early 1940s, still along the western shore of Cole Harbour but on a new site on the west side of Bissett Road. County Council had set a special committee concerning the County Home. On August 18, 1938, the committee had recommended that council accept a tender of $245,391 for a new home to be known as the Halifax County Home and Mental Hospital. The new structure, built with reinforced concrete, was considered the most modern institution of its kind in Atlantic Canada. Like its predecessor, the new facility, which was also partially supported by a farm, created a number of new employment opportunities for the area.

The tide of battle abroad slowly began to turn with the entry of Russia and the United States into the war as allies against Germany, Italy, and Japan. The invasion of Normandy in June 1944 finally turned the war towards its conclusion with the unconditional surrender of Germany on May 7, 1945. The war with Japan ended in August with the dropping of atomic bombs on Hiroshima and Nagasaki.

The end of the war in Europe was marked with celebrations and dancing in the streets everywhere across Canada. However, VE Day celebrations in Halifax and Dartmouth turned to drunkenness, rioting, and looting, which resulted in heavy property damage and injuries to innocent victims. Some members of the armed forces and the civilian population received prison sentences and paid heavy fines for their part in what were coined the VE Day Riots.

A short time later, residents of Halifax and Dartmouth suffered through a night of terror that started in the early evening of July 18, 1945, when the Bedford Magazine that stored military ammunition and high explosives caught fire and exploded. The fire broke out on the magazine jetty, where ammunition had just been unloaded from a corvette. Within minutes the entire jetty as well as a barge tied along the wharf was in flames. At 6:30 P.M. the jetty and barge exploded, shattering windows and flattening some houses in nearby Burnside and Tufts Cove. The blast was felt throughout Dartmouth and across the harbour in Halifax. The fire spread from the jetty to other areas of the Bedford Magazine property, threatening other buildings where explosives were stored.

Most residents of north Dartmouth were finishing their evening meal when the explosion occurred. Roads in and out of the area were soon choked with people in cars trying to flee from the scene and thus creating problems for fire engines, police, and ambulances trying to get to the magazine.

Explosions continued throughout the early evening, threatening the entire area. People who had lived through the 1917 explosion had premonitions of a new disaster. By 9:00 P.M. a convoy of military vehicles began evacuating residents from north Dartmouth to a safer location at the Hartlen Point A-23 Training Station near Eastern Passage. Approximately 2,000 residents from the north end were taken to safety. The evacuees spent a sleepless night on barracks floors. Some Dartmouth residents fled the town to stay with family and friends living in nearby Cole Harbour, Woodlawn, Lawrencetown, and communities along the Eastern Shore.

Don Harris remembered that the driveway to his father's farm on the Cole Harbour Road was lined with the cars of Dartmouth residents who had left the town to seek safety elsewhere. Community and church halls opened for overnight shelter, and many gratefully accepted the offer.

Firefighters continued battling the raging inferno throughout the night and into the next morning. The last explosion occurred just before dawn and was heard as far away as Eastern Passage and Cole Harbour. Many evacuees feared north Dartmouth was in ruins similar to the 1917 explosion.

After nearly 10 hours, tired and exhausted firefighters finally brought the fire under control. By the following afternoon, residents returned to their homes and were happily surprised to find them and other buildings still standing with only minimal damage – cracked chimneys and broken windows – all easily repairable. Unlike the earlier explosion, in which 1,951 people died and about 9,000 were injured, only 1 person was killed as a result of the Bedford Magazine explosion.

Within months of the end of World War Two, soldiers, sailors, and airmen returned home to their wives or girlfriends, and to their civilian jobs or further education. Others never returned. By the end of war, Cole Harbour was still very much a rural farming community, but the winds of change were blowing, and within a few decades the serene rural life would vanish as the area was transformed into a bustling suburban community.

26

FARMING 🍏 A COLE HARBOUR TRADITION

Cole Harbour's young men returned from war to their farms and a way of life that had been part of the community's heritage for almost two centuries.

In the late 1940s and 1950s, Cole Harbour was still untouched by the residential housing boom underway in the nearby Town of Dartmouth and its adjacent communities. Rural families were still able to make a decent living from farming. The family farm and farming methods had modernized over time, improving farm production, and farming remained the core activity.

Traditionally, Cole Harbour was a market garden area from the early nineteenth century until farming ended in the 1970s. There were other types of farms – dairy, pork, and poultry – but market gardening was the mainstay for most farmers. Market gardening developed and prospered on the outskirts of most urban growth centres. Before the advent of modern transportation and storage and processing capabilities, city dwellers relied on small backyard garden plots for fresh vegetables or trips to surrounding country farms, weekly visits to green markets, or door-to-door peddlers. As cities and populations grew, the production of perishable garden products for a market of urban dwellers became a way of life for farmers living on the fringe of these urban centres. Most vegetables were seasonal. Some were highly perishable and had to be sold within a couple of days.

One way to get a jump on the growing season was to plant seeds indoors before it was time to plant them outdoors, so that the plants were well established by the time the frost was out of the ground. Greenhouses made this possible. They often overlapped and co-existed with hotbeds. Greenhouses eventually took over, but for many years hotbeds were the practical but labour-intensive choice. With hotbeds, a market gardener could realize a good income from a relatively small acreage.

Leslie MacDonald perches on a hotbed, perhaps to absorb some of its warmth. Plants were normally set out in March, so it was commonplace that they would be growing while snow surrounded their protected beds. (RE/1920s?/Melvin Harris album)

Some Cole Harbour farmers set out as many as 100 hotbeds, which measured three feet by six feet each and were covered over with panes of glass. The heat came from the fermenting animal manure filling the beds. Planting vegetables and flower seeds in this manner went as far back as the Roman times.

The preparation of the manure and soil, the setting up and maintenance of the beds required a high level of experience and skill. Hotbeds were planted around mid-March before winter frost and snowstorms had ended but while temperatures could sometimes reach midsummer highs. Farmers responded to these temperature changes by covering and uncovering the hotbeds to protect their precious crops for the six to eight weeks they resided there. Then as many as 100,000 small plants were transplanted in the fields, a process that required many hands and was best done in the evening to avoid the heat of the day. With a summer of weeding, cultivating, and good weather a farmer could bring a hefty crop to harvest and deliver it to customers in fine condition.

Working together on the Murray Ritcey farm are, from left, Bob Ritcey (Murray's son), Cornelius Van de Rijt (farmhand), Anna Maria Van de Rijt, Lorne Ritcey (Murray's brother), Murray Ritcey, and Stanley Ritcey (Murray's father). (Marj Ritcey, spring 1958/Ritcey collection)

Marketing crops depended on the farmer's skill in establishing customers and reliably servicing them, whether citizens at the Halifax City Market or wholesalers or exporters. Gordon Eisener, who sold exclusively to wholesalers, spoke of deliveries of 500 fifty-pound bags of cabbages. Keeping the harvested crop cool was essential in maintaining quality. By the middle of the twentieth century Eisener and Stuart Harris had both installed cold storage units for the temporary storage of their crops. Before the advent of these units, root cellars were typically used to store longer-lasting vegetables. Other produce, such as lettuce and green peas, simply had to be sold immediately.

Eisener's lettuce was considered of such superb quality that he was once given a special order for a dinner in Halifax during World War Two for Britain's Prime Minister Winston Churchill, who stopped off in the port city on his way to Quebec for a high-level meeting with U.S. President Franklin Roosevelt and Canadian Prime Minister Mackenzie King.

Gordon Eisener loads a truckload of cabbages in the 1950s, when they were often exported. Lloyd and Gerald Eisener are on top of the truck. (ca. 1965, courtesy of Lloyd Eisener)

When the T. Eaton Company opened its Halifax department store on Granville Street in the late 1920s, it featured a grocery store on the basement level. Ira Settle offered to supply fresh vegetables to the store. He later recalled that the manager was less than enthusiastic about the idea, until Ira promised to bring fresh produce each day and remove anything not in prime condition. The manager readily accepted this offer. Settle's relationship with Eaton's continued for as long as they had their grocery store. He had a similar arrangement with other Halifax grocery stores.

For market gardeners, fertilizer was an important aspect of crop growing, and for many years this meant livestock manure for most farmers. Many Cole Harbour farmers also used kelp, called sea manure, which they collected from nearby beaches. Eastern Passage and Cow Bay were favoured locations for collecting sea manure, as was the Cole Harbour beach and adjoining shore.

Maurice Strum recalled that after a storm there could be 30 to 40 teams on the beaches collecting the washed-up kelp. Farmers rose early, fed their horses, and were ready to leave for the beach a little after 5:00 A.M. As soon as they arrived at the beach they staked out their area by putting their horse and wagon parallel to the shoreline. Farmers weren't allowed to harvest the kelp until sunrise because of a Halifax County bylaw; without the bylaw some farmers would be at the beach all night.

The Halifax County bylaw dealing with sea manure stated, "[N]o person shall be allowed to collect, pile, or haul, or otherwise remove kelp or sea manure from the shore, coves, or beaches within the limits of Halifax County before sunrise or after sunset. Any person violating the foregoing regulation shall be fined not less than two dollars or more than eight dollars."

Another supply of animal manure was from businesses such as Ben's Bakery in Halifax, which used horse-drawn wagons in the early part of the twentieth century to deliver their products to customers. The bakery maintained stables in the city, which produced large quantities of horse manure. In some cases they gave the manure to farmers who were willing to go to their stables and cart it away regularly. As the demand for manure increased, some businesses began charging the farmers for what they hauled away. On the return trip to Cole Harbour the manure was frequently off-loaded and piled at the foot of Breakheart Hill. The farmer might return to the city for another load and often made several more trips to get the load over the hill. Sometimes a third horse was used to lighten the burden for the other horses.

Eisener credited agricultural representative Art MacLaughlin with the suggestion that farmers using hotbeds and greenhouses sterilize their manure and soil at the Woodside sugar refinery. To do this, a wagon or truckload of manure was tightly covered then it was driven over the steam outlet at the refinery and kept there for at least 20 minutes. The scalding refinery steam at 180°F raised the temperature of the manure and killed most of the unwanted organisms. This practice continued until the sugar refinery closed down at the start of World War Two.

If market gardening was the predominant type of farming throughout the Cole Harbour area, dairy farming was probably next most important. In the early twentieth century about 20 small milk

Cyril and Stewart join their father Tom Bissett before he sets out on his Dartmouth milk route in the late 1930s. The Bissett home in the background is now Maryann's Gift Shop. (Stewart Bissett album)

producers in the area sold their product door to door each day. To compete successfully at that time, farmers had to provide bottled milk. Many had their own embossed bottles, a few of which still exist in private collections. Ira Settle said his father Robert was the first dairy farmer in the area to use glass bottles. Robert's son Charles Settle, who eventually took over the business, became one of the largest milk producers in the area. Nat Patterson, another local dairy farmer, specialized in cream and purchased additional cream from other farms in the area to boost his own supply. Tom Bissett collected milk from other farms in the area for his customers and Peter Max Kuhn also operated a successful retail milk delivery business from his farm in Woodlawn.

Although dairy farms used various types of fodder for their cattle, one popular source of food was brewer's grains – the malted barley that remains after it has gone through the mashing process at the brewery. The mash was filtered to separate the liquid, known as wort. The spent grain was of no further use in the brewing process, though still a nutritious food supplement for cattle. Before trucks came into regular farm use, some dairy producers took their horses and wagons to the Halifax and Dartmouth breweries and hauled away the brewer grain for their milk cows. It was another heavy load for the horses to drag over Breakheart Hill.

Operating a successful dairy demanded skilled labour, an ever-increasing outlay for equipment, and constant attention to sanitation. When pasteurization and other refinements became law, only the larger dairies could compete profitably.

One of the largest dairy operations in the area was Woodlawn Dairy. Started in 1895 by John and Norman Morash, they operated as the Morash Brothers Dairy until 1912 or 1913. J. R. Morash operated the business until 1928, when his sons took over and changed the name to Woodlawn Dairy. Most of the smaller milk producers in the area gave up selling their milk door to door and instead sold their milk wholesale to Woodlawn Dairy, which came out to the farms to collect it. The company provided door-to-door milk delivery throughout Dartmouth and surrounding area using horses and wagons until the late 1940s. The brothers moved the operation from Woodlawn to Pleasant Street in Dartmouth and operated at that location until 1946, when they built a completely modern processing plant on Canal Street. Woodlawn Dairy operated as a separate company until 1967, when it became part of the Twin Cities Cooperative Dairy.

One very important aspect in the life of Cole Harbour farmers during the late nineteenth and early twentieth centuries was their involvement in the Dartmouth Agricultural Society. The organization came into existence on June 28, 1880, when a group of Dartmouth and area farmers met in the Anchor Lodge in Cole Harbour. The purpose of the society was to hear lectures on the various topics and trends in agriculture, exchange ideas with other members, and engage in friendly competition.

Several of the founding members were Cole Harbour farmers; these familiar names appear in the early records: Settle, Beck, Turner, Kuhn, Lawlor, Farquharson, Lloy, Eisener, Cross, and Elliot. The first president was John G. Bissett; Edward Foster was secretary; and James A. Beck was treasurer. The first directors were: W. H. Keeler, J. Morash, Charles Bissett, W. K. Angwin, and Peter McNab. Other Cole Harbour family names involved in the Agricultural Society in later years were Bell, Baker, Roche, Patterson, Tulloch, Peverill, and Lydiard.

The society's minutes book, now in the Cole Harbour Rural Heritage Society's archives, records numerous programs and events from the date of the first meeting until November 5, 1907. The annual membership fee was one dollar. Early
meetings, attended by 40 to 50 farmers, alternated between Anchor Lodge, which charged $1.50 for the use of the hall, and Brookhouse in Woodlawn. Later meetings took place at various locations, including the Dartmouth ferry building.

By 1895, the Agricultural Society listed more than 100 farmers in its membership. There were several other agricultural societies scattered around the province, and the Dartmouth group kept in touch with most of them. Dartmouth president G. J. Troop was a delegate in 1895 to an Antigonish meeting to organize the Nova Scotia Farmers' Association.

One of the first projects discussed by the society was the purchase of a purebred bull to be kept in the area so that farmers could upgrade their dairy herds. On January 27, 1881, John Beck was picked to go to Major Curack's farm in Cornwallis to look at a purebred Ayrshire bull named "Lord Cornwallis," which he subsequently purchased for $50. He kept the bull at his farm, for which he was paid nine dollars a month for the bull's upkeep. The fee for stud services was 50¢ for members and 75¢ for non-members of the society. A few months later, society members realized that they were losing money on the bull and decided to sell him to the highest bidder. In September 1881, R. Settle bought "Lord Cornwallis" for $32. In the eight months the bull was owned by the society, "Lord Cornwallis" earned only $23.50 in stud fees. Over the next few years, the Society continued to purchase bulls, cows, and stallions in an effort to improve and upgrade the local livestock.

On October 11, 1881, a plowing match and exhibition was held at James Farquharson's Preston farm. This was the first attempt to hold an exhibition and many more would follow in succeeding years. Secretary Foster wrote of the first exhibition, "The day was very cold and windy, still there was a large number present. It was on the whole a successful exhibition."

Five plows competed in the plowing match. Charles Bissett won the prize of $10. The four-page prize list includes prizes for early Rose

The exhibition building and rink on Synott's Hill in Dartmouth was for many years the site of the Dartmouth Agricultural Society's annual exhibition and also saw tug-of-war competitions. The building was destroyed in the 1917 Halifax Harbour Explosion. (top, 1884 DHM; above, 1884 DHM)

potatoes to D. Donovan and R. Settle Jr.; for drumhead cabbage to E. Cross, Peter McNab Kuhn, and Jud Baker; for long blood beets to C. J. Keilor and R. Settle Sr.; for winter apples to C. J. Lydiard and Henry Baker. At this exhibition prizes for butter went to Mrs. D. Donovan, Mrs. J. Morash, and Mrs. G. Kuhn. At subsequent exhibitions the butter-makers weren't acknowledged even as "Mrs."; their entries were under their husband's names.

There were numerous discussions on the locations of exhibitions, joint exhibitions with Halifax, representation on exhibition committees in other areas, the provincial exhibition, and the ongoing rivalry with Middle Musquodoboit as to the site for the Halifax County Exhibition. By 1889, Dartmouth gave up hosting the Halifax County Exhibition in favour of Middle Musquodoboit, where it continues to be held to the present day.

Prizes headed the list for discussions over the exhibitions, but there were also discussions regarding the entertainment program, tenders for refreshments, and arranging special rates on the ferry for Halifax visitors. In 1890, the society held a raffle during the exhibition offering a parlour organ as the prize for the holder of the winning 25¢ ticket.

The minutes book in the spring of 1884 records discussions for the building of an ice rink, which could double as the location for the annual agricultural exhibition. Society president G. J. Troop presented a set of plans prepared by architect Henry Elliot for a suitable building estimated to cost $2,500.

The members decided to open a stock list at $10 a share. A committee was appointed to solicit subscriptions, and within a short time members purchased approximately $1,800 worth of stock. Additional minutes book entries record that repairs to the building in 1891 were estimated at $700. Located at the top of Synott's Hill on the Dartmouth Common, the building was totally destroyed in the 1917 Halifax Harbour Explosion.

The last list of members in the minutes book is for the year 1905–06. At that time membership in the society had dropped to just 40. At times they had difficulty getting enough members for a quorum in order to conduct business. The president and executive in the final days of the society were G. J. Troop, president; S. W. Lydiard, vice-president; A. S. Wolfe, secretary-treasurer; and Maynard Tulloch, assistant secretary. Directors were Henry Baker, C. J. Keeler, J. M. Henneberry, Arthur Giles, and W. W. Peverill. The Livestock Committee, which had been increased to five members, included M. Tulloch, R. Settle, W. W. Peverill, George A. Hall, and C. J. Keeler.

For the farmers of Cole Harbour and surrounding area, attending the weekly Farmers' Market in Halifax to sell their goods was a way of life that began in the 1700s and continued well into the twentieth century. Some farmers began their weekly market visits when they were young children, which allowed them to help contribute to the family's income.

One woman who went to market at an early age was Rose Faucher of West Chezzetcook, known to most market regulars as "Big Rosie." She recalled later in an interview that she had started attending the Halifax Market when she was only four years old. Like many of the Chezzetcook women, she was a proficient knitter and was still turning out socks well into her eighties.

The majority of Chezzetcook residents walked to the Halifax Market carrying or pulling their load, or sometimes pushing it in a wheelbarrow. Maurice Strum remembered hearing them pass his house on Long Hill at dawn, chattering away in French, sometimes singing and usually knitting as they walked. John Giles said his grandfather told him that he remembered seeing a group of Chezzetcookers skating past his home on the Cole Harbour Road, which was ice-covered. They were pulling hand sleighs loaded with socks and mitts as well as smelts and eels.

Not all the horses pulled plows and wagons. Donnie Turner of Westphal became well known all over the province for his horse-racing exploits. His headstone in the Woodlawn Cemetery has a racehorse and sulky on it. Younger brother George Turner was involved with horses from a very early age, and by the 1920s was travelling around the countryside with a draft stallion providing stud services for farmers' mares. George bought his first racehorse in 1934 and became one of the top breeders, trainers, and drivers in the Maritimes. Although he raced on many Canadian and American racetracks, he was known locally for racing his horses on the ice at Lake Banook during the winter.

George Turner drives Josedale Clansmen over an ice-covered Lake Banook in Dartmouth during a winter harness-racing event. Turner, involved in horse racing for many years, bought his first racehorse in 1934 and became one of the top horse breeders, trainers, and drivers in the Maritime provinces. This photo was taken in 1959, the last year for the International Ice Championship on Lake Banook. (1959/courtesy of Shirley Turner)

Sportscaster Colleen Jones of CBC interviews George Turner during a special horse-racing meet on Lake Banook in 1987 to celebrate the popular winter pastime. Turner was 86 at the time. (1987, courtesy of Shirley Turner)

When a special ice-racing meet was staged in 1987 to commemorate the popular winter activity, George Turner at age 86 was on hand to take part. George Turner also operated a general store and gas pumps on the No. 7 Highway opposite the Lake Major Road.

One interesting period in Cole Harbour farming history was the participation by some of the community's young men on the "harvest trains" to the Prairie provinces at the beginning of the twentieth century. The harvest trains came about due to the need for extra hands to help harvest the grain crops on the Prairies. It was a federal government program that subsidized the fares for trainloads of young men from both the east and west coasts of the country. The program started in the 1890s and continued without interruption until 1928. Some of the Cole Harbour area men who participated were Harry Joe Giles, Peter Max Kuhn, Wilfred Kuhn, Harvey Patterson, and Charlie Negus.

The trains that carried the young men left from Halifax and Sydney and stopped at centres in New Glasgow, Truro, and Amherst to pick up other workers. Other trains left from New Brunswick centres. A few veterans went back year after year to help with the harvest, but for most one year in their late teens or early twenties was enough.

One or more young men from most of the farming families in Cole Harbour, Westphal, Woodlawn, and Eastern Passage ventured west on the harvest trains at one time or another. For some it was an adventure, an opportunity to see more of the country, but for most the main attraction was the relatively high wages. While some squandered their earnings, many others were able to save most of what they earned and return home with a substantial nest egg.

As the trains rolled west picking up more and more workers, the rough accommodations in special cars grew crowded. During the several days' journey, there was little to do but drink and play cards – a combination that often resulted in arguments and fisticuffs. At the infrequent stops, workers left the trains to buy food and drink. Although theoretically a good business opportunity for local merchants, the visits often deteriorated into drunkenness and looting. According to A. A. MacKenzie's *The Harvest Train*, "Haystacks were set on fire, cars were overturned, and merchandise was stolen from the stores." Experiences on the train coupled with the hard work of the

After a hard day's work, the young farmers of the Cole Harbour area often enjoyed pitting their strength and skill against their counterparts from other communities in a tug-of-war competition. Teams were known by the combined weight of their 10 members. Here is the Cole Harbour 1,400-pound team, front row (left to right): Bob Settle, Charles Settle, Harvey Patterson, and Fred Bissett. Back Row (left to right): Bill MacKenzie, John Giles, Tom Bissett, Dick Owens (coach), Harry Elliot, Jim Beck, and Charles Elliot. (1920s, Harry Elliot album)

harvest were two reasons that many young men participated for only one season.

Nova Scotia had a farm program in which high school students were employed on local farms from late spring through the summer. During the last year of World War One, raising food for the burgeoning army and civilian population was given a high priority by the government. Participating students were given the assurance that their past year's work would be used as the graduating standard rather than the usual June examinations. One Dartmouth student involved was Ian Forsyth, who later became superintendent of Dartmouth schools. Forsyth spent a summer at an Upper Lawrencetown farm owned by Peter McNab Kuhn, who also ran a grocery store in Dartmouth, and

Rogation Services were held in the spring of the year by the Anglican Church to bless the seeds, crops, animals, and anything related to farming. This particular service took place in the 1960s on the Stuart Harris farm, now the Cole Harbour Heritage Farm Museum. (Robert Tulloch album)

operated by his son Peter Max Kuhn. Forsyth lived at the family's farmhouse and spent his days carrying out farm-related chores.

In the early twentieth century, tug-of-war competitions were popular recreation among area farmers. After a hard day's work, the young men got together to practise, usually on a level piece of road. Maurice Strum remembers practising at the intersection of the Bissett and Cole Harbour Roads, where St. Andrew's Church stood at that time. Ira Settle said his team practiced at the intersection of Cole Harbour Road (now Portland Street in Dartmouth) and Gaston Road. The actual tug-of-war pulls were usually held indoors, most often at the old Dartmouth rink. Prizes consisted of clocks, chairs, and sets of china – one of the more popular prizes.

Teams were known by the total weight of its 10 members. A heavyweight team was usually 1,500 pounds, a lighter team approximately 1,200 pounds. Harvey Patterson coached a very strong team in Woodlawn. Dick Owen coached a successful heavyweight Cole Harbour team.

The Dartmouth Kiwanis Club organized the Bell K Calf Club in 1950. The service club purchased calves for boys and girls living on Cole Harbour farms to look after. Several of the young people showed their calves at field days and exhibitions. The club was named for Laurie Bell, who was president of the Kiwanis in 1950. Shown here are (left to right) Sinclair Giles, William Giles, Harold Elliot Jr., Donald Harris, Alfie Giles, Keith Settle, Stanley Giles, Doug Harris, Robert Ritcey, Harold Turner, and Dora Giles in front. (Benjamin's Studios/courtesy of Maurice Strum)

In 1962, the congregation of St. Andrew's Anglican Church revived a farming tradition known as the Rogation Service to ask the Lord's blessing on the crops, animals, seeds, and everything else to do with the farmer's year. It appears to have been held on the Stuart Harris farm. Much later, the Cole Harbour Rural Heritage Society organized five Rogation Services from 1979 to 1981 and again in 1993.

By the mid-twentieth century area farmers were well served by the Department of Agriculture Extension Service, which supplied representatives for the area. The men, and later women, helped local farmers by bringing them the latest ideas and advice, particularly in promoting co-operation among producers, marketing strategies, and long-term planning. Some representatives who worked in the area were Peter Stewart, Tim Haliburton, and Art MacLaughlin.

In 1949–50, Peter Stewart was involved with the Bell K Calf Club. The name of the club came from long-time Dartmouth Kiwanian, Laurie Bell, and the K was for Kiwanis. Dartmouth Kiwanis Club members went to other parts of the province and purchased a number of purebred Guernsey calves to give to farm children in Cole Harbour, who raised and trained their animals and were judged on the results. Some exhibited their animals at the Halifax County Exhibition in Middle Musquodoboit.

Upper photo, Maurice and Willow (Henneberry) Strum proudly display some of their bountiful harvest in the 1930s. Willow was the daughter of J. M. Henneberry, superintendent of the County Home from 1899 to 1906. (Maurice Strum collection)

Lower photo, Ervin Clayton shows off some good-size potatoes grown on Bryden Bissett's farm in 1953. (1953/ courtesy of Frank Bissett)

Although farming has nearly disappeared from Cole Harbour, a few families continue the farming tradition. Kenny Conrad raises beef cattle. Melvin Harris operates a market garden near the end of Bissett Lake Road. Stewart Bissett produces vegetables and keeps some livestock at his Bissett Road farm. Mary Ann LaPierre grows produce at her farm on No. 7 Highway in East Preston, which she sells at the Halifax City Market as did her father, mother, sister and grandmother. LaPierre has been an active supporter of the Halifax Market, serving as president and helping to keep it going when it was without a home. The market is thriving at its current location in the Keith's Brewery.

Until the early twentieth century, Cole Harbour was considered one of the best farming areas in the province. By the 1950s and 1960s, its close proximity to Halifax and Dartmouth, which had served it so well for two centuries, became one of the reasons for the decline of its farms. There were other reasons that farming declined, even before the surge in residential development began in earnest – the limited size of the Cole Harbour farms and the competition brought about by improvement in transportation and storage methods for fresh produce. There are still a few farmers in Preston, Lawrencetown, Seaforth, Grand Desert, and Chezzetcook, but the golden years of farming in Cole Harbour are over. The tradition will fade into the mists of time, unless future generations keep it alive.

VI
CHANGES AND CHALLENGES
MID-TWENTIETH CENTURY TO 2003

27
POST-WAR YEARS

28
A DECADE OF CHANGE 1960S

29
THE ROYAL COMMISSION

30
MR. COLE HARBOUR

31
THE COLE HARBOUR RURAL HERITAGE SOCIETY

32
VOICES FROM THE PAST

33
THE BULLDOZING ERA

34
POLITICS THEN AND NOW

35
A CENTURY ENDS

27

POST-WAR YEARS

Dartmouth's population growth begun during the war years accelerated in the years immediately following the war. By the start of the 1950s, most of the vacant land in the town was rapidly turning into housing and apartment projects.

Construction of the Angus L. Macdonald Bridge, the dream of many politicians and business leaders for more than half a century, finally became a reality. Talk of a replacement bridge across the harbour began shortly after the old railway bridge collapsed during a summer night and silently floated away in 1893. There were discussions and feasibility studies and more discussions on the importance of a cross-harbour bridge to the future economic development of the area. War and the Depression made the project financially unrealistic until the 1950s. Premier Angus L. Macdonald turned the sod in March 1952 to start construction. Unfortunately, the premier did not live to see the bridge that would carry his name completed and opened.

Almost immediately after the sod-turning, clearing land began on both sides of the harbour for the necessary approach roads. Once the land was cleared, the concrete uprights were put in place, and slowly a steel suspension span crossed the harbour linking the two communities. Most of the sand needed for the concrete foundation came from local beaches in the area, including Rainbow Haven Beach.

The first vehicle to cross the new bridge even before it was officially opened was driven by Leslie MacDonald of Cole Harbour who was a driver carrying supplies of steel for George H. Day. The vehicle travelled from Dartmouth to Halifax.

The bridge was completed and officially opened with great fanfare on April 2, 1955, by Premier Macdonald's widow. The new bridge was an instant success with motorists and pedestrians alike. The only group unhappy with the bridge was the Dartmouth Ferry Commission, which watched its motorized traffic quickly evaporate in favour of the faster bridge crossing. Within months of the bridge opening, the car ferries were retired and replaced with smaller passenger ferries.

The bridge was a boon to farmers in the communities adjacent to Dartmouth because it relieved them of the early-morning rush to line up for the Friday and Saturday morning ferries to the Halifax Market.

The bridge further accelerated residential and commercial building in Dartmouth. By the mid-1950s, the Town of Dartmouth had run out of available land, and the population began spilling over the town boundaries into the adjacent communities of Tufts Cove, Port Wallace, Westphal, Woodlawn, and Woodside. Woodlawn and Westphal experienced the greatest residential growth as the once fertile farmland was almost instantly transformed into subdivisions. These new housing developments without paved streets were served by wells and septic tanks instead of water and sewer lines. School construction could not keep pace with the mushrooming population.

In the late fifties, the residents of suburbia began pushing the County Council for services similar to those provided in the adjacent town: water and sewer, paved streets, better educational and recreational facilities. The County Council, set up to provide services to mainly rural communities, was ill-equipped to deal with the demands. To the suburbanites the only solution to the problem was amalgamation with the Town of Dartmouth.

Cole Harbour continued as a farming community throughout the 1950s and most of the 1960s, but the idyllic rural lifestyle enjoyed by the residents would soon be disrupted; the population boom that had transformed Westphal and Woodlawn to urban suburbs was creeping into Cole Harbour's farming community.

One women's organization that played an important role in the life of the Cole Harbour community following World War Two was the Women's Institute of Nova Scotia. The organization, started in 1913, was largely centred in rural farming communities throughout the province. In 1935, the Westphal Women's Institute president, Frances Turner, organized a petition to have the area adjacent to Woodlawn, known at that time as the Preston Road, changed to Westphal in honour of brothers George and Phillip Westphal, who

His truck loaded with produce, Cole Harbour farmer Murray Ritcey heads off to participate in Dartmouth's Natal Day Parade. Farming was a business that Cole Harbour farmers were good at and proud of. (ca. 1948/Ritcey collection)

were born near Salmon River and left home as teenagers to join the Royal Navy. Both men rose to the rank of admiral.

The Cole Harbour branch of the Women's Institute of Nova Scotia, formed on November 25, 1946, operated for several years as both service and social club, carrying out several worthwhile community projects. They supplied drinking water fountains and cleaning supplies to the Cole Harbour School. In later years, the Cole Harbour branch bought a projector and screen and other supplies for the Caldwell Road School. They also supported the Boy Scouts and Cubs in the community and undertook numerous projects to assist the patients at the Halifax County Home and Mental Hospital.

Women's Institute members held regular dances at Victoria Hall and split the profits with the organization that operated the hall. They raised extra money by catering for weddings and banquets. In the early years the members met in Victoria Hall. When the hall was not available they met in members' homes.

The Institute's early minutes books have been lost, but those that have been saved begin in 1954 and offer a detailed account of the meetings, the names of the women involved, and the various projects carried out by the group. In the formative years as many as 25 women attended meetings, but in later years as few as 6 attended. The remaining minutes books are in the archival collection of the Cole Harbour Heritage Farm Museum. The last minutes book entry is dated May 15, 1975.

Another improvement that Cole Harbour residents applauded was the paving of the Cole Harbour Road. The pavement meant the end of dust in the summer, muddy ruts in the spring, and easier snow removal in the winter. Gordon Eisener, who moved to Cole Harbour from Woodlawn in 1939, said the road into Dartmouth was a dirt road until 1954, when it was finally paved. He also remembered that every man over 18 years old had to take his turn to help clear the unpaved road of snow following a winter storm; failure to help with the shovelling could result in a fine. At that time, local road overseers were appointed to look after the area roads.

By the end of 1955, the Cole Harbour Road was paved from Dartmouth to the vicinity of the County Hospital. This ribbon of black asphalt running through the community made the journey into town faster and easier. It also opened up the farming community to more residential construction. The modern new bungalows and two-storey houses made an interesting contrast on the local landscape to the farmhouses and barns that had been built more than a century ago.

One new and different building erected in the area by young farmer Eric Geldart in 1950 was described in the local newspaper as an "apartment house for hens." These pampered chicks, 1,500 in total, were housed in a new three-storey thermocrete building measuring 50 feet by 36 feet. An automatic water distribution system was incorporated into the structure along with a lighting system, which turned on in the morning and off late at night by a special control. The hens lived on the top two floors, while the basement section was used for a garage, storeroom, and egg room.

Geldart had started in the egg business as a boy in the 1940s with 100 hens on his father's farm. His father, Walter Geldart, operated a dairy farm of 100 cows. Eric built the modern henhouse on his own five-acre farm, next to his father's.

Left, Eric Geldart as a young man. Above, these henhouses at the Geldart farm on the Cole Harbour Road in the 1950s were not the "apartment house for hens" variety, but probably shelters used in raising chickens to the laying stage. Across the road at the left is Victoria Hall, a landmark in the community for many years. (left, RE/Geldart collection; above 1950s)

Stuart Harris and his sons Douglas and Melvin reportedly tried for a couple of years an addition to their farm of 100 young turkeys. The Harrises were primarily market gardeners, but they also kept dairy cows on their 50-acre Cole Harbour Road farm.

With an active credit union available to assist the farmers with their financial matters, the next logical step for mutual assistance among the farmers was the formation of a co-operative, which began in the early 1960s. The seeds for the co-operative movement had been sown in the 1950s, when a buyers' club was organized. A dozen or so farmers had banded together to purchase feed and fertilizer by the railway carload in order to get a better price. The train brought the feed and fertilizer into the railway station in Dartmouth, where the local farmers drove in to pick it up in their trucks. Some of the first men involved in the buyers' club were Murray Ritcey, Stuart Harris,

John Giles, Harold Giles, and Bob Davies. The buyers' club eventually evolved into the Eastern Halifax County Co-operative, which continued buying supplies for the farmers and arranged the sale of the farmers' produce to wholesalers and stores in order to a obtain a better price.

The Dartmouth Rod and Gun Club, one of the oldest in the Maritime provinces, had been located on Dartmouth's Lake Banook before it moved to Gaston Road. In 1942, members of the Dartmouth club won the Maritime Trap Shooting Championship. The growing residential population in south Dartmouth made the Gaston Road site impractical. In 1955, the Dartmouth Rod and Gun Club announced their relocation to Strawberry Island in Cole Harbour. For years, Strawberry Island had been a popular berry-picking spot for residents. The Cole Harbour property, which was leased from Harold Horne, permitted fly casting, duck hunting, and trap shooting for its members. The club held its first shooting competition at its new home in Cole Harbour in April 1955, and the following year it hosted the Nova Scotia Trap Shooting Championships.

Philip Morash of Cole Harbour enjoys shooting at the Dartmouth Trap and Skeet Club near Rainbow Haven Beach. (Scott Morash March 1977/courtesy of Scott Morash)

In the Halifax County 1955 municipal elections, District 14, which included the communities of Tufts Cove, Cole Harbour, Port Wallace, Westphal, and Woodlawn, became a dual constituency, allowing for two elected members. Councillor Ira Settle of Cole Harbour, the incumbent councillor, was re-elected by acclamation. Capt. John Matthews won the second seat on council.

The *Dartmouth Free Press* reported in 1955 that a company incorporated as the Silver Sands Company had purchased Silver Sands

Beach in Cow Bay from the estate of Robert Stomford for $50,000. The company planned to use the beach area for recreational purposes.

Early the following year, there were reports that Trynor Construction Company was removing sand from a portion of Silver Sands Beach. The company maintained that the area from which the sand was being removed was a section of the beach unused by picnickers and swimmers. Later in the year, more complaints were made that Trynor Construction Company's removal of the sand to build the runways at the nearby Shearwater Naval Air Station would eventually destroy the beach. The owner of the construction company assured his critics that the beach would be restored during the winter months by the action of the sea. Nevertheless, Dartmouth businessman Jake Creighton, speaking to a meeting of the Dartmouth Kiwanis Club, urged provincial and municipal governments to take a greater interest in the preservation of local beaches. (The sand did not return over the ensuing decades.)

The Halifax County Home and Mental Hospital, which had opened at the start of the 1940s and had been hailed as the most up-to-date mental hospital in the Atlantic region, came under fire for overcrowding. A report from the Halifax County's Welfare Committee stated that during the day there were only 20 staff members on duty to care for nearly 600 patients. During the night shift there were even fewer staff members.

In February 1956, members of the hospital's official Visiting Committee, led by the Rev. P. C. Jefferson of Ship Harbour, made an unannounced visit. Other committee members were A. C. Pettipas, the Rev. Gerald B. Murphy, the Rev. J. D. N. MacDonald, and John Crookshank. The committee, too, criticized the overcrowding. Their report alleged that there were 30 per cent too many inmates for the size of the building. Their report recommended more recreational facilities, a trained social worker on staff, and a full-time chaplain. The report praised the work of local service clubs and their visiting programs.

The hospital's problems continued when six nurses resigned in 1958 over salary disputes. Hospital Superintendent E. V. Smith said three more had threatened to leave until salary adjustments were made. At the same time, the farm manager quit and was replaced by C. Mooy from Holland.

Victoria Hall continued to be an important facility in the community throughout the 1950s as a popular place for meetings and social gatherings. Some residents, who criticized the hall's officials for running into debt, urged a change in the rules for its operation and new means to raise money to maintain the hall. Some feared that the hall might have to be sold to pay its debts unless changes were made.

Regular users of the hall included the Farm Forum, Farmers' Federation, and the Russell Credit Union. Some residents belonged to all three organizations. The Farm Forum held regular discussion groups on what was needed to make Cole Harbour an ideal community. These groups boasted the fact that Cole Harbour was a most productive and fertile market garden supplier, and that from its very beginning the area's market gardeners had fed the garrisons at Halifax and Dartmouth as well as residents of both communities. Members expressed concern that the rich farmland was slowly being diverted by land developers.

During the 1950s, serious discussions occurred between the Halifax County Council and the Department of National Defence for permission to use the then vacant buildings of Elkins Barracks at Hartlen Point for a seniors' nursing home.

The building boom that had engulfed the Town of Dartmouth in the early 1950s continued at a rapid pace into the adjacent communities. Ratepayer Associations in Tufts Cove, Woodside, Port Wallace, Westphal and Woodlawn met regularly and pressed for amalgamation with Dartmouth. Petitions were circulated and signed by ratepayers with the vast majority favouring union with the town. Finally in October 1958, the Nova Scotia Department of Municipal Affairs gave its blessing for the amalgamation of Dartmouth and the adjacent communities. All that was needed was to work out the fine details before the municipal marriage would be a fact.

In the Halifax Municipal County elections in 1958, Councillor Ira Settle was returned to office in District 14 with a vote margin of 962. The second councillor for the area, John Matthews, went down to defeat at the hands of a feisty community activist, Eileen Stubbs. Stubbs, one of the leading promoters of amalgamation with the town, had a long and successful political career; she was eventually elected mayor of the City of Dartmouth.

Everett Giles plows the land on his farm for the spring planting with his horse Queenie. Everett and his brother Fred were the last of the Giles family to work the original farm. (Dartmouth Free Press 195?)

Frank Bissett with a tractor and stone boat clears rocks from his land for the last time in 1974. The farm is now the site of the Sobey's Shopping Mall on Forest Hills Drive. (RE)

By the end of 1958, the threat of land development, about which the Farm Forums had expressed concern, became a stark reality. A Saint John and Montreal Company, Community Enterprises, announced its plan to build a 400-home development on the 122-acre Bell farm on the Cole Harbour Road near present-day Bel Ayr subdivision. The 3-bedroom homes would have landscaped lots and would sell for $13,000 to $14,000. All the streets within the development would be paved. The company hoped to start construction on the first 25 homes by Christmas of 1958. The new housing development eventually became part of Dartmouth after amalgamation.

The credit union, which had begun humbly in the 1930s, was growing in popularity among the area farm families, and in 1957 Russell Credit Union hired Ross Osborne as manager. When Osborne took over the credit union, its assets totalled $55,000. Osborne recalled years later that the credit union operated smoothly. Cole Harbour at that time was a close-knit community, Osborne said. Most of the people were related to each other either through blood or marriage. Most of the farmers had inherited their farms from their parents. Farmers borrowed money in the spring and paid it off in the autumn when the harvest was in.

In the very beginning, the credit union opened one night per month, and then it opened every two weeks, then every Friday night to serve its customers. Most of the loans in later years were for trucks and farm equipment. The farmers borrowed money at a fairly low rate of interest. "We never had any trouble with the repayment." During the years Osborne managed the credit union, from 1957 to 1972, Russell Credit Union wrote off only $17.

In March 1959, the Silver Sands Company announced plans to turn the Cow Bay Beach site into a Disneyland-style recreational area with a swimming pool, canteen, restaurant, dance hall, trailer park, and cabins. The company pledged to spend $25,000 initially with more money to follow. Although some development of this type occurred later, the announcement was merely a dream that never materialized.

The summer of 1959 was so wet that crops of the area market gardeners were threatened. Murray Ritcey, president of the Nova Scotia Federation of Agriculture, said the damage to the crops by mid-July had cost farmers $25,000. They were replanting and keeping their fingers crossed in the hope that they might recoup some of their losses. That wet summer weather had detrimental effects on farmers all along the Eastern Shore and as far away as Cape Breton.

Canadian National Railway (CNR) applied to the Board of Transportation Commissioners in August 1959 for permission to terminate

A once familiar sight in the area was the train chugging through the community that linked Cole Harbour with Dartmouth, the Eastern Shore, and the Musquodoboit Valley. The passenger service ended in the early 1960s, and the freight service ended in the 1980s. The rail bed that once held the tracks is now the Salt Marsh Trail, part of the Trans-Canada Trail. (RE 1977)

the passenger rail service from Dartmouth to Upper Musquodoboit. The very first train had arrived at Upper Musquodoboit with great fanfare on January 2, 1916, and proved an essential transportation link for both passengers and freight from the Musquodoboit Valley along parts of the Eastern Shore to Dartmouth. The rail line set an all-time record for carrying freight in 1948, when 12,224 tons of freight were shipped out of the Musquodoboit Valley area. Freight included lumber, Christmas trees, pulpwood, limestone, and dolomite.

As highway systems improved and automobiles became more accessible, passenger usage on the line declined, and by the late 1950s it had virtually vanished. The once daily service to and from the area was now only operating on a thrice-weekly basis. CNR indicated that the company had received only $300 in passenger revenue during the preceding year. Ruth Morton, a reporter and editor for the *Dartmouth Free Press,* later confirmed CNR's claim of low passenger usage when she rode as the lone passenger from Dartmouth to Upper Musquodoboit and back. The one-way fare by then was $2.60. When the line opened in 1916, the fare was 25¢. A few passengers climbed on board for the train's historic final run through the valley.

Residents of Cole Harbour were surely noticing the rapid changes to their community and surrounding area. The next two decades would bring even greater changes to the face of the land and the lifestyle of the people who lived there.

28

A DECADE OF CHANGE 🍂 1960S

For Cole Harbour area farmers, the 1960s proved to be a pivotal period of transformation. The fertile farmland was vanishing beneath profitable housing developments. In the previous decade, most of the farmland of Woodlawn and Westphal had been sold, subdivided into building lots, and resold as home sites.

By the start of the 1960s, the new suburbanites were disillusioned with the services offered by Halifax County, and they enthusiastically opted to leave the county and join the Town of Dartmouth. By 1960, amalgamation was a *fait accompli*. On January 1, 1961, the town and its suburbs became one. Three months later Dartmouth became the province's third city.

At the start of the 1960s, Cole Harbour area residents lost their passenger rail service when the last passenger train, affectionately known as the "Blueberry Express," made its last run to the Upper Musquodoboit Railway Station.

On February 1, 1960, a new facility for indigent senior citizens opened in the former World War Two army barracks at Hartlen Point, near Eastern Passage. Previously, these seniors had been housed in the Halifax County Home and Mental Hospital in Cole Harbour, a facility that served mentally challenged patients as well.

The new facility was called the Ocean View Manor. A total of 43 residents were transferred from the county hospital to the new home, which had a staff of 28 under the guidance of Mr. and Mrs. J. T. Lynch, the superintendent and matron. The pensioned residents paid $47 monthly for their care and upkeep. Federal government paid two-thirds of the operating costs, and the county paid the remaining one-third. By the time the facility was officially opened in May, there were 52 residents living at the former army base, which was designed to accommodate 60 residents in its new function.

One of the first businesses unrelated to farming to locate in the Cole Harbour area was Eagles and Radcliffe Limited, a commercial art and design company that opened on Bissett Road in 1960. Owned and operated by Richard Eagles and Geoffrey Radcliffe, the company began producing architectural renderings for local architect firms. A silkscreen printing plant was built on the property and they became one of the top silkscreen printers in Nova Scotia. The company was sold in 1990 and became a division of Day Nite Neon Signs Ltd.

In August 1961, Councillor Ira Settle, by then chair of the Halifax County Planning Board, announced a project to clean out nine years' accumulated silt from Little Salmon River. The project came on the heels of many years of complaints from both summer and permanent residents that Cole Harbour's fishing and swimming were being destroyed by the silt buildup. The cause of this ecological problem was sand and gravel companies' practice of washing gravel in the river, sending silt downstream to the harbour.

Councillor Settle also suggested that the project include cleaning of the harbour, so that it might be restored to its former role as one of the major clam harvesting areas on the Eastern Shore. He noted that the planning board was paying particular attention to the Ross Road area, where many new housing units were being built. "Restoration of the Little Salmon River was essential and necessary for the area." The sand and gravel companies assured the Planning Board that the granite silt would be cleaned out. Cleaning Little Salmon River began in October 1960 and continued into 1961. Councillor Settle said in an interview he hoped various levels of government would acquire the land bordering the river and reforest it, then restock the river with fish.

Also during the summer of 1961, the Dartmouth Rod and Trap Club on Strawberry Island underwent a major facelift as well as a name change. The members opened a brand-new clubhouse on August 13, with the new name, Dartmouth Trap and Skeet Club. The name change was part of a new constitution and charter, which allowed members to form a limited company in order to purchase shares to reduce the construction costs. The enlarged clubhouse, designed and built by club member Gerald Leverman, Maintenance Supervisor for the Dartmouth School Board, permitted more social as well as shooting activities. Additional future features such as a swimming pool and tennis courts were being considered. Cyril (Todds) Beazley was the president of the club. Dr. Wylie Verge was the vice-president.

The summer of 1961 started dry, jeopardizing the fall harvest; however, several days of rain mixed with days of sunshine saved the day, according to Councillor Ira Settle, who was also a farmer. In a *Dartmouth Free Press* interview, Settle said area farmers were starting to specialize. One of the main crops was iceberg lettuce. "The trend now is away from planting a little of this and a little of that. Dairy herds were now playing an important role in the agricultural picture of Cole Harbour, and a few farmers were also turning to beef production."

In 1961, the small Meeting House on Long Hill on the Cole Harbour Road that had served the Methodist community for over a century and the United Church of Canada since church union in 1925 was retired and replaced with a new building. The new church at the corner of Bissett and Cole Harbour Roads was prefabricated and formed a complete unit of church, hall, office, and washrooms. The Cole Harbour congregation rented the new building from the Board of Home Missions for about five years, until the congregation grew large enough to afford to build and maintain a church on its own. The Rev. Ward MacLean, Chair of the Halifax Presbytery, dedicated the new church on October 9, 1961. The Rev. Eric Fullerton served as minister of the church.

Halifax County Municipal Elections were held in 1961. Councillor Ira Settle was re-elected by acclamation.

Removal of silt from Little Salmon River apparently hit a snag, for the Maritime Sand and Gravel Company was ordered by the Nova Scotia Government to cease dumping waste into the water. According to the *Dartmouth Free Press,* the company at first ignored the order and continued washing gravel for the next few days until the minister in charge of the Nova Scotia Water Act, W. S. Kennedy Jones, sent a formal order to the company to cease operation. The government action followed a formal protest by the residents, who produced a petition carrying 700 signatures.

In 1962, Woodlawn Dairy opened its new facility and headquarters on Canal Street in Dartmouth. Brothers N. A. Morash and J. R. Morash had started the company in 1894 in the Woodlawn area. When the dairy moved from Woodlawn to Pleasant Street in Dartmouth in 1928, it operated at that location as Woodlawn Dairy. Cole Harbour dairy farmers were among its major milk suppliers.

One unpredictable enemy of farmers of any ilk was fire, which was too often financially ruinous. It could take years to rebuild a farm and the stock. Over the years, several Cole Harbour farmers lost barns, homes, and livestock in fires. When a fire broke out in the area, farmers relied solely on the Dartmouth Fire Department; before the telephone they had relied on bucket brigades organized by helpful neighbours. With new homes being built in the area, the need for local firefighting organization became crucial.

In 1962, the Cole Harbour Volunteer Fire Department was organized by the District 14 Service Commission to purchase essential firefighting equipment and to train members for firefighting. The initial volunteer fire department consisted of 30 members who elected the chief and other officers. They turned out every Tuesday night for training, which was conducted by members of the Dartmouth Fire Department. St. John Ambulance provided first aid training. Members of the volunteer department did all their own mechanical work on the trucks and the equipment.

Cole Harbour resident Murray Elliott, who later became fire chief, recalled that the department was strictly volunteer in the beginning, but eventually full-time paid staff were hired to operate the station day and night. "There were not a lot of house calls in the beginning; most of the calls were for brush fires, particularly in the spring of the year."

A ladies' auxiliary formed to help raise money to buy a pumper truck and other equipment. One of the main fundraising events was a bingo. Chief Elliott recalled another important source of fundraising

Jack Settle's barn was consumed in a fire in 1911, about 70 years before modern firefighting equipment came into use in the area. At the time of the fire, the barn was full of hay, 15 milking cows, 5 horses, and a pig. Many of the farmers were attending church services in the Meeting House when the alarm was given. They left the church at once to help put out the fire. The family started to rebuild the structure on July 22, 1911. Shown are (left to right) Sophie (Bissett) Whitehouse, Jack Settle, Clara Settle, Dave Settle, John Settle, and the contractor and his helper who built the new barn. (July 22, 1911/Roy Settle Album)

in the early years was hauling water to fill wells during the dry summer months. At first the department received $7 to fill a well, then the price increased to $8 and before the department ended the service it was up to $10.

Chief Elliott said the Cole Harbour volunteers serviced Westphal and the Preston-Cherry Brook area and made mutual aid calls to assist fire departments in neighbouring areas. Chezzetcook formed a volunteer fire department about the same time as Cole Harbour, and Lawrencetown formed one about a decade later.

In May 1963, Halifax County Hospital, formerly Halifax County Home and Mental Hospital, announced a major reduction in its farm operation. Various management boards had tried different methods of creating a self-supporting farm without success. Institutions in most

Murray Elliott was the Cole Harbour fire chief for many years. He began his firefighting career as a when the department was all volunteer. In later years he became one of the paid members. The department was first organized in 1962 and is now part of the HRM firefighting service. (RE 1980s)

provinces of Canada had abandoned their farm operations before the 1960s. The pig farm, which was self-supporting, continued. It produced enough pork for the hospital's use and a surplus for sale to local wholesalers. The hen operation was curtailed and small vegetable gardens would continue as a tool for the occupational therapy department.

In July 1963, the hospital auctioned off the farm's livestock and equipment, which did not fetch the anticipated high prices. The auction did realize $12,000, of which $7,000 was used to clear debts.

Criticism from several people targeted a huge dredging operation in the area in the autumn of 1963. They argued it was tearing away the sand barrier that protected the shoreline from Cow Bay to Three Fathom Harbour. H. J. Baker, a prominent Dartmouth businessman, maintained that if the operation continued it would destroy Cow Bay Ocean Park and the prime hunting and fishing area of Cole Harbour, and would open up Porters Lake to the ravages of the ocean and allow salt water into the Lawrencetown-Mineville area, ruining a valuable duck and geese habitat. Lands and Forests Minister E. D. Haliburton was urged to set up a commission to assess the current damage, take the necessary corrective steps, and develop a 25-year plan for the proper use of the land in the area.

In March 1964, a local newspaper reported an explosion in the wellhouse of Cole Harbour farmer Stuart Harris that blew off the door, shattered windows, and split the eaves on the roof of the 7-foot by 12-foot shed located about 25 feet from Mr. Harris's house. The explosion shook the farmhouse of Charles Settle about a quarter of a mile away. He thought an airplane had crashed nearby. The best suggestion as to the cause of the explosion was that methane gas, formed from rotting animal and vegetable matter, had leaked into the well area, and when the ground around the well froze during the winter it shut off the escape route for the gas.

Halifax County Hospital opened a new 400-seat auditorium and devotional centre on October 7, 1964, which saved county taxpayers about $200,000. The story of the new facility had begun three years earlier, when various groups advocated more recreational space in the hospital. Early in 1964, the hospital's board of management submitted plans to build an auditorium and chapel at an estimated cost of $235,000.

However, Deputy Warden Settle proposed a more economical solution. He suggested that the county purchase the former St. Thomas More Church, located then at the MicMac Rotary, which was offered for disposal by the Department of Highways for $500. The board purchased the steel frame and brick structure and then moved it to the hospital property where it was re-assembled. The new addition, which ultimately featured a projection room and storage area, was completed at a cost of $40,000, considerably less than the original $235,000 estimate.

Ira Settle, who had been elected warden of Halifax County, suggested in January 1965 that the county erect several small housing units for elderly couples on some of the 9.2 acres at Ocean View Manor near Eastern Passage. As a centennial project for 1967, if accepted, it would have received federal and provincial matching grants. However, this project did not materialize.

The Cole Harbour two-room school became a community hall, replacing Victoria Hall, in 1965. The Halifax Regional Municipality eventually used it for recreational programs. Now used primarily for programs for the young people of the community, it is familiar to them as "The Box." (1946, courtesy of Melvin Harris)

In May 1965, the owners and operators of Victoria Community Hall entered into an agreement with the District 14 Service Commission, owners of the 1940s Cole Harbour two-room school, to transfer the assets of the community group to the Service Commission and to purchase the two-room school as a replacement for Victoria Hall on Cole Harbour Road. This school stood on the site of an earlier one-room school on the north side of Cole Harbour Road between Ashgrove Drive and Bissett Road.

The community group agreed to pay the Service Commission $5,674 over a six-year period to maintain the former school as a community hall. A five-member management committee was set up – three trustees from the Victoria Community Hall and two from the Service Commission. The management committee was authorized to make bylaws and regulations to allow all groups within the Cole Harbour District and the District 14 Volunteer Fire Department fair and equitable use of the jointly operated community hall. This building has remained in use as a community hall to the present.

In December 1965, Robert Tulloch, secretary of Russell Credit Union, wrote to William Bonn, chair of the trustees of Victoria Hall requesting the board consider selling the hall to the credit union for $3,000. The following year, a meeting of the Victoria Hall trustees was held in May to consider the credit union's offer. There were more meetings and letters between the two groups, but in November 1966, the sale became final; the former community centre became the property of the credit union, which had used the hall regularly for meetings and banking sessions since the late 1930s.

County Council was presented with a proposal in August 1965 for the construction of a new seniors' home. The proposed complex would house 150 patients – 50 spots would receive nursing care and the remainder would be for welfare patients. At $10,000 a bed, the estimated cost of the new facility was $1.5 million. The present facility at Ocean View, formerly an army base during World War Two, needed extensive repairs to upgrade the building. The architect firm of Leslie Fairn and Associates was asked to prepare a proposal for the institution.

Cole Harbour farmer and businessman Murray Ritcey provided some excitement in the community, when he thwarted a robbery at the Eastern Halifax County Co-op Store before dawn on March 28, 1966. Ritcey received a telephone call about 2:30 A.M. from his neighbour Harold S. Morash, informing him that there were three suspicious men lurking about the store. Ritcey, a director of the co-op and the owner of the building that housed the store, got up, armed himself with a shotgun and shells and sped to the nearby store, where he caught the three men rummaging through the office. Ritcey held the men at gunpoint until the RCMP arrived to take the men into custody.

During the preliminary hearing, Judge Martin D. Haley praised Ritcey for his conduct and his courage. "More people should have that kind of courage. If they did we wouldn't have so much crime." The three men – Henry James Roache, Richard Wayne MacPhee, and Peter Daniel Walsh, all of Halifax – were each charged with breaking and entering with intent and committed to stand trial in County Court.

In 1967, Canadians across the nation celebrated their country's 100th anniversary with a variety of special events and community

Cole Harbour women, mostly farmers' wives and daughters, were generous with their time and talents in shedding light on rural life in the community. Shown here (left to right): Muriel Morash and Margaret Kuhn Campbell enjoy a tea party at the Heritage Farm Museum. (RE 1989)

Two other women who assisted the Cole Harbour Heritage Farm Museum with information on rural life in the community were Bernice Settle (left) and Donna Kuhn. The two women attend a harvest church service in the former Meeting House. (RE 1990)

projects. It was a year-long gala celebration with Expo '67 in Montreal and travelling events such as the Military Tattoo and the Centennial Train. Canadians began to realize that their nation was blessed with a rich heritage that should be preserved in books, plays, artwork, and community museums.

The Cole Harbour Women's Institute made a start in gathering and saving some of the local heritage by organizing a public meeting on Saturday April 15 in the Colonel John Stuart School hall. Older residents of the community were especially asked to attend in order to be interviewed by Barbara Pollach. Their stories about the history of Cole Harbour were to be taped for future reference. Well-known Canadian folklorist Helen Creighton of Dartmouth was the special guest.

As part of the Cole Harbour centennial celebration, a cairn whose plaque bears the names of 32 of the area's early settlers was unveiled in

September 1967 in the front of the former Meeting House. Warden Settle said in a *Dartmouth Free Press* report:

> Preserving our heritage may not be very popular with the public, but I believe in it. The plaque commemorated the memory of the pioneers of the community, who during Canada's first 100 years of living with faith and trust in God, built churches, homes, cleared the land, and produced food for their families and Canada.
>
> It's unfortunate that histories weren't kept alive. As these areas become developed and new people come into the district it doesn't take long for all signs of its history and heritage to disappear.

In November 1967, Mr. Settle was re-elected to County Council and re-elected warden of the municipality – a fitting way to cap off a year of centennial celebrations.

A federal election was one of the big events of 1968. The new leader for the national Progressive Conservative Party was Nova Scotia native Robert L. Stanfield, a former premier of the province, but most of the nation at that time was spellbound by the wave of Trudeaumania.

For the first time the dual constituency for Halifax County was divided into three with Dartmouth and the Eastern Shore forming one constituency. The main combatants vying for the right to represent the new Dartmouth-Eastern Shore riding were two former journalists, Arnie Patterson for the Liberal Party and Michael Forestall as Conservative standard-bearer. When the dust finally settled on election night, Trudeau had been swept to power in Ottawa, while Nova Scotia had gone Conservative, save for one lone Cape Breton constituency. Mike Forestall was the new Member of Parliament for Dartmouth-Eastern Shore, which included Cole Harbour.

The need arose during 1967 for a new junior high school to serve Cole Harbour and Eastern Passage due to the serious overcrowding at Graham Creighton. Plans were made for the new school to be expanded later with 8 additional classrooms to accommodate students from Westphal, Preston, New Road (in the Preston area), and Lake Loon. County Council decided to locate the new school in the Cole Harbour area. At a County Council meeting in the spring of 1968, Eastern Passage Councillor Thomas Tonks objected to the new junior high school being built in Cole Harbour and suggested that the Tallahassee School in his riding be expanded instead. Council rejected his request.

The school was originally planned as a 16-room facility with room for expansion, but Cole Harbour area residential growth was so rapid that 8 additional classrooms were build immediately. Cost of the school with all its teaching facilities was estimated at $1 million. It was expected that the school would be ready for the 760 students at the opening of the 1969 school year.

The Eastern Halifax County Co-op, which had been serving the Cole Harbour farming community in equipment and supplies for the past number of years, opened a general retail store on the Cole Harbour Road on November 7, 1968. In addition to groceries, the new store offered through a new illustrated catalogue about 8,000 different hardware items – paint, bathroom fixtures, farm hardware, electrical appliances, batteries, and car tires. People involved in the operation of the store were Roy DeWolfe, store manager; D. Wayne MacKinnon, grocery manager; and Bill Bonn, meat manager. Opening day was a huge success with line-ups at the cash registers and a full parking lot during most of the day. The first 100 women through the checkouts received a free pair of nylons.

Residential construction was picking up in the Cole Harbour area near the end of 1969, prompting County Council to investigate the cost of extending the water and sewer lines from Dartmouth to serve parts of Cole Harbour Road. The cost to bring the lines to Caldwell as far as Astral Drive and Nova Terrace and to the Halifax County Hospital was estimated at $902,100 with the county's share at $325,680. Council was asked to make a formal request to the city.

In May 1969, work was underway to develop a canoe club on the eastern side of Bell Lake by the residents of Bel Ayr subdivision, now part of Dartmouth. The boat club, which drew its members from the surrounding area, was named Abenaki.

The opening of the new junior high school was in fact delayed a month because the water and sewer extension from Dartmouth was not completed, and some of the school's gym equipment and desks hadn't arrived. By mid-October all the classrooms were filled. The new junior high was named Sir Robert Borden Junior High School in honour of the Nova Scotia-born prime minister of Canada.

29

THE ROYAL COMMISSION

At the official opening of the Halifax County Home and Mental Hospital on October 23, 1941, it was considered the most modern and up-to-date hospital of its kind in the Maritime provinces. Built on a hill overlooking Bissett Lake, the concrete structure replaced the Poor Farm, which had burned in 1929.

When the Department of Health began sending patients from the Nova Scotia Hospital to the Halifax County Home and Mental Hospital instead of local asylums, serious overcrowding arose. An additional building was erected at a cost of $963,150 next to the 1941 structure. The new builing opened January 9, 1952, and provided 200 more beds, x-ray and operating rooms, and improved day room space. By the time the new addition opened, the institution's name had been changed to the Halifax County Hospital. The hospital came under criticism from time to time in the late 1950s for overcrowding, a lack of recreational facilities, and the need for an on-staff psychiatrist and chaplain.

When the province started paying one-third of the operating costs in 1958, it insisted that all sane but indigent patients be removed from the mental hospital. In order to comply, the municipality opened a welfare home at the former World War Two army base at Hartlen Point, near Eastern Passage, in 1960 and transferred those patients to the new facility, called Ocean View Manor.

In January 1962, under the guidance of new Superintendent Eric J. Davies, the hospital met with considerable praise for the much improved conditions. Patient care, according to one newspaper report, had been lifted out of the "dark ages." Three-quarters of the patients were placed in open wards allowing them the freedom of the hospital and the grounds. There were only two locked wards for the severely ill. Under Eric Davies, there was an extensive occupational therapy program. Many of the patients helped out on the farm during the summer months, if only to weed and clean rocks from the field. At the beginning of the 1960s, the patient population at the hospital exceeded 500 with only about 30 per cent coming from Halifax County.

Conditions at the hospital took a turn for the worse in 1968, when the RCMP were called in to investigate a fire as well as acts of cruelty and homosexuality, which required Superintendent Davies and the Chief Medical Officer Dr. J. W. Barteaux to make a public statement to the media. Their joint statement indicated that the RCMP investigation revealed that a patient, not a staff member, had committed the burning incident mentioned in the press.

Further, acts of cruelty and homosexuality involved a very limited number of patients on one ward and three staff members responsible for that ward out of 260 staff members. One staff member was immediately suspended; the decision on the other two staff members awaited the report from the RCMP investigation.

The report emphasized that the acts of cruelty and indecency involved only a few members of the non-professional staff on weekend shifts. The hospital authorized the Attorney General's office to proceed with appropriate charges. "Very definite and strong steps have been taken by the administration and the medical staff to ensure against similar incidents. The patients in the institution will be given every personal protection."

A month after the RCMP were called in, Councillor Percy Baker, speaking during a County Council meeting, called for a judicial inquiry into the operation and management of the Cole Harbour hospital. Originally, his motion called for an inquiry into the operation and management of all such county hospitals in the province. Council amended his motion to deal with only the Halifax County Hospital. Councillor Baker said at the time he was concerned with the peace of mind of the patients' relatives.

A Royal Commission, headed by Halifax barrister H. P. McKeen, was appointed on July 23, 1968, to inquire into all aspects of the organization, establishment, operation, and administration of the Halifax County Hospital at Cole Harbour with emphasis on the competence of the staff and the care and treatment provided to the patients. David Waterbury was appointed counsel and secretary to the commission; Dr. F. A. Dunsworth was named psychiatric consultant; and Henry Bourgeois was named social work consultant.

The commission carried out considerable preliminary research and investigation before public hearings were held. The first public hearing took place on November 25 and 26 in the Red Chamber of Province House. Other sessions were held at the hospital itself and at the citizenship court.

During the hearings, briefs were presented by the Rev. L. F. Hatfield, Institute of Pastoral Training and the Halifax-Dartmouth Council of Churches; Harland Clark, on Sections 28 and 29 of the Municipal Mental Hospitals Act; Andrew Crook and George Levatte, Canadian Mental Health Association; Peter Greer, Nova Scotia Barristers' Society; Alderwoman Eileen Stubbs, City of Dartmouth; D. W. Tingley, Union of Nova Scotia Municipalities; four Dalhousie law students: W. C. Hoskinson, W. E. McKeown, John D. Romans, and W. M. M. Thoms; L. T. Hancock, The Welfare Council; and Gilbert Levine, Local 1028 Canadian Union of Public Employees. In all, 52 witnesses gave evidence under oath.

Superintendent Eric Davies resigned from his position on February 13, 1969, and was succeeded by Leslie Havers, the former director of nursing services at the hospital, as acting superintendent.

The McKeen Commission made 25 recommendations concerning the operation of the hospital, 6 of which involved amendments to the Municipal Mental Hospitals Act. Among those recommendations were better training for the nursing staff, particularly in the area of psychiatric nursing; additional staff psychiatrists, as well as two full-time chaplains; a public relations and information service for the hospital. Other recommendations involved budgetary and accounting procedures. County Councillor Percy Baker, Chair of the Hospital Board at the time, left politics and became the full-time superintendent at the hospital in May 1971. (Baker, first elected to County Council in 1958, had been appointed chair of the Halifax County Hospital Management Board the following year. He remained in that role for the next 12 years.) He superintended the hospital through the 13 years following the Royal Commission.

Speaking during a taped interview years later, Baker reflected on the Royal Commission, its aftermath, and his role in putting things right. He said the abuse at the hospital involved beatings of the patients by staff members, one was given a hot foot and severely burned, some were made to perform homosexual acts, and two female patients were pregnant by staff members. At the conclusion of the inquiry, which began in 1968 and ended in 1969, a total of 28 staff members were dismissed and one went to jail for three months for his part in the atrocities. "When I took over as hospital administrator I held regular weekly meetings with the department heads, and together we mapped out a five-year plan for improvements at the facility. Many of the changes involved buying new furniture, painting, and replacing curtains and drapes. When that five year plan was completed we started on another five-year plan."

Under his administration the hospital developed an extensive crafts program for the patients, and the money received from the sale of the crafts went back to the patients to fund other projects.

The hospital bought a summer camp at Musquodoboit for the patients for $30,000, which was raised without the aid of government financial assistance. "We also purchased a bus that was used to take patients on day trips to the Annapolis Valley and other areas of the province, to visit museums, and for weekly bowling matches."

During Baker's administration the hospital population averaged about 200 patients; although at one time the hospital population was 600 patients. He conceded that he played a major role in cleaning up the Halifax County Hospital.

The institution continued to serve the mentally challenged into the twenty-first century and underwent one more name change – to "Halifax County Regional Rehabilitation Centre" – before it closed its doors finally in 2002.

30

MR. COLE HARBOUR

Ira Settle was a most unlikely person to enter the rough-and-tumble arena of municipal politics. He was quiet and unassuming, and unlike many politicians, he listened patiently to the opinions of others. It was perhaps his friendliness and his conscientious devotion to public service that made him loved and respected by an electorate that kept him on County Council for 27 years. Even after his retirement from politics, he continued to serve the people of the Cole Harbour community where he was born, educated, and lived his entire life.

Ira Settle was a man of the soil, a farmer, descended from a long line of farmers that came to the area from Lancashire, England, in the early nineteenth century. Ira was born on September 6, 1908, the youngest child of Robert and Edith (Turner) Settle. His mother, the daughter of James Turner and Eunice Ross, was born in Westphal in 1870. Ira's father, the son of John E. Settle, was born in Cole Harbour. Ira's parents were married on January 1, 1895, and had five other children: Charles, Eunice, Clara, William, and Robert. William died at the age of 19 months. When Ira was born, his mother was battling tuberculosis, a battle she would lose three years later at age 42.

His father (1867–1955) was a market gardener as well as a dairy farmer with a herd of 30 to 40 cows. The family rose before daybreak to milk the cows by hand and cool the milk before setting off on their door-to-door milk route in Halifax by 7:30 A.M.

Ira recalled years later that his family was the first in the area to deliver bottled milk to their customers. They sold about 300 quarts a day in an area from Inglis Street in south Halifax, west to Oxford and north to Black Street, and all the streets in between. His brother also had several customers in Dartmouth.

He received his early education in Cole Harbour's one-room school, where the teacher taught everything from primary to grade

A young Ira Settle sits on the back of the Clover Bank Dairy wagon. Both Ira's father Robert and his brother Charles were involved in dairy farming for many years and claimed to be the first to sell milk in glass bottles. (ca. 1918, Ira Settle album)

10. From the community school he went to the Halifax Academy. There he wrote and passed his provincial examinations.

The young Ira Settle took an active part in sports, especially baseball, and when he grew older he was an active participant on tug-of-war teams. On several occasions he was a member of championship teams.

From a very early age Ira Settle's ambition was to be a farmer like his father and brother, and he became a market gardener. Although his father at one time made regular trips to the Halifax Market to sell produce, Ira instead sold only to stores in the Halifax-Dartmouth area.

Ira and his family farmed through the difficult Depression years, and when World War Two broke out in 1939 it generated a boom to the local farming industry. Most of the farms in Cole Harbour, Woodlawn, Cow Bay, and Lawrencetown were busy growing produce, much of which was shipped overseas to feed service personnel.

Farming remained fairly steady until air service came to the area. Ira recalled in later years, "The air service meant that they could fly in produce from anywhere in competition with local farmers. It was no longer a closed market."

In the 1950s, two important events occurred in Ira's life – his marriage to Bertha Sparks and his entry into politics. Ira and Bertha, a native of Newfoundland, were married in 1950 at Woodlawn United Church. She died January 8, 1969, and was buried at the same church where they were wed. The did not have children. Ira never remarried.

When his cousin Fred Settle, the sitting county councillor, died of a heart attack just before Christmas in 1951, a by-election was called for early in the new year to fill the vacancy on the municipal council. A meeting was held in Woodlawn a few weeks into 1952, at which Ira was urged to run for the vacant seat. Ira's sweeping victory in the February election was the first of many such electoral successes he would enjoy.

One of his first jobs on the County Council was to chair the Halifax County Planning Board. Ten years later Ira was elected as deputy warden. In 1964, a dozen years after he first ran for council, he was elected warden of Halifax County, a position similar to mayor. Ira held that position for the next 15 years.

During his years on council, several new projects were undertaken in the county – Rock Head Prison was closed down, and a new correctional centre opened in Lower Sackville; a new county courthouse was built on Water Street in Halifax; and new county offices and council chambers were built on Dutch Village Road in Halifax. Serious flooding that occurred each year along the Musquodoboit River was rectified. Numerous roads throughout the county were paved.

In 1979, after 27 years of political life, Ira Settle retired from politics and returned to full-time farming for a while. "It was time for younger people with new ideas and a new vision to come forward," he said.

Ira continued to play an active role in his church, community, and the Cole Harbour Rural Heritage Society. He was the honourary fire chief when the local volunteer fire department was organized in 1962, and he was instrumental in having a new fire station built to serve the area.

In 1984, Ira Settle was the first person selected by the Cole Harbour Kiwanis Club to receive their Distinguished Citizen Award. In

As warden for Halifax County, Ira Settle welcomed numerous visitors to the area with his friendly handshake. Here he welcomes Princess Alexandra of Great Britain, while Premier and Mrs. Gerald Regan and Lieutenant-Governor Victor deB. Oland look on. (photographer, date unknown/courtesy of Marie Arnold)

The new Cole Harbour Fire Station under construction. Ira Settle, whose house is visible in the distance, donated land to the fire department for the building. (RE spring 1987)

Ira Settle, retired from politics, hoes his lettuces. (RE 1989)

a tribute to Ira at the time, Kiwanis president, David W. Ritcey, wrote, "The contributions of Ira Settle to public life and to better government for the residents of Halifax County are well known. Less well known are his private acts of generosity and his loving devotion to the betterment of the community served by our club. He is truly deserving of the title – Mr. Cole Harbour."

Ira Settle died in 1995 at the age of 87.

31

THE COLE HARBOUR RURAL HERITAGE SOCIETY

Plans by government and land developers to dump sewage from two massive housing developments into the virtually land-locked Cole Harbour threatened destruction of the centuries-old salt marshes and sparked a community protest that eventually led to the birth of the Cole Harbour Rural Heritage Society. In order to halt the pending ecological disaster, a few residents banded together and enlisted the help of neighbours and professionals in an effort to preserve the salt marshes for future generations. An organization called the Cole Harbour Environmental Committee was formed, which had two main objectives: to inform the public and enlist the help of experts, particularly scientists who could identify the extent of the problem and its long-range effects.

Countless volunteer hours were spent eliciting support through telephone calls, in research, in writing briefs to government, letters to government officials and newspaper articles, and in CBC interviews. The residents' strong opposition paid off – government officials and developers finally came to their collective senses, and the harbour was spared. Arrangements for funding were eventually made with government to build a line to carry the raw sewage to Eastern Passage, where it could be treated and then emptied directly into the ocean. The federal government, through the Department of Regional and Economic Expansion, paid $1 million towards the project.

Residents involved in the battle for environmental preservation decided to take on another equally challenging project – preservation of the area's culture and heritage. A few members of the Environmental Committee contacted other community activists who had been involved in the campaign to stop the sewage dumping in addition to people they knew would be interested in local history. Notices were sent out to the community inviting anyone interested in forming an historical society to come to an organizational meeting.

On the evening of July 3, 1973, they met at the Cole Harbour Road home of Barbara Bell to form a society that would record some of the area's heritage before it was lost. In Miss Bell's house on Long Hill, overlooking the harbour, this new organization agreed that "the view" must be preserved for posterity. There were approximately 15 people at the first gathering. Not all those present joined, but it was the beginning of the Cole Harbour Rural Heritage Society.

The new organization not only agreed to continue the role of community environmental watchdog but to research, record, and tell the story of Cole Harbour. Members of this group would attempt to interest the rapidly growing population of the area in their goals, in hope that a greater appreciation of the natural and cultural history would improve the community's long-term outlook.

Barbara Bell sits by a large picture window in her home overlooking the harbour. It was at her home in July 1973 that residents gathered for an exploratory meeting, which resulted in the formation of the Cole Harbour Rural Heritage Society. (RE 1993)

David Morash, left, and his brother Scott ride the tractor with their father Norman. Scott became the first president of the Cole Harbour Rural Heritage Society. (ca. 1948/courtesy of Eva Morash Kuhn)

The first president was Scott Morash, who was born and lived all his life in Cole Harbour. Morash's father, Norman, and his grandfather farmed in Cole Harbour on land adjoining the Morash/Strum property, latterly the Bishop property, overlooking the harbour. Scott Morash and his brother David have remained members of the society throughout its 30-year life.

One of the strongest supporters of the fledgling organization was Rosemary Eaton, who had the vision of what the Cole Harbour Rural Heritage Society could be. She believed that the community's rural heritage should be remembered. She hoped that the society could capture the spirit and flavour of what once had been predominantly a farming community. She also felt strongly about protecting the harbour and its wildlife and was intrigued by the way farmers used the salt marsh. The Halifax Market was another of her special interests.

For three decades Rosemary Eaton was, in many ways, the glue that held the organization together. She was tireless in arranging meetings and getting people out to see what the society was doing. She wrote letters and briefs, spent hours on the telephone arranging for articles and photographs in various publications. In the early days of her collecting, a few of the residents continued to pursue some of the traditional ways; she recorded and photographed them whenever possible: Johnny LaPierre cutting salt hay, George Kuhn making sauerkraut, Joe Diggs making witherod brooms, Wilfred Bissett collecting eelgrass, and Helen Horne playing the pump organ in the Meeting House (photo page 80).

John Slater, originally from western Canada, was a charter member and keenly interested in establishing a farm museum. Murray Ritcey was also a charter member and another early advocate and promoter of the farm museum. Some other members who played leading roles in the society's formative years were Joan Slack, Barbara Mackintosh, Barbara Bell, Norwood (Akie) Akerlund, Fraser Conrad, Frances Nixon, and Sally King.

The newborn heritage society immediately took on the task of saving a heritage property. The former Methodist Chapel, now called the Meeting House, located on top of Long Hill, had deteriorated since the United Church had moved to a new building on Bissett

Road. The society made an agreement with the church to take on maintenance of the building, which required money – and so began the continual search for funding. The society began using the building, which was without heat and water, for its regular meetings. Twenty-five years later, the United Church of Canada deeded the building to the society.

Shortly after rescuing the Meeting House, Halifax County Warden Ira Settle, who was not a member of the society at the time, gave the members another and even greater challenge – to save the Giles House, which was scheduled for demolition. This house might have been overlooked as an important heritage site, except that Warden Settle was aware of its age and its role in Cole Harbour's history.

At the same time the idea of a farm museum was beginning to take concrete form; the museum's board of directors was looking for a museum site. Giles House was relocated to the eventual site of the Cole Harbour Heritage Farm Museum.

The first Joseph Giles settled in Cole Harbour about the 1780s. The society has been unable to pinpoint the exact date of Giles House. It appears to date from the 1780s, but any structural details that could prove this tentative date conclusively have been lost over the past two centuries as various generations of families have altered and renovated the building to meet their particular needs.

At times the Giles House must have been stretched to the limit, as in 1827, when 16 people lived there. In contrast, during the late 1800s and early 1900s, another Joseph Giles (who died in 1919) and his sister (who died in 1924) were the sole occupants, followed by their nephews Everett and Fred Giles, the last private owners. All four were direct descendants of the early settler.

Since the first Joseph Giles purchased his land in the area from his

As traditional methods and skills fall out of use, demonstrations and photo records become important. On facing page, Cole Harbour resident George Kuhn makes sauerkraut according to tradition brought from Germany by his ancestors in 1752. (RE 1990)

At top, Wilfred Bissett gathers eelgrass along the shore of Cole Harbour in the 1970s, as Cole Harbour residents had done for generations, to bank the foundation of his home before winter sets in. He is just south of the present Salt Marsh Trail, where the ferry to Lawrencetown departed in the early nineteenth century. (RE ca. 1974)

Frank Conrad makes a witherod eel pot for the Cole Harbour Heritage Farm Museum in 1974. (RE 1974)

John Slater, a board member of the Cole Harbour Rural Heritage Society, presents the organization's first honourary membership to long-time Cole Harbour resident Maurice Strum for his help in providing information about its history. The young lad in the photo is Graham Fyfe, Mr. Strum's great-grandson. (Dartmouth Free Press 1974)

father-in-law, Jacob Conrad, it's quite likely the house was already on the property. The suggestion exists that Jacob Conrad may have brought the building by water from Lunenburg, where he owned land and is known to have frequently bought and sold properties.

No one period in the history of the Giles House stands out from the others. Of the many artifacts in the building, only a few are associated with the Giles family. It was agreed early on that no attempt would be made to restore the interior of the house or furnish it to a particular period or date. Instead, the house features many periods and the changes that it underwent during its long history. The artifacts on exhibit represent life in Cole Harbour generally, and span the whole period of Cole Harbour settlement rather than the life of any one family.

Of course, saving the old farmhouse from the wrecker's ball and moving it to a new location involved hours of meetings, research, regular visits to the site and hours of manual labour, plus fundraising and promotion. The Nova Scotia Department of Housing supplied the site for the building plus funding for the move.

Ernie Clark, Chief Planner for the Nova Scotia Housing Commission, was influential in helping the society preserve Giles House. It had been rented out for several years since Everett Giles had built a new house next door, but it became vacant when the property was taken

The Giles House is moved along Cole Harbour Road. The photo looks eastward from near the intersection of Forest Hills Parkway, Cumberland Drive and Cole Harbour Road, down Beck's Hill toward Bissett Road. St. Andrew's Anglican Church shows in the distance on the right. The Cole Harbour Road was receiving its first widening. See Beck's Hill 25 years earlier on page 295. (RE Sept. 2, 1976)

over by the Nova Scotia Housing Commission as part of the Forest Hills Land Assembly. Under Clark's influence, Giles House was used as the Forest Hills sales office from 1975 to the summer of 1976, which kept the old house heated and occupied.

After considerable discussion, Giles House was moved on September 2, 1976, to the Stuart Harris farm, which was by then part of the Forest Hills Land Assembly.

The Harris farm became the new location for Giles House; the existing house, barns, outbuildings and land would form part of the proposed farm museum. Society member Murray Ritcey helped organize the move of Giles House to its new location in many ways, including directing and stopping traffic when necessary. Murray Filmore, who owned a flatbed truck, carried out the move. There were a few glitches such as forgetting to inform the RCMP until the

Mrs. Andrew Settle feeds the chickens in the early twentieth century beside the Settles' mid-nineteenth-century barn, now part of the Cole Harbour Heritage Farm Museum. Settles farmed here for over a century, but it became known as the Harris Farm after Stuart Harris inherited it from the Settles. In the distance is the Bell farm, now the site of Bel Ayr subdivision. (Melvin Harris album, ca. 1920s)

move was underway, and when the house nearly toppled off the flatbed as it moved up the Harris farm driveway.

With Giles House now situated on a ready-made farm, the Cole Harbour Heritage Farm Museum slowly began to take shape. A few years later, the deeds to 2½ acres of land plus all the buildings were transferred to the Cole Harbour Rural Heritage Society. The buildings as a group were later designated a Provincial Heritage Property.

The Harris house and barn had been built by the Settle family in the mid-1800s and had been in continuous use. Household artifacts were displayed in Giles House, agricultural equipment in the upper main barn; the lower barn housed the livestock. Harris House was used for an office and storage space, a caretaker's apartment, and a tearoom. Remaining buildings provide storage, display and program space.

Repairs and renovations to the museum buildings continued in the following years, which involved considerable commitment of the resources of the society. A small area rate was levied on the taxpayers by the Municipality of Halifax County and, in addition to a small operating grant from the Nova Scotia Museum, provided the basic funding for the society's operation of the farm museum. Through large contributions of volunteer time and skills plus financial donations, the society has invested heavily in maintaining the site.

One of the major jobs undertaken by the society in its ongoing preservation of Giles House was fumigating the entire building for powder post beetles in 1987. The house was built of solid logs, so the damage inside several of the timbers went unnoticed for many years, probably since the time of the renovations in 1976 and 1977. At that time some timbers from other old buildings in Cole Harbour were used for repairs, and the beetle may have been introduced inadvertently. The only solution was to treat the entire building.

Akie Akerlund obtained a sheet of plastic large enough to completely envelope the house in an airtight package. He picked up a discarded mattress in front of a house on garbage day to cover the brick chimney and prevent it from tearing the plastic shell. Then, methyl bromide was pumped into the house, and left for 24 hours, sealed by the tightly wrapped plastic cocoon.

After 1974, Cole Harbour farmers generously donated scores of pieces of farm equipment and artifacts as barns in the area gradually fell to the housing developers' bulldozers. In addition to artifacts, the society began collecting a variety of documents, audio tapes of oral histories, and photographs. It also collected plants from disappearing farms, as well as herbs, bulbs, and fruit trees. Eventually, a few farm animals were added to the museum's collection.

After three decades, tthe Cole Harbour Rural Heritage Society considers education its most important role. It has developed numerous exhibits, programs, and promotional and fundraising projects. The society, with the help of a grant from the Department of Tourism and Culture, developed an inventory of pre-1914 buildings in the area. Although many have disappeared since the inventory, the exercise produced considerable useful information. The society continues to

Fourteen years after it was moved to its new location at the Heritage Farm Museum, the Giles House was found to be infested with powder post beetles. To remedy the situation the house was completely wrapped in a plastic cocoon in 1987 and fumigated to rid the structure of beetles. Norwood (Akie) Akerlund who arranged for the donation of the plastic from Guildfords, designed the cocoon, and rounded up 15 able-bodied volunteers to install it. (E. Corser 1987)

advocate long-range environmental planning and habitat conservation and foster understanding and respect for nature.

One rewarding outcome of the society's initiative was the establishment by the province of the Cole Harbour-Lawrencetown Coastal Heritage Park, the acquisition of large tracts of land around the harbour by the park, and the restoration of the barrier beach at Cole Harbour's mouth. The idea of creating the natural wildlife park encompassing most of the undeveloped land from the foot of Long Hill, where a public landing place is located, around the western side of the harbour to Rainbow Haven Beach, came about in the 1960s, when it became evident that the harbour and environs were extremely vulnerable to the weight of the land development that was taking place.

Halifax County Council, at the urging of the Cole Harbour Rural Heritage Society, placed a special area designation on the property to

Interpreters Christian Chaddock (left) and Maria Driscoll, summer students in 2002, polish their wool-working skills in the Giles House to prepare for the many school groups that visit the farm. (Darren O'Neil 2002)

Local farmers (from left) Gordon Eisener, Melvin Harris, and Sandy Farquharson enjoy reliving the days when woodcutting was common practice. The woodcutting machine was often transported from farm to farm. A couple of days' work was sufficient to cut a winter's supply of wood. (RE 1978)

One of the many projects of the Cole Harbour Heritage Farm Museum was collecting flowers and plants that once grew on the former farms in the area. Fanny Foster Kuhn's double daffodils, planted almost a century ago at her home in Upper Lawrencetown, now thrive at the Heritage Farm. (left, Carolyn Gesner, 2003; right, courtesy of the Kuhn family)

Paul Brunelle has repaired, restored, and refurbished several artifacts in the Heritage Farm Museum's collection of farm implements. He is shown repairing a hay rake. (Terry Eyland 2003)

the south of Long Hill and on Lawlors Point, which is located in the immediate foreground as viewed from the hill. A condition of the designation was that construction or any other change could take place only through special development agreement.

Members of the society appeared regularly before the county planning board and Halifax County Council to argue for the continued preservation of lands around the harbour as land development proposals were put forward. They continued to press the park idea by bringing it to the attention of local politicians at all levels of government as well as local residents.

By the early 1980s, the society had made a number of converts to the park proposal, most notably the Department of Lands and Forests (now the Department of Natural Resources), which realized the

Fraser Conrad (centre) and Chris Trider (right) of the Nova Scotia Department of Natural Resources look over some of the land that eventually became part of the Cole Harbour Heritage Park. Mr. Conrad was instrumental in convincing some family members to contribute land and was a major supporter of the park. Also in the photo is Helen Fletcher, a Cole Harbour Rural Heritage Society Board Member. (ca. 1984)

value of protecting the area. The process of acquiring properties around the harbour took several years.

By the mid-1980s the Cole Harbour-Lawrencetown Coastal Heritage Park was beginning to take shape, and the beaches at Lawrencetown and Rainbow Haven were designated provincial parks. However, an important section of the park reserve properties still remained unprotected. The former site of the county Poor Farm and all the land adjoining it as far as the old railway tracks to the south remained park reserve only, which offered no real protection for the land.

Rosemary's Way, part of the Salt Marsh Trail, was named for Rosemary Eaton in recognition of her many years of service on behalf of the Cole Harbour Rural Heritage Society. Rosemary and husband Mike, both committed to preserving the marsh, first came to Cole Harbour in the 1960s. (right, mid-1960s/courtesy of RE; below, Eva Mackay 2002)

The Peter McNab Kuhn Wildlife Management area, consisting of 2,315 acres or 930 hectares, covers 3.6 square miles. Descendants of Peter McNab Kuhn, who owned and operated the dyke for many years, donated the land to the Province of Nova Scotia. Attending the formal handover are (left to right) David Kuhn, grandson, Mollie Kuhn Campbell, daughter (age 101 at the time), Mary Kuhn Osborne, granddaughter, and Natural Resources Minister Ken MacAskill. (Ross Osborne 1998)

Throughout the 1990s, the Cole Harbour Rural Heritage Society continued to lobby the Natural Resources minister and other politicians to give the property full park status. After a few years, when the Cole Harbour Parks and Trails Association and the Harbour East Community Council of Halifax Regional Municipality also voiced their support, the park designation was granted.

All the land that was reclaimed by the ocean when the dyke was destroyed in 1917 has since been taken over by myriad plant, animal, and fish species. It is now a nursery for numerous commercial fish species. Trout have returned to the harbour, and a few local people still catch gaspereau heading up Little Salmon River in the spring. It is again possible to set nets under the harbour ice for smelts or spear eels as was once common in the harbour. Since it was neither suitable nor desirable to consider the marsh area a park, it became a wildlife management area and has been named the Peter McNab Kuhn Wildlife

Management Area. The Salt Marsh Trail has opened up the marsh to a whole new group of people who enjoy hiking and cycling during the spring, summer and autumn, and cross-country skiing in the winter. It's also a popular locale for birdwatchers and photographers year-round.

Another Cole Harbour site with historical significance and affiliation with the society is situated at the foot of Long Hill and is known on older maps as simply "public landing place." There was considerably more boat traffic in and out of the harbour due in part to the generally poor condition of the roads in the late eighteenth and early nineteenth centuries. The main channel was deeper and there was neither a dyke nor a railway trestle to impede navigation. There are references to Bissett's boat-building operation and shipping ventures, and Jacob Conrad, one of the earliest settlers to the area, is known to have owned a vessel.

The public landing place was located where Smelt Brook enters the harbour on its western arm. Collyer's map of 1808 has the Cole Harbour Road touching the water's edge at this location then narrowing as it continues on towards Lawrencetown. From the late eighteenth century another road – Miller Road, named for Tobias Miller, a Hessian soldier who owned land in both Cole Harbour and the Preston area – connected the harbour from the landing point to the interior.

Governor John Wentworth is thought to have used the harbour regularly to get to his estate in East Preston, and he may have used this landing place. He is known to have landed further east near Robinson Road, which appears on some early maps as Wentworth Road. However, only the Smelt Brook site has been found marked "public landing place" on an official map.

Although generally forgotten with the passing of time, the area of approximately one-third of an acre still remains a public landing place. When the last transfer of the adjacent land took place from Strum to Bishop in the 1960s, this piece of land remained as part of the Strum estate. When Robie Strum died, each of the two Cole Harbour churches – Cole Harbour-Woodside United Church and St. Andrew's Anglican – received one half of the one-third acre. In the late 1990s, both churches agreed to donate their interest in the property to the Cole Harbour Rural Heritage Society.

Music and afternoon tea in the Rose and Kettle Garden at the Heritage Farm Museum is one of the farm's many summer activities combining fundraising with enjoyment of the farm's relaxing environment. (RE 1999)

Over the years, numerous men and women have given time, talent, money, and artifacts to promote and continue the work of the society and the farm museum. Rosemary Eaton helped create a vast library of oral history tapes and photographs. Ira Settle was a leading proponent in saving Giles House and having it moved to a new location for safekeeping, in addition to donating a number of artifacts. Murray Ritcey, Frank Bissett, John Giles, Robert Tulloch, and a host of others all played an integral part in building the Cole Harbour Rural Heritage Society.

Elizabeth Corser, who joined the society in 1973, had become involved with farm museum activities when the first annual Farm Days, involving children and farm animals, were held in 1978. They were continued for the next four years. In 1988, with the help of an operating grant from the Nova Scotia Museum and other funding sources, the society hired Elizabeth Corser, who had been working as a volunteer or as a term employee for 10 years, as full-time director/curator.

In following years, Sean Smith was hired full time as assistant curator. In 1991, he moved away, and Connie Holland was hired in that capacity. In the mid-1990s, titles became executive director and curator/archivist. In 1995, Terry Eyland was hired for the latter position. By this time, the museum was open daily from mid-May to mid-October.

The society continues to sponsor fundraising dinners and social events such as corn boils, strawberry festivals, plant days, and three church services in the old Meeting House – a sunrise service at Easter, a harvest service and a Christmas service – and it publishes a quarterly newsletter.

In July 2003, the Cole Harbour Rural Heritage Society marked its 30th anniversary, celebrating three decades of unstinting service in gathering and preserving the culture and history of the community.

The Rev. Lester Settle, left, has often officiated at special services held in the Cole Harbour Meeting House. On this occasion, he donned a costume and took the part of the Rev. William Croscombe, one of the first Methodist ministers to serve the area. In the interest of authenticity, the Reverend Settle arrived on horseback. He is shown going over his sermon notes with Gary Gibson, a member of the Heritage Society who has conducted extensive research on the Meeting House, culminating in the building's designation as a Provincial Heritage Building. (Eric Carlson 1998, courtesy of Ed Carlson)

Above right, the Rev. George Russell, who ministered to the Cole Harbour community in the late 1930s and early 1940s, returned to take part in special church services in the Meeting House sponsored by the society. In his first harvest service in Cole Harbour he exhorted his congregation to bring lots of produce to decorate the church, unaware that the produce was given to the presiding minister. (RE 1987)

In 1993, Verna (Giles) Osborne and Beatrice Geldart invited all Cole Harbour residents and former residents age 65 or over to the farm for a strawberry tea. Several of the people in attendance were in their 90s. It was a well-attended event with lots of food and good music supplied by drummer Vince Cribby, the Armstrongs, and the Kazoo Kuties, a spirited group of singing seniors. Above, Emily Greatorex, wife of a former Cole Harbour minister, shares strawberry shortcake and memories with Gerald Strum. (RE 1993)

Popular local fiddler Ron Noiles has also performed for society events on several occasions. (RE 1989)

The farm museum attracts thousands of visitors and schoolchildren each year, who take a step back in time to experience life in Cole Harbour when it was an active farming community.

Above, Connie Holland, assistant curator at the Heritage Farm 1992–94, explains to visitors how a hotbed operates. Several thousand schoolchildren visit the farm museum annually. (RE 1992)

Cole Harbour Heritage Farm Museum's tearoom and gift shop attract visitors to the museum and raise money to maintain the heritage buildings. The farm ambience and period buildings also make the farm an attractive location for filming.

One production brought Gordon Pinsent to the farm. At left, he stands in costume outside the tearoom. (Terry Eyland 1998)

32

VOICES FROM THE PAST

Over the years, the Cole Harbour Rural Heritage Society has amassed a storehouse of archival material in the form of maps, deeds, subdivision plans, newspaper cuttings, books, and photographs, which have been catalogued and filed for present and future generations of historical researchers. One very important asset is the society's oral histories, a collection of about 90 taped interviews with area residents, who helped create a living history of the community.

These living voices from the past evoke days of yesteryear in a special way. They include stories of market days, the social life of the community, the origins of the credit union, the co-operative, the Temperance Society, churches, life on the farm, the Halifax Explosion, the Cole Harbour dyke, the railway, and family trees of some of the early families who settled the area and whose descendants still live nearby.

The tapes are not historically pure in that exact dates of events are often omitted; the memories of those interviewed have dimmed with the passing of time. Rosemary Eaton, an early instrumental member of the society, conducted most of the interviews. Students employed at the farm during the summer months and other volunteers also conducted interviews. Many of the interviewees have since passed on, but their voices and their stories are captured on tapes that form a permanent record of the life and times of Cole Harbour.

Effie Nieforth, who grew up in Three Fathom Harbour, talked about going to the Saturday night dances held in the various community halls of the area. In Seaforth, she said, there was always a dance the day after Christmas and on Easter Monday. Most times they walked the road to the hall, but sometimes they walked over ice or even rowed to the dances. She recalled dances at Cole Harbour, Lawrencetown, and Three Fathom Harbour. There were about 40 to 50 people crowded into the halls. It was lively toe-tapping music

Rosemary Eaton spent many hours interviewing older Cole Harbour residents and collecting information on the history and life of the area. As a result of her efforts, the Heritage Farm Museum has a large collection of oral history tapes for future researchers. She is shown here interviewing Russell Sellars. (photographer uknown 1980s)

served up sometimes by the Conrad Brothers and other times by the LaPierre boys from Grand Desert.

"Sometimes we danced all night and until early in the morning. There were waltzes, polkas, plain sets, and quadrilles. We never did the shaking that they do today. Some of the boys had drinks but they never drank in the hall. If they wanted a drink they went outside. The girls never drank nor smoked," she added. Sometimes the dances were box socials to raise money for the community hall, the school, or one of the churches.

Wilfred Bissett spoke of a young Prince of Wales, later King George v, who went hunting in the Cole Harbour area. The prince at that time was serving on a British naval ship that came into port at Halifax. He expressed a desire to go hunting and was brought to Cole Harbour for a day's outing.

Florence (Bissett) Hartlen in a 1981 interview talked about her grandfather, John George Bissett, who served the area on the Halifax County

Maurice Strum lived and farmed most of his life at the family farm on Long Hill. Mr. Strum, while in his 90s, could recall 80+ years of personal experiences as well as stories he remembered from his uncle and grandfather. Mr. Strum, seen here with his dog Rosie, shared his memories on several oral history tapes now in the Heritage Farm Museum's archives. (RE ca. 1974)

Council for about 40 years. At that time the constituency covered an area that included Cole Harbour, Woodlawn, Lawrencetown, Cow Bay, and Eastern Passage. Councillor Bissett died at the age of 96. Florence Hartlen also remembered a shipwreck off Cole Harbour that was carrying a cargo of tobacco. Many of the men in the village went down to the wreck to gather up tobacco. They were able to collected enough to last for months.

She recalled a time when she and family members picked raspberries and cranberries that grew wild in the dyke area, and they later sold them at the Halifax Market. As a child on Sundays she did double duty, attending first the Anglican Sunday school at St. Andrew's because her father was Anglican and then attending the Methodist church service with her mother in the evening. As an adult she joined the United Church of Canada.

Many of the interviewees mention the small ferry that operated between West Lawrencetown and Cole Harbour in the early 1800s. None were old enough to have actually seen the ferry service in operation, but they were passing on stories from their parents and older residents of the area.

Opinions differ among some of the interviewees as to the geographical boundaries of Cole Harbour. One person suggested the community extended from Little Salmon River on one side to where the railway tracks crossed the other side of the harbour and from the harbour to the top of Breakheart Hill. Another person maintained the width of the community was about the same but stretched its length from the harbour all the way to Gaston Road at the pre-1961 Dartmouth town boundary.

Vinie Patterson, who came to Cole Harbour in 1937 from Eastern Passage, remembered cutting ice with a saw on Bell Lake around the new year and hauling it home in a horse and wagon. Most people who cut ice did so for their own use during the summer months. The ice was covered in sawdust and stored in a barn.

Rosemary Eaton interviewed Eugene Bellefontaine of West Chezzetcook in 1976 on his 81st birthday about his involvement in the clam-digging industry on the Cole Harbour flats during the Depression years. At that time he was digging clams for General Seafoods of Yarmouth, a company that exported the product to markets in Boston and New York. The seafood company sent their trucks to pick up the clams, which were shelled and in buckets. He said he also dug and sold clams to Sunnyside, a fast-food outlet in Bedford.

Cole Harbour was an excellent area for clam digging at that time, Eugene Bellefontaine said. He had about a dozen men working for him then. One of his men, Joe Baker, dug 65 buckets of clams in one day. The diggers usually received 25¢ a hod – there were two buckets to a hod, which measured approximately one bushel. A good digger could make up to $3 a day, which was considered good money at that time. Eugene Bellefontaine said a good digger could dig up to seven or eight hods to a tide, which usually lasted about four hours; a spring tide lasted a little longer. Since Cole Harbour seldom froze during the winter months it was possible to dig clams year-round. In the early years the diggers used a shovel to dig clams, but later they switched to a hoe with a short handle.

By 1936, the clams in the area were starting to die out. No one was really certain as to the cause, but most seem to agree that it was a disease of some kind because every harbour along the Eastern Shore was affected. Bellefontaine gave up clamming early in the 1950s, and clams finally died out by the late 1950s.

Mrs. Jessie Joslin, originally from England, came to live in Cole Harbour in 1918 following the 1917 Harbour Explosion. She remembered Jersey Jack, who wandered into the area as a 16-year-old boy following a shipwreck at the turn of the century or earlier. He was a cabin boy on a sailing ship bound for Halifax when it was wrecked in a storm off Cole Harbour dyke. He came from Jersey, one of Britain's Channel Islands, hence the name bestowed by the locals. He had a French name that translated loosely to Vincent. Jersey Jack married Alice Costley, a local girl, and they had a number of children before she died in 1929.

Jessie Joslin recalled Jersey Jack was a real character who came regularly to her family's home on Saturday night and drank rum, sang songs, and step-danced for them. He was in his 90s when he died.

Another familiar figure in the Cole Harbour community was Jerry Lonecloud, a member of the Mi'kmaq Truro band, who came regularly for sweet grass. Helen Horne remembered Jerry Lonecloud staying at her home when she was a child, and he sat up late into the night talking to her uncle Jim Beck. She said he rose early in the morning, had breakfast, and went down to the dyke to cut and dry the sweet grass he used to make the baskets he sold at the Halifax Market.

"As little children we would sit with our mouths open listening to his fascinating stories." She couldn't remember any of his stories but she did remember seeing him swing off their feet two grown men holding on to his braids.

Jerry Lonecloud would indeed have had a vast repertoire of interesting tales. He was born in Belfast, Maine, to Nova Scotian parents, Abram and Mary Anne, who made a living selling tonics and medicines. His father joined the Union Army during the American Civil War and was one of the 25 New York cavalrymen who captured John Wilkes Booth, the man who assassinated Abraham Lincoln. Afterwards, his father went to New York City to claim his share of the reward money; he never returned. His mother died shortly after his father left.

As head of his family, Jerry Lonecloud moved his two brothers and sister back to Nova Scotia, a journey that took almost two years. In Nova Scotia he supported his family by hunting, trapping, and fishing, but he returned to the United States in the 1880s to join a Wild West Show. He worked for a time in Buffalo Bill's show before forming his own touring troupe, the Kiowa Medicine Show. His travels brought him to New Brunswick, where he married Elizabeth Paul.

Together they travelled the Maritime provinces hosting shows and selling medicines.

Others in Cole Harbour remember seeing Lonecloud in the community and at the weekly Farmer's Market. He died April 16, 1930, at 76. Lonecloud's life was the subject the 2002 book, *Tracking Dr. Lonecloud: Showman to Legend Keeper*, by Ruth Holmes Whitehead.

The society's audio tape collection is a valuable asset, featuring stories from the people about life as they once knew it in the Cole Harbour community.

33

THE BULLDOZING ERA

The residential development boom that began during the 1960s accelerated throughout the 1970s and continued into the next decade with more and larger housing projects. It was a time of transition – the end of rural living and the start of a new era of suburban living. Along Caldwell Road, previously known as Indian Road and then Lodge Road, about 1,200 acres of farmland, once under the plow, were giving way to the bulldozer and turning into residential housing developments.

As the 1970s opened, Halifax County was negotiating with the City of Dartmouth for an extension of the city's water and sewer lines into the new housing development. The city wanted the county to provide a proper development plan for the Cole Harbour area and assume the capital cost of the water and sewer extension. The county agreed to the city's terms by May 1970. The county also agreed to widen the Cole Harbour Road from 20.1 metre (66 feet) to an eventual 30.5-metre (100-foot) right-of-way. The housing development, when completed, would accommodate 15,000 to 20,000 new residents and include schools, parks, a neighbourhood commercial area. The city asked the county to amend its subdivision regulations to plan for the orderly development of Cole Harbour as well as to conform to Dartmouth's subdivision regulations.

The Joslin farmhouse, originally owned by Hezekiah Bissett, was one of the early farmhouses in the Cole Harbour area. It, like so many others, is now only a photographic memory. (RE 1983)

In July 1970, the Federal Department of Regional and Economic Expansion (DREE) approved a cost-sharing arrangement with Halifax County for the water and sewer extension program from Dartmouth to the Cole Harbour area. A 61-centimetre (24-inch) pipeline would bring city water from Dartmouth to the Caldwell Road, then 30.5-centimetre (12-inch) and 35.6-centimetre (14-inch) pipes would carry the water to homes in the Smith and Dickson subdivisions and to the Halifax County Hospital. Atholea subdivision was not included.

The cost of the project was estimated at $620,000 with a 50-50 cost-sharing arrangement between the federal government and the county. A sewage treatment plant was to be erected near Bissett Lake.

A little more than a week after the DREE water and sewer announcement, Clayton Developments Ltd. announced another major housing and commercial development to be known as Colby Village. It was to begin at the junction of the Caldwell and Cole Harbour Roads and continue down the south side of Cole Harbour Road to Bissett Road.

The development featured 1,260 single-family homes, 25 acres of low-density multiple residential housing, a shopping centre, a recreation centre, and land for school construction. It was estimated that

8,000 to 12,000 people would live in the new development. Five model homes were built on the site and opened for inspection by October 1970. Cost of the homes in the new development was considerably lower than in Clayton Park, the company's Halifax housing development. Colby Village offered prospective homebuyers all the essential services: paved roads, streetlights, and landscaped lots. Prices for the homes started at $23,700. The first 25 homes were built and ready for occupancy in the spring of 1971.

In the municipal elections of 1970, Ira Settle comfortably defeated Ken Robb and Russell Miller to retain his seat on County Council. He later edged out Councillor Sylvia Hudson by a nine to seven vote to retain his position as warden of the county.

During a County Council session, Eastern Passage Councillor Tom Tonks exposed a plan by Canadian Plant and Process Engineering Ltd. to pump treated sewage into Cole Harbour with the blessing of the Nova Scotia Water Resources Commission.

It had been previously suggested that a treatment plant be built at Bissett Lake and a second one be built later near Morris Lake. The new amended plan suggested eliminating the other plants – sewage from the surrounding area would be collected and pumped into an existing treatment plant at the Halifax County Hospital, which would be enlarged to accommodate the additional flow.

However, as pointed out in a local newspaper, the mouth of the harbour had a very narrow opening, creating very poor water circulation. The tidal flow was concentrated in one main channel. The dyke area also had one of the few sandy beaches remaining in the area, and it was popular for swimming. The harbour, according to the newspaper, was a stopover for migrating geese, ducks, and shore birds. In the spring and autumn as many as 2,000 black ducks and 2,500 Canada geese and hundreds of teal and goldeneye visited the area. Although the sewage entering the harbour under the proposal would be treated, without proper drainage the phosphates in the effluent would allow for the rapid growth of eelgrass and algae, depleting the supply of oxygen and destroying the delicate balance in the harbour.

Area residents quickly banded together to fight this proposal. They warned County Council that a serious pollution problem would

Prevention of sewage discharge preserved a key wildlife area. Many bird species, like these Greater Yellowlegs (Tringa melanoleuca) *depend on Cole Harbour as a rest and feeding stop as they migrate south in the autumn and north in the spring. During the fall migration, the harbour becomes a major bird-watching site. Japanese Foreign Minister Kono, an avid birdwatcher, managed to fit in a visit to the area during the G7 Summit held in Halifax in 1995.* (RE 1980s)

occur in the harbour if sewage were discharged into it without proper treatment. A letter was also sent to Alan Sullivan, the minister responsible for the Nova Scotia Water Act, outlining the serious ecological threat to the harbour. "In effect the harbour is a shallow lake at high water and a river (the main channel) passing between the mud flats at low water," the letter stated.

Warden Settle told the delegation attending the council meeting that a government task force was studying the problem and would report back in the near future. In July 1971, Metropolitan Area Planning Commission released its report on the Cole Harbour Pollution Study, which confirmed everyone's worst fear: "Cole Harbour was unable to support effluent of secondary and even tertiary treatment on a long-term basis." The residents had won their battle; the government would have to look elsewhere for a solution to the sewage problem that the many new housing developments in the area were creating.

Eventually, a sewer line was built overland from the community of Cole Harbour to a treatment plant in Eastern Passage and the plant's product was pumped directly into the Atlantic Ocean.

Another sign of the changing way of life in the area from rural to suburban was the closure of the Co-op grocery store near the entrance to Bel Ayr Park and the end of the co-operative movement. The store had opened in 1968 but closed within a few years. Some attributed its failure to the fact that most people in the area could by then drive into the city for their grocery needs and other essentials. The building became an IGA grocery store, but that also closed.

The area rate for Cole Harbour District was increased in the spring of 1971 from 10¢ to 15¢ to help pay for a $20,000 addition to the fire station and other essentials for the department. The volunteer fire department, which had started 10 years earlier, by then owned two pumpers and a tank truck. In addition to its volunteer members, the department had a full-time chief and three paid firefighters. Cole Harbour Fire Department was responsible for fire protection in Cherry Brook and Westphal, as well as the ever-growing Cole Harbour area.

Councillor Percy Baker resigned his council seat in May 1971 to take over the full-time administration of the Halifax County Hospital at an annual salary of $10,680.

By June 1971, Colby Village was beginning to take shape; tenders were called for a contract to connect city water and sewer facilities to the new development. The first 20 homes were ready for occupancy by the end of August, and 75 more homes were ready by year's end.

In November 1971, the Nova Scotia Government had acquired almost 1,000 acres in the area for a major housing development it hoped would alleviate the housing shortage for low- and middle-income families. Housing Minister D. Scott MacNutt, making the announcement, said the construction of the homes would not begin before 1974. Developers would build the houses to a point at which people could move in and complete them on their own time. He stated that apartments as well as townhouses could also be part of the overall housing mix. He explained that expropriation by the government of some land in the area was essential in order to prevent a spate of land speculation and the type of problems that had plagued the Sackville land assembly years earlier. "About 30 to 35 people were affected by the expropriation," he said. The new housing development, Forest Hills, to be situated on the opposite side of the Cole Harbour Road from Colby Village, was expected to accommodate an additional 20,000 people when completed.

In 1972, Ross Osborne retired from his post as the full-time manager of the Russell Credit Union, a position he had held since 1957. When he took over the credit union, its assets had totalled $55,000. When he retired, they had reached almost $300,000. "Sometimes we had to wait for two years for a loan to be repaid, but we eventually received the payment," he remarked.

In 1972, Cole Harbour residents were confronted with yet another government-inspired problem for the community – the expansion of Cole Harbour Road to a four-lane highway. The four-lane highway was expected to solve an ever-increasing traffic problem caused by the residential developments already underway and those planned for the future. The government's proposal would have expanded Cole Harbour Road from Bel Ayr Park all the way to Ross Road.

The proposed highway expansion met stiff opposition from local residents. A group of approximately 60 citizens, led by Murray Ritcey, met with Highway Minister Garnet Brown to protest and to offer alternate suggestions. If the highway went ahead as planned, they argued, a cemetery in front of the old settlers' Meeting House would have to be moved to another location. Residents were also concerned that a four-lane highway running past their doors would decrease their property value. Minister Brown assured the residents that the design work for the upgrading of the road to a four-lane highway was incomplete, and any opposition at that time was premature.

The four-lane highway was postponed pending further government study. Following the completion of the study, the four-lane highway proposal was abandoned for the time – another battle with government that residents had won. However, the road was eventually expanded to a four-lane highway as far as Bissett Road (see photo page 267).

Throughout the 1970s and into the 1980s, construction company bulldozers continued clearing the fertile farmland to put in subdivisions with new homes, schools, shopping centres, recreation areas, and paved streets. Farming had all but disappeared by the mid-1970s, ending an era that had begun with the European settlers and United Empire Loyalists. The only reminder of the past way of life in Cole Harbour was the Heritage Farm Museum created and maintained by people with a vision of preserving the past for the future.

34

POLITICS THEN AND NOW

The people of Cole Harbour have been active players on the local political stage for more than a century. Their involvement in politics has run the gamut from elected representatives, to backroom political strategists, to political appointees. In past years, Cole Harbour was part of a much larger political arena. Recently, Cole Harbour became a separate political entity on the municipal and provincial level. On the federal scene, Cole Harbour is shared between the Dartmouth riding and the Sackville, Musquodoboit, Eastern Shore riding.

Halifax County, stretching from Ecum Secum in the east to Hubbards on the South Shore, became a municipal political unit in 1880, when a set of bylaws were approved for the general operation of the municipal government.

The bylaws set out the time for council meetings, the conduct at meetings, duties of the warden and councillors. It also set out laws relating to the eight standing committees of council: Public Accounts and Finance, Tenders and Public Property, Licences, Roads and Bridges, Assessments, the Lunatic Asylum, Law Amendments, and Jury Lists. The bylaws also set out the duties of the various district officers such as assessors of poor and county rates, collectors of county and poor rates, overseers of the poor, overseers of statute labour, health officers, and surveyors of logs and lumbers. The bylaws covered such items as dogs, stud horses, bulls, rams, animal pounds, ferries, sea manure, peddlers, burning brush, firing guns, thistles and noxious weeds, and Sabbath Day desecration. It was unlawful for anyone to carry a gun or a fishing rod or to be found shooting or fishing in any part of the county on the Sabbath Day. The fine for such an offence was not less than $5 and not more than $20.

When County Council was formed, Cole Harbour was part of District 31 and was called Dartmouth. The first representative on council for the district was Daniel Donovan. The following year, District 31 was renamed Cole Harbour, and John George Bissett, locally known as Squire Bissett, became the council representative for the district. Squire Bissett continued to serve the people of the district for the next 17 years. Samuel L. Lydiard took over in 1899 and continued until 1910.

In the overall operation of the municipal government there were a host of officers and minor positions to which the elected representative often appointed local people as a reward for loyal support. Those appointed could expect remuneration in the form of an annual stipend. When new representatives were elected to council, new people were appointed to these positions.

One of the appointed positions was that of road overseer, charged with the task of ensuring the roads within the community were in good condition. During the winter months the road overseer was responsible for getting local farmers out to shovel the snow off the highway. The overseer usually went door to door and continued the practice long after telephones came into general use in the area. Many times when a snowstorm hit the area, telephones were left off their hooks.

Fence viewers had the task of ensuring that all fences in the community were kept in good repair to prevent cattle and other livestock from roaming and causing damage. Fence viewers also ensured that fences were erected on the property of their owners and not over the line infringing on another property. The position of fence viewer began in 1885, when Judson Baker and James Turner were appointed for Cole Harbour. The position was terminated in 1940.

Pound keepers were appointed from time to time, depending on need, and their job was to pick up stray animals, particularly livestock that got loose, and were invading another farmer's land or roaming the roads. The first pound keeper appointed in 1881 was Judson Settle.

Hog reeves and sheep valuers are positions whose duties appear to have been lost with the passing of time. The first hog reeve appointed in 1885 was John Thornham. The position appears to have been terminated after one year.

Wallace Peverill represented Cole Harbour on the County Council for 22 years, split over two separate periods, the first 1911–19. Joseph Fassett was the council representative from 1920 to 1922. When Peverill returned to council in 1923, he was elected as the first county warden to come from Cole Harbour. He continued to serve on council until 1937.

In 1938, Cole Harbour became part of District 14, which included Tufts Cove, Port Wallace, Woodlawn, and Westphal. The first councillor for the new district was Fred Settle. He represented the area until he died in 1951. His cousin Ira Settle was elected to council the following year in a by-election. Ira Settle later became the second county warden from Cole Harbour. Warden Settle represented the area until he retired in 1979 with a record 27 years. District 14 was greatly reduced in size and population in 1961, when most of its area became part of the new City of Dartmouth.

As population increased in the area, the district was split in the early 1980s, giving one seat to Woodlawn and one to Cole Harbour. Wes Topple was the first elected council member for Woodlawn. Ray DeRoche replaced him in 1982 and served until 1991. Ben Bates won the seat then. Rick Stewart replaced Ira Settle on council for the Cole Harbour area. Stewart resigned from council before completing his term. Harry McInroy won the seat in a by-election.

In 1982, the Cole Harbour area was given a second seat on the municipal council, which was won by Steve Mont. In 1988, Ron Cooper replaced Mont. Dennis Richards also represented part of the Cole Harbour area on council from 1988 until 1993, when he was elected to the Nova Scotia legislature.

In 1996, when Halifax, Dartmouth, Bedford, and Halifax County were amalgamated to form the Halifax Regional Municipality, the Cole Harbour-Woodlawn elected representatives were reduced from

The Cole Harbour Road, looking west up Beck's Hill, during a winter's day in the 1940s. On the right is Charlie Bissett's milk stand where empty milk cans are stacked by the mailbox. A local dairy would have picked up the full milk cans earlier. (ca. 1950/CHR-SU)

For many years the men of Cole Harbour were responsible by law for keeping the road free of snow following a snowstorm. Rudolphe (surname unknown) heaves a hefty shovelful off the Long Hill road while Bob Davies digs in. Leaning on their shovels in the background enjoying a moment's rest are (left to right) Maurice Strum, Stanley Ritcey, and Norman Morash. (ca. 1950/Davies collection)

Ira Settle, with the help of Fraser Conrad and Lloyd Eisener, restored a small building at the Cole Harbour Heritage Farm Museum for use as a blacksmith shop. Mr. Settle is seen at the completion of the project with County Councillor Ray DeRoche (left), Ron Giles, and his son Joseph. The latter are descendants of Joseph Giles, first resident of the Giles House. (RE 1986)

three to two. In the election for seats on the new regional council Ron Cooper beat out Ben Bates, and Harry McInroy was elected to council as well. Both men continue to represent the Cole Harbour, Eastern Passage, and Woodlawn area into 2003.

With a sudden increase in population in the late 1960s and through the 1970s, Cole Harbour became a separate provincial constituency. Before that, Cole Harbour had been part of the Eastern

Elizabeth Corser, executive director of the Heritage Farm Museum, chats with Leader of the New Democratic Party Darrell Dexter, MLA for Cole Harbour, over a cup of tea at the farm's tearoom. (Michael Creagan 2002/courtesy of Darrell Dexter)

Shore constituency, which stretched from Dartmouth city limits to Ecum Secum on the Eastern Shore and was represented for many years by A. Garnet Brown, a member of Gerald Regan's Liberal Cabinet. David Nantes represented Cole Harbour as a Progressive Conservative member in the John Buchanan Government throughout most of the 1980s. When Nantes retired from politics, Dennis Richards, Liberal member in the John Savage government, won the seat. Alan Mitchell also represented a section of the Cole Harbour area in the Nova Scotia legislature.

The current MLA is Darrell Dexter, a Dartmouth lawyer, who was elected as an New Democratic Party member. In 2002, he was elected as NDP party leader and is now the Leader of the Opposition. Kevin Deveaux, an NDP member in Eastern Passage, also represents a part of Cole Harbour in the legislature.

On the federal level, Cole Harbour was in the dual riding of Halifax until 1968, when it became part of the new Dartmouth-Eastern Shore riding. The first Member of Parliament for the new riding was J. Michael Forestall, a member of the Progressive Conservative Party, who defeated Arnie Patterson, the Liberal candidate. Forestall won re-election over Dartmouth's Dr. John Savage and a second time over Arnie Patterson and yet again in another campaign with Dr. John

Savage. Forestall lost the seat to Ron MacDonald, a Liberal candidate. Forestall was subsequently appointed to the Senate. When Ron MacDonald retired from the political arena, well-known playwright Wendy Lill won the seat for the NDP. She was re-elected to the House of Commons in the general election of 2000.

Politics and the players involved at the municipal, provincial, and federal levels continue to shape Cole Harbour life.

Member of Parliament for Dartmouth and Cole Harbour Wendy Lill (fourth from left) visits the Heritage Farm Museum with a group of high school students and parents from the area involved in an exchange program with Quebec high school students in 1999. Ms. Lill has actively promoted the student exchange for several years. (1999 photographer unknown)

35

A CENTURY ENDS

The last half of the twentieth century was a time of unprecedented growth in Cole Harbour, not only in terms of population but also in the area's infrastructure. During the first half of the century, the community perhaps had 2,500 people. During the 1970s and 1980s, the major housing developments along Caldwell Road, Colby Village, and Forest Hills pushed the population figures to almost 25,000, The area became the fifth largest population base in Nova Scotia and had the ninth highest growth rate in Canada.

The new residents, like the early settlers, came to the area with dreams of a life for their families in a secure community environment. Most of the new arrivals in the 1970s and 1980s were young married couples with young families requiring the municipal amenities of schools, recreation areas, churches, parks, and shopping centres.

Cole Harbour Road, which received its first coating of asphalt in 1954 after about 200 years, only needed about 2 decades to blossom from a simple two-lane road into a four-lane thoroughfare between Bissett Road and Dartmouth. The area was also served by a much-improved transit system that connected the community with the ferry service as well as other transportation links in the Metro area. The scene along the road had changed dramatically – the farmhouses and barns, the grazing animals and the fields of vegetables were replaced by shopping centres, strip malls, gas stations, and fast-food outlets.

School construction received high priority during this period of rapid population growth. The two-room school on the Cole Harbour Road near Bissett Road, which had served the population for years, became the first Cole Harbour fire hall. It is now a recreation centre known by Cole Harbour teens as "The Box" (1965 photo on page 247). A number of elementary, junior high, and high schools have since supplanted that early two-room school. Several of the schools names

James Frederick Bissett at age 92 attended the formal opening of the George Bissett School on October 18, 1981, with his great-grandson Bradley Bissett. James Bissett, a carpenter, was the grandson of the James Frederick Bissett who built a gristmill on the Cole Harbour Road in 1835, and a relative of Squire John George Bissett for whom the school was named. (Shirley Robb Dartmouth Free Press 1981)

honoured former residents – Colonel John Stuart, Joseph Giles, Robert Kemp Turner, and George Bissett. Others were named geographically – Caldwell Road, Astral Drive, Colby Village, and Cole Harbour. By the start of the 1990s, Cole Harbour area had nine elementary schools with a combined population of 3,211; three junior high schools with a combined population of 1,414; and a crowded Cole Harbour District High School with a population of 1,719, for a total of 6,344. In 1994 Auburn Drive High School was opened. It remained the most technologically advanced school in the province for several years.

For almost a century, the farm families' spiritual needs had been served by two churches in the community – the Methodist Chapel, which became Cole Harbour United Church in 1925, and St. Andrew's Anglican Church. In the 1960s the United Church moved from its historic site at the top of Long Hill to a larger but temporary facility on Bissett Road near Cole Harbour Road. This pre-fabricated building was replaced by a more permanent structure, which was dedicated on June 7, 1970. The Rev. Garth Casely was the minister at the time. The pre-fab structure was sold to the St. Thomas More Men's Club for one dollar and moved to North Preston, where it was used for a medical clinic and daycare centre. In 1999, Cole Harbour United Church amalgamated with the Woodside-Imperoyal United Church to become the Cole Harbour-Woodside United Church.

Since 1870, St. Andrew's Anglican Church had been part of the parish of Eastern Passage, but in 1950 it became a member of the parish of Westphal under the Rev. B. Fream. Seven years later St. Andrew's was made part of the Church of the Holy Spirit in Dartmouth. In 1982 the congregation became a parish in its own right under the Rev. Wayne G. Lynch. As the community of Cole Harbour continued to grow, so did the congregation of St. Andrew's, requiring the parish to seek a larger gathering place. In 1980, a decision was made to move family Eucharist and the Christian Education classes to the Colonel John Stuart School until a more suitable accommodation could be arranged.

A new church building was built on Circassion Drive and dedicated on June 6, 1987. Three years later the Rev. Melvin Langille arrived as the second rector of the parish. He was followed by the Rev. Peter MacDonald, who was followed by Canon David Reid in 1998. The former church building on the Cole Harbour Road across from Bissett Road was sold to developer Sinma Investments Ltd., which incorporated the former house of worship into an apartment and commercial structure. It can still be clearly seen as a church-like structure.

The Forest Hills Fellowship Baptist Church was organized in November 1971, with the first services held in the parsonage chapel at 22 Hughallen Drive. In the spring of 1972, the new Baptist community with a membership of only 17 people established a building fund for the eventual construction of a more permanent structure. On October 20, 1974, the membership increased to a point that forced the congregation to move to the Bel Ayr Elementary School for Sunday services.

The Baptist congregation purchased land on Cole Harbour Road from the Nova Scotia Housing Commission on February 20, 1975. On May 29, 1977, the sod was turned for the construction of a new church building, which began on June 9, 1977, and was completed and dedicated on March 4 and 5 the following year.

Roman Catholics living in the rapidly growing community of Colby Village were required to go to either St. Thomas More or St. Clement's parishes, both in Dartmouth, for Sunday Mass and the sacraments, until a separate parish, Pope John XXIII, was established in July 1973. Archbishop James M. Hayes appointed the Rev. Joseph Pottie parish priest. In the fall and winter of 1973 and 1974, Father Pottie, who lived at St. Clement's rectory, celebrated Sunday Mass in peoples' homes. In April 1974, Sunday Mass was celebrated in the Colonel John Stuart Elementary School. When that building became too small, the congregation moved to the Colby Village Elementary School, until the parish church opened for worship in 1976.

With the development of Forest Hills subdivision in the mid-1970s and into the 1980s, a second church was needed for the expanding Catholic community. A new parish, St. Vincent de Paul, was formed with Father Thomas White as the first parish priest. Sunday services for the new parish were first held in Joseph Giles Elementary but moved to Cole Harbour District High School in 1986. On September 27, 1987, a new $1.3 million church with a seating capacity of 500 was officially opened and dedicated. At the time the new church opened, the congregation consisted of 450 families. The Rev. Martin Currie, pastor at the time, was later appointed Bishop of Grand Falls, Newfoundland. The large metal statue of Christ that had been affixed to the outside of the former Halifax Infirmary building on Queen Street in Halifax was relocated to the grounds of St. Vincent de Paul Parish.

Grace Lutheran Church unofficially began when the Lutheran Church purchased land at 40 Caldwell Road in 1985. In October of 1986, the Rev. Stephen Jasch started pastoral development by knocking on doors and making visits in the community. Five months later, the first worship service was held on March 8 in Joseph Giles Elementary. On November 13, 1988, Grace Lutheran Church was officially organized. A charter was drawn up listing the purpose and mission statement of the new congregation, which consisted of 64 adults and 26 children. Pastor Jasch was officially called as pastor of Grace Lutheran Church on January 29, 1989.

After various fundraising projects the Lutheran congregation made a decision on June 14, 1992, to construct a church building and assume a mortgage. The groundbreaking service was held on September 6, 1992. The cornerstone service was held two months later on November 15, and the following month the first worship service was held on Christmas Eve. Official dedication service took place on October 24, 1993. By 2003, the church building was being used extensively for both religious and community programs.

One very distinctive building in Cole Harbour is the all-white Temple of the Church of Jesus Christ of the Latter-Day Saints (Mormon) with a statue of a golden angel gracing the top of the structure. The Mormon community moved to Cole Harbour in the early 1980s, after the congregation outgrew its Dartmouth facilities. Ground was broken for a new chapel in a ceremony on October 6, 1984, and the first worship service was conducted the following September. At that time the Mormon community had approximately 400 members.

On Thanksgiving, October 12, 1998, about 700 church members throughout the area participated in the groundbreaking ceremony for the temple, which was conducted by Elder Jay E. Jensen, president of the North American northeast area. The temple was completed and dedicated by President Gordon B. Hinckley the following year on November 14, 1999.

Church members regard the temple as the house of the Lord, the most sacred place on earth. The temple is set apart from the outside world, and only the most important religious ceremonies are held there. The chapel is used for weekday activities and regular Sunday worship services. Since the temple is a unique place, only the finest materials and craftsmanship are used in its construction. Church members wear white clothing while inside the temple to symbolize purity, cleanliness, and the setting aside of earthly things. To date, there are 6 temples in Canada and 114 temples throughout the world. The temple and chapel stand near each other on Cumberland Drive.

Hillside Wesleyan Church was established in September 1974, under the leadership of its first minister, the Rev. H. C. Wilson. Services during the next year were held in the Colonel John Stuart Elementary School. The present church building on Cole Harbour Road was formally opened and dedicated in 1975. During the 1970s, the church had six school buses in operation at one point and was known as "the church on the grow." The church has won numerous Sunday school awards, including Fastest Growing Sunday School. By the start of the twenty-first century, the congregation consisted of 100 families.

Forest Hills United Church on Forest Hills Drive came about as the result of the rapid population growth in the Cole Harbour-East Dartmouth area during the 1970s and early 1980s. A Presbytery Calling Committee was formed and given the mandate to call a minister to the East Dartmouth New Church Development Ministry. On April 15, 1985, the Rev. Blake C. Caldwell was inducted into this ministry. After a door-to-door canvass by the minister during the spring and summer of 1985, the gymnasium of the Robert Kemp Turner Elementary School was rented in September for Sunday services and Sunday school.

The following year 2 hectares (4.9 acres) of land were purchased along Forest Hills Drive as the site for a new church building. A Building Committee was formed under joint chairs Jim and Sharon Lisson to raise money and make the necessary financial arrangements for the construction of a new church building. MacFawn Rogers were appointed as architects, and D. B. Stevens Construction Ltd. was the contractor.

The Forest Hills United Church was formally dedicated on September 18, 1994. By 2003, the congregation had grown to 230 families and was still growing.

The rapidly growing residential developments of young families with children also increased the need for athletic and recreational facilities. The entire Cole Harbour area was a "hotbed" for summer and winter sports as evidenced by the success of the minor hockey and ringette program. Baseball, softball, and soccer also enjoyed the same rapid growth and popularity at all age levels. The community

Cole Harbour Junior Colts, the Metro Valley Junior Hockey League finalists in the 1976–77 season, front row (left to right): Gary Knickle, Jack Gray, Jamie Yates, Rick Knickle, Bob Hendrie, Don Pearson, Allen Beaver, and Scott Baker. Back row (left to right): Eric Thomson (trainer), Rick Ruddock, Darren Fraser, Steve Storey, Jim Allen, Bill Darrach, Moochie Friesan, Mike Clarke (assistant coach), Dean Mitchell, Randy Brooks, Joe Winchester, Mike Connors, and Graham Henderson (coach). (1977 photographer unknown)

did not have the facilities to meet the current demands. With approximately 1,200 new homes scheduled for construction during 1983 and 1984, which would result in an additional 4,000 people, the demand for recreational facilities would intensify.

In 1983 the Bissett Lake Park Development Committee under the leadership of Gary Illsley proposed a major recreational park. The committee had already worked for over a year, holding meetings with the District Service Commission, the County of Halifax, and the Provincial Department of Culture, Recreation, and Fitness.

The park proposal covered a 15-hectare (38-acre) parcel of land with 1,219 metres (4,000 feet) of water frontage on Bissett Lake – the largest freshwater lake in the area; comparable in size to Lake Banook in Dartmouth. Recreational uses for the proposed park included softball and baseball, beach and marina, play areas, hiking/exercise trails, cross-country skiing, skating, and passive enjoyment of the surrounding lake and grounds. The proposal also made provision for off-street parking for 180 cars.

Cole Harbour was a pioneer in the sport of ringette, winning a provincial championship. The Grantham's Fair Faucets 1977–78 team includes, front row (left to right) Gail MacDonald, Suzie MacIntosh, Lisa Gomes, Stephanie Bruce, Kerry Alexander, Melanie Stewart, and Kelly Mercier; and back row (left to right) Shirley MacDonald, Bernetta Stewart, Janice Hart, Dawn McIntosh, Wanda Steele, Shelly Langille, Louise Freeman, and Gerry Bruce. (1978 photographer uknown)

A public meeting was held on June 22, 1983, with representatives of the county and elected councillors to discuss the park proposal along with the timing of the development and the funding method. Over time, most of the Bissett Lake Park proposed in 1983 was put in place for the benefit of the entire community.

As proposals were put forth for a major park along Bissett Lake, planning was also underway to develop a recreation and cultural centre for the community. The Cole Harbour-Westphal and Area Cultural and Recreation Foundation was formed in 1984 by a group of community-minded individuals to develop Cole Harbour Place. The foundation had an executive committee and two major committees: a Building Committee and a Capital Committee. The latter consisted of a number of subcommittees that conducted fundraising projects with major corporations, community businesses, individuals, and the overall community. Members of the foundation and its various committees were all community volunteers, including engineers, lawyers, chartered accountants, bankers, senior government officials, and several people with business and community experience.

Cole Harbour Place architects were Sperry/MacLennan of Dartmouth. They had previously excelled in sports and recreational facilities such as the Dartmouth Sportsplex, the 1985 Canada Games Aquatic Centre in Saint John, New Brunswick, and the Canada Games Arena in Sydney in 1987. Project managers were Dineen Construction (Atlantic) Inc.

Cole Harbour Place was built on the Community Central Commons on Forest Hills Drive, the geographic centre of the Cole Harbour-Westphal Community. The central commons was a 18-hectare (45-acre) parcel of land bordered on two sides by the two annexes of Cole Harbour District High School. The complex itself was located on 4 hectares (11 acres) of land and involved a wraparound design to encompass the existing Scotia Stadium.

Existing recreational facilities on the Commons in addition to the Scotia Stadium consisted of two ball fields (one with lights for evening use), a soccer field, a paved running track, three tennis courts, and a nature trail with a walkway system. The additions included a regional library, a community social hall, offices, a daycare, a multi-purpose room, a swimming pool, a health club, an aerobics and weightlifting room, a second ice surface, and an upgrade of the existing surface, and kitchen and canteen facilities. The overall cost of the facility, which was built in three stages, was estimated at $15 million.

In June 1986, Municipal Affairs Minister David Nantes, MLA for the area, announced a $5 million provincial grant, which would be paid in two instalments over the next two fiscal years. Nantes said at the time that Cole Harbour Place filled a vital need in the community. Stephen Mont, District 21 Councillor representing the Cole Harbour area, hoped Halifax County would provide $1.5 million towards the project. Cole Harbour Place opened in the autumn of 1988.

In 1993 the Cole Harbour Rural Heritage Society celebrated its twentieth anniversary amid the evidence that their advent had been timely. The neat suburbs, new churches, influx of new residents and

Cole Harbour Place a popular recreational facility in the community since 1988, has recently accommodated a modern skateboard park provided by the Halifax Regional Municipality to accommodate a popular pastime. (Terry Eyland 2003)

Education Minister Ron Giffen snips the ribbon to officially open the new library in the Cole Harbour Place complex in 1989. Assisting the minister at the opening are (left to right) County Councillors Harry McInroy and Ron Cooper, Ira Settle, the minister, and Municipal Affairs Minister David Nantes, MLA for Cole Harbour, who arranged a $5 million grant from the provincial government towards the construction of the building. (RE 1989)

As part of its twentieth anniversary celebrations in 1993, the Cole Harbour Rural Heritage Society presented a Bissett Rose to Margaret Bishop. Scott Morash looks on with MLA David Nantes, daughter Heather and Dianne Nantes enjoying the scene. The society has propagated and distributed this rose, believed to have been brought from France by the first Bissetts, so that it will always be found growing in the Cole Harbour area.

thriving sports leagues that meant Cole Harbour in the late twentieth century could be well-served by a organization that gave the community continuity with its past.

In 1995, there was another critical shortage of playing fields and the Cole Harbour-Westphal Recreation Advisory Council asked Halifax County to acquire an additional 20 hectares (49 acres) of land to create new playing fields. Most of the leagues in the area had hit a ceiling and couldn't grow any more due to the lack of available field time, according to Blair Blakeney, regional manager for the Halifax County Parks and Recreation Department, in a *New Dartmouth News* article. John Russell, president of the Cole Harbour Minor Baseball Association, said his organization had been forced to turn away 40 to 50 children in 1994 because of the shortage. They expected to have to turn away more children in 1995. In 1995, the association had 1,100 players ranging in age from 5 to 18, a dramatic increase over the 500 players in the 1988 season. At that time the community had 13 baseball and softball fields and 11 soccer fields serving 20,000 to 27,000 people. The area needed 3 to 5 more baseball fields, 4 or 5 soccer fields, a rugby field, outdoor tennis and basketball courts.

The drive to provide the community with more playing fields and recreational facilities was paying off in terms of the many young people who were excelling in various sports. Craig Hillier moved up from Cole Harbour in 1996 to play for the Ottawa '67s in the Ontario Hockey League; he was the Pittsburgh Penguins' first-round draft pick in the same year. In October 1997, the Cole Harbour boys under-15 team represented the province at the Canadian Soccer Championships held in Charlottetown. David Detienne, a 20-year-old Cole Harbour man, was drafted by the Los Angeles Dodgers and played for the Dodgers farm club, the Great Falls Dodgers of Montana, where he had .215 batting average with one home run and 16 RBIs. Janice Campbell was picked to play on Canada's Junior Women's softball team in the World Championships in Taipei. In 1999, a Forest Hills team won the Nova Scotia Soccer League Women's Division. In the same year Morgan Williams was selected to Canada's National Rugby team for the World Cup held in England. The following year the young rugby star played for Canada in the United States-Hong Kong Seven-a-Side Rugby Tournament. Cole Harbour baseball pitcher, 18-year-old Steve Nelson, signed a one-year contract with the Los Angeles Dodgers. The terms of the contract were not disclosed, but he did receive a signing bonus.

Although only a few made it to the "big leagues" by signing professional contracts, playing in world competitions, or winning provincial championships, the Cole Harbour athletic program provided thousands of young boys and girls with the opportunity to participate in sports, be fit, and learn about teamwork and sportsmanship.

On April 1, 1996, Cole Harbour District along with the cities of Halifax and Dartmouth, the Town of Bedford, and Halifax County all lost their individual municipal status and were rolled into one huge municipal unit by the Nova Scotia Government. The new municipality, known as Halifax Regional Municipality (HRM), was comparable in size to Prince Edward Island but with a larger population. Elections were held in December 1995 to elect a mayor for the supercity and a 23-member council. Ron Cooper and Harry McInroy, incumbents on the abolished Halifax County Council, were elected to represent the residents of Cole Harbour.

The amalgamation, which merged the police and fire services, and the planning, recreation, and public works departments, also joined the four separate school boards into one large board to serve the entire municipality. One of the early problems that the new school board had to contend with was a brawl at Cole Harbour District High School, which shut down the school for a week. The school at the time had 1,020 students from Eastern Passage, Lawrencetown, North Preston, and Cole Harbour.

The fight, which broke out on Thursday, October 10, 1996, between two students in the schoolyard over stolen drug money, drew in more students then divided along racial lines. The fight moved from the school grounds into the cafeteria then continued back in the schoolyard. Principal Gary Hartlen shut down the school at 10:00 A.M., hoping the closure and the Thanksgiving holiday weekend would ease tensions. According to a local newspaper account, "the scene was reminiscent of a racial brawl at the school that involved 60 people in 1989."

The night before students returned to their classrooms, approximately 100 people gathered in the school for a prayer service. The following Thursday, students returned under the watchful eyes of five or six uniformed police officers. One student later remarked that the fight wasn't about race at all but drugs and money.

Almost a year to the day later, another confrontation broke out at the school, this time involving about 40 students. Two students were injured and were taken to hospital, and a male teacher was assaulted. Again the school was closed down and the students were sent home.

School Superintendent Donald Trider met with the school staff, who were concerned for their own safety as well as the students' safety. Consideration was given to closing the troubled school for a year and sending the then 950 students to other schools in the metro area, but that idea was rejected.

School board members agreed to implement an extensive set of recommendations from a study conducted by Mount Saint Vincent University educator Blye Frank, aimed at easing racial tensions at the school. The study cost $399,000, of which the school board paid $234,000 and the province paid the remainder. Frank suggested hiring more visible minority teachers and a director of school improvement as well as adding anti-racism courses and literacy programs. A zero tolerance policy was also adopted at the school, which meant that a student involved in trouble would be suspended automatically.

At least six students were expelled because of the violence the previous week and more than a dozen were given five-day suspensions. Security teams of three and four persons headed by the RCMP were placed in strategic locations throughout the school along with security cameras. Tensions eventually eased and things returned to the status quo for the balance of the year; the school operated without incident during the years that followed.

In February 1997, area residents banded together to take on the planners of the newly created HRM to stop a proposed ring road from the No. 7 Highway through Cole Harbour and Cow Bay to Eastern Passage and Shearwater. The proposed highway would stretch from the No. 7 Highway just south of Ross Road, cross Cole Harbour Road at Long Hill. Then there were two options. Either pass through land east of Bissett Road that the province had declared part of the Cole Harbour-Lawencetown Coastal Heritage Park System in the early 1980s ago or run along Bissett Lake, turning towards Shearwater and meeting up with the Circumferential Highway.

Approximately 100 residents turned out for a public meeting at Prince Andrew High School in Dartmouth to air their views. Several speakers gave impassioned speeches about how the road would destroy the parkland, ruin people's peaceful country lives, and jeopardize the Nova Scotia portion of the Trans-Canada Trail.

Gerry Geldart, whose family had lived on land at Long Hill since 1805, said, "People moved to Cole Harbour to get away from existing highways. Our property values will go down if the road is built."

President of the Cole Harbour Rural Heritage Society, Beverley Brucha, told the meeting, "We do not think a ring road is needed now nor in the future. We feel the land is too valuable as parkland to be considered for a road or any other kind of development." Residents' strong arguments won the day and kept the ring road out of Cole Harbour.

In May 1997, members of the Cole Harbour Rural Heritage Society made a presentation to the Harbour East Community Council supporting Councillor Harry McInroy's motion to preserve the name "Cole Harbour Road" from Caldwell Road to Ross Road. Elizabeth Corser, who made the presentation, pointed out that settlers in the 1760s began to clear the land on the shores of Cole Harbour. Homes and barns began to appear on Long Hill and on both sides of the dusty road leading to Dartmouth. Farmers from other settlements used the road year-round to get their produce to the Halifax Market. The road was kept up and cleared of snow by the settlers' own labour. As the development of modern Cole Harbour covers the former market farms, the name "Cole Harbour Road" is gradually being lost. The process started in Dartmouth, where Portland Street swallowed the part in town, then extended to Breakheart Hill, and finally paused at Caldwell Road.

"Thousands of cars now carry people from Cole Harbour north and south (current population 30,000 and growing) to town over this road. We ask you to remember the old Cole Harbour Road and the farm families who cleared and cultivated the land that made the modern community." The presentation concluded asking that the council members remember Cole Harbour Road by saving what was left of it. Council acceded to the Heritage Society's request and saved the name for the remaining portion of Cole Harbour Road.

While community battles were waged and won in the name of preserving local history, Cole Harbour residents, like many other people around the world, anxiously awaited the end of the twentieth century – a century of two world wars, economic depression, and finally the end of the Cold War. They eagerly anticipated the dawn of the twenty-first century and the new millennium.

36

POSTSCRIPT ❦ THE TWENTY-FIRST CENTURY

Surprisingly, the twenty-first century and third millennium opened in a similar vein to the start of the previous century, with a war involving Canadians. The war against terrorism was initiated when members of al-Qaeda, a terrorist group based in Afghanistan, hijacked passenger planes out of Boston's Logan Airport and crashed them into the World Trade Towers in New York City and the Pentagon in Washington, D.C., on September 11, 2001. The twin towers in New York immediately caught fire and soon collapsed in a pile of smoking rubble, killing 3,025 people and injuring thousands of others.

International air traffic into the United States was promptly shut down, diverting overseas flights to Canadian airports. Halifax International Airport received 44 international flights, stranding about 8,000 weary passengers who were housed in high school gymnasiums, ice arenas, and private homes. Some of the stranded passengers found temporary lodging in Cole Harbour homes.

The United States, Great Britain, and Canada responded by sending planes and warships to the Persian Gulf and ground troops to Afghanistan to hunt down and destroy terrorist cells and capture their leaders. Canada sent the Princess Patricia Light Infantry Regiment, and four of its soldiers were killed when two American warplanes mistakenly dropped bombs on the Canadian troops during a night exercise. Two of the four soldiers killed were Nova Scotians: Pte. Anthony Green of Mill Cove, and Pte. Nathan Smith of Ostrea Lake on the Eastern Shore. Canada withdrew the ground troops after several months but continued sending warships to the area.

While international war raged in distant lands, on the local scene in June 2001, community radio station CHCN went on the air, giving a broadcast voice to Cole Harbour, the Preston area, Lawrencetown, and Eastern Passage. Broadcasting at 106.9 FM, the station, the brainchild

Cole Harbour Rehab Centre (formerly the Halifax County Hospital) was closed in 2002, and the residents were moved to other facilities in the area. In 2003, the vacant buildings were used in filming a mini series called "Shattered City," about the 1917 Halifax Harbour Explosion. Bissett Road crosses the foreground. (RE 1983)

of Mike Whitehouse, offered its listeners a mix of music, talk shows and community news. Veteran radio broadcaster Freeman Roach was station manager. Most of the on-air announcers and disc jockeys volunteered their time and talent.

During the summer of 2002, the Halifax County Rehabilitation Centre, formerly the Halifax County Hospital, closed its doors. The building at one time had been overcrowded, housing several hundred, but in more recent years it had been home to slightly over 100 patients. In 2001, there were 60 residents but by the time of closure that number had been scaled back. Eleven of the adult residents were relocated temporarily to Sunshine Manor in Halifax, and six other residents were placed in small options homes in Dartmouth.

About 35 employees were given jobs at Sunshine Manor. The remaining staff were let go without severance packages, prompting the Canadian Union of Public Employees (CUPE) to get involved and call for a strike vote. Councillor Harry McInroy, chair of the board for the Rehab Centre, said at the time that the union had waived its right to severance. The contract that CUPE had negotiated in 1999 contained monetary enhancement, which the union had accepted in lieu of severance. However, CUPE national representative Linda Thurston-Neeley denied that the union had waived its right to severance pay.

According to a spokesperson for the Department of Community Services, there were no immediate plans to replace the Rehab Centre with a new long-term facility. The trend at the time was to move away from large institutions. The building and the land were owned by the HRM. There were indications at the time of closure that the property would be sold for a housing development.

A serious fire broke out at a recycling depot in North Preston in June 2002 that burned for 48 hours, threatening nearby woods. The fire started in a 5-metre (16-foot) high mound of construction and demolition debris. Thirty-five firefighters from six stations in the area battled the blaze. A helicopter spent most of the afternoon dropping water from a nearby lake on the fire. The fire was finally brought under control and extinguished after firefighters dumped more than 40 million litres (about 42 million quarts) of water on the burning debris. The billowing black smoke was seen as far away as Brookfield, near Truro.

In July several residents from the Preston communities made the annual pilgrimage to the Town of Pictou to participate in the 10th annual celebration to commemorate the formation of the 2nd Construction Battalion, which consisted solely of Black soldiers during World War One. Members of the battalion did most of their training in the Pictou area before being sent overseas. A number of young men from Preston had served in the unit.

The North Preston community received almost $3 million in government funding during 2002 to build a new community centre to replace the one destroyed by fire in 2000 – $1.98 million from the Canada-Nova Scotia Infrastructure Program plus $990,000 from the HRM. A series of public meetings held throughout the area had placed the need for a community centre at the head of everyone's wish list. When completed, the new multi-purpose centre will serve up to 5,000 people in the area, contain space for recreational facilities, health and social services, and an office for the RCMP.

Michael MacKinnon of Cole Harbour was one of three Nova Scotians in July 2002 selected to greet Pope John Paul II when the pontiff arrived at the Toronto Airport to participate in the World Youth Day. The 20-year-old Cole Harbour man not only met the Pope but also talked with him, "Your Holiness it's amazing to see you; I'm really glad you're here." When the Pope learned that Michael was representing the Archdiocese of Halifax, which hosted a papal visit in 1984, he sent a special blessing to Nova Scotia.

Caldwell Road resident Bill Stratton, a member of the Cole Harbour/Westphal Kiwanis Club, was named Kiwanian of the Year in 2002 for his work as site coordinator for the Kiwanis Centre Beach and Park on Morris Lake. He won out over members in 287 clubs in Ontario, Eastern Canada, and the West Indies. (2003 courtesy of Bill Stratton)

In October 2002 Caldwell Road resident Bill Stratton, an active member of the Cole Harbour-Westphal Kiwanis Club, was named Kiwanian of the Year from among the members of 287 clubs in the district, which included Ontario, Eastern Canada, and the Caribbean. Bill Stratton had had five strokes since 1991, the last one in 2000, but he worked continually on numerous community projects. As site coordinator he helped build the Kiwanis Centre Beach and Park on Morris Lake. The park, although not completed, attracted more than 5,000 young people to the area for swimming and other activities during the summer of 2002. A Torontonian by birth, Bill Stratton had come east when he became a leading seaman radar plotter in the navy. After he retired from the service, he joined the Department of Supply and Service in 1976. He retired from the department in 1990, when his health began to fail. He joined Kiwanis in 1985. He was elected club secretary in 1988 and president in 1991. When his term as club president ended he returned to the club's secretary position.

Early in December, the Big Leagues Beverage Room in Cole Harbour made a record-breaking donation of $37,600 to the annual Christmas Daddies telethon. Two employees and a committee of volunteers raised the money. They held a road toll, a 28-kilometre (17-mile) walkathon, and a charity auction in the weeks leading up to the telethon. The auction sold off merchandise donated by local businesses, including a "returnable" teddy bear, which brought in $1,100 from the staff of a local Tim Horton's. Over a period of 14 years, the Beverage Room has raised a grand total of $275,000 for Christmas Daddies, a fundraising event that helps children at Christmastime as well as throughout the year.

Catherine Coyle made headline news in December 2002, when her Air Canada flight to Newfoundland took her there by way of London, England. The Cole Harbour mother of two was on her way to visit her mother, who had been recently diagnosed with cancer. She settled into her seat and fell asleep shortly after takeoff. It was a 90-minute flight to Newfoundland, but when she awakened about four hours later, she was on her way to England. Apparently, when the plane landed in Newfoundland, the flight attendants had neglected to wake her. Air Canada returned Coyle to Halifax free of charge, apologized for the inconvenience, and provided her with a free flight to Newfoundland to visit her mother. During her second trip, Coyle stayed awake.

At the start of 2003, the Cole Harbour community had a large enough population – between 25,000 and 30,000 – to be a town in its own right. Considerable residential development is ongoing in the area, which will continue to increase the population.

One sure sign of population growth in the area was a $600,000 expansion program planned by the Cole Harbour-Woodside United Church at Bissett and Cole Harbour Roads. The addition will include a new sanctuary to hold about 260 people, a new choir to hold 50 people, and a small chapel to accommodate 40 to 50 people. The present church sanctuary holds only about 150 people. When the new sanctuary is completed the older section of the building will be converted for additional Sunday school and office space.

The two councillors first elected to the HRM Council at the time of amalgamation, Ron Cooper (Cole Harbour North-Cherry Brook) and Harry McInroy (Cole Harbour South-Eastern Passage), continue to represent the people of the area on municipal council at the time of publication. As mentioned, Darrell Dexter, MLA for Cole Harbour, was elected leader of the Nova Scotia New Democratic Party in June 2002 and is the Leader of the Official Opposition in the Nova Scotia

Tug of war is just as intense and exciting for competitors and audience in 2003 as when it was a mainstream athletic activity in Cole Harbour. At the Cole Harbour Rural Heritage Society's thirtieth-anniversary Field Day at the Cole Harbour Heritage Farm, Falmouth pulled against Stewiacke Valley. Both teams gave it their best, and Falmouth was overall winner for the day. Off camera to the right is Falmouth anchor Jeff O'Leary. From right, Ian Patterson, Alex Patterson, Andrew Patterson, Mike Payzant, Chris Turnbull, Brian Huntley, Randy Payzant, and Darren Peach. Coach Gordon Patterson kneels in the foreground. (Terry Eyland 2003)

legislature. And playwright Wendy Lill continues to represent the electors of Cole Harbour and Dartmouth as their Member of Parliament.

The year 2003 marks the 30th anniversary of the Cole Harbour Rural Heritage Society. The society is celebrating the event with an appropriate schedule of events, one of which is the publication of this history of the community.

Cole Harbour Road, with its long and storied past, will surely continue as an important highway link for present and future generations of Cole Harbour residents. New developments are still underway and the community continues to evolve.

Stewart and Florence Bissett celebrated their fiftieth wedding anniversary at a special gathering at the Heritage Farm Museum on June 29, 2003. They are shown with their great-grandson Austin Bissett, the latest in a long line of Bissetts that stretches back to the arrival of the first Bissetts in the province in 1752. (June 2003)

Andrew Henry was one of the performers in the Colby Village Elementary School's Historical Review of Cole Harbour staged at Auburn High School and sponsored by the 4Cs Foundation. (This photo was taken at a special performance at Alderney Landing.) Andrew Henry is the great-grandson of the late Davie Settle, a long-time Cole Harbour resident. Young Andrew seems to have inherited his great-grandfather's sense of fun and joie de vivre. (right, Mrs. Fram, May 2003; left, RE ca. 1975)

TIMELINE OF COLE HARBOUR AND AREA HISTORY

1691 Mathieu de Goutin received land grant in the Chezzetcook area named Mouscoudabouet
1749 Founding of Halifax
1750 Founding of Dartmouth
1751 Protestant settlers arrived from Germany, Switzerland, and France
1751 Capt. Charles Morris surveyed land from Liverpool to Chezzetcook for new settlements
1754 Twenty land grants made for Lawrencetown settlement
1759 Lawrencetown land grants subdivided
1759 Capt. James Cook charted waters around Nova Scotia; named inlet Cole Harbour on his chart
1764 Permanent French settlement established at Chezzetcook
1765 Six land grants of 500 acres each were given in the Cole Harbour area
1783 United Empire Loyalists arrived in Nova Scotia and settled on land in Dartmouth, Woodlawn, Preston, Lawrencetown, and Cole Harbour
1792 Black Loyalists sailed for Sierra Leone in Africa
1796 Maroons arrived from Jamaica and settled on land in Preston and Cole Harbour
1800 Maroons left for Sierra Leone in Africa
1814 First school established at Woodlawn; Edward Potts first teacher
1814 First school established in Cole Harbour, Edward McNamara first teacher
1832 First Methodist Chapel established at Lawrencetown
1830–35 First Methodist Chapel established at Cole Harbour
1835 Temperance Society organized in Cole Harbour
1840 Presbyterian Church established in Lawrencetown
1842 "Babes in the Woods" buried in Woodlawn Cemetery
1842 Cole Harbour Dyke Company established
1846 Construction of dyke begun but ended in failure
1847 Temperance Society joined Independent Order of Good Templars, became Anchor Lodge
1862 Gold discovered at Mineville
1872 St. Andrew's Anglican Church consecrated
1875 Second Methodist Chapel built at Lawrencetown
1876 Second company formed to build a dyke at Cole Harbour
1877 Work begun on second dyke
1879 Dyke and roadway across Cole Harbour completed; company went bankrupt
1879 Dyke company assets sold to George Baden Crawley of London, England
1886 County Council bought land from Harriet Roche for a Poor Farm

1887 Poor Farm built; opened with two patients; James Turner first superintendent
1891 Dyke company and deed to land grants sold to Peter McNab Kuhn
1899 Poor Farm superintendent James Turner died; J. M. Henneberry new superintendent
1910 Dyke damaged by dynamite but repaired
1914 World War One began
1916 No. 2 Construction Battalion formed with all Black soldiers; men from Preston and Cherry Brook signed on for overseas duty
1916 New Farmer's Market building opened in Halifax
1916 Railway came to Cole Harbour and Eastern Shore
1917 No. 2 Construction Battalion left for overseas duty
1917 Cole Harbour dyke dynamited beyond repair
1917 Halifax Harbour Explosion, December 6
1918 World War One ended on November 11
1920 Prohibition began; rum-running and bootlegging also began
1921 Victoria Hall opened
1923 Rainbow Haven Fresh-Air Camp opened
1925 Union of Methodist, Presbyterian and Congregationalist Churches to form the United Church of Canada
1929 Fire destroyed the Poor Farm; nobody killed or injured but residents relocated
1929 New York Stock Exchange crashed; Great Depression began
1938 Credit Union Study Club organized
1939 Russell Credit Union opened for business
1939 Construction begun on new County Home
1939 World War Two broke out in Europe
1940 Radar station at Bell Lake
1945 World War Two ended; VE Day Riots
1945 Bedford Magazine exploded
1954 Cole Harbour Road paved
1955 Angus L. Macdonald Bridge opened
1955 Dartmouth Rod and Gun Club moved to Strawberry Island in Cole Harbour
1955 Silver Sands Beach purchased by Silver Sands Company
1957 Russell Credit Union hired a full-time manager
1958 400-home subdivision planned for Bell farm on Cole Harbour Road
1960 End of passenger rail service to Cole Harbour and Eastern Shore
1960 Indigent patients at County Home transferred to new facility at the former at Hartlen Point army base, called Ocean View Nursing Home
1961 Rod and Gun Club changed its name to Dartmouth Trap and Skeet Club and opened new clubhouse
1961 Methodist Meeting House on Long Hill closed; new pre-fab church opened at Bissett and Cole Harbour Roads
1967 A cairn and plaque with names of the first 32 families to settle the area

erected at the old Meeting House as a centennial year project
1968 Co-op grocery store opened on the Cole Harbour Road
1968 Royal Commission investigated abuse at Halifax County Hospital
1969 Abenaki Canoe Club established at Bell Lake
1969 Sir Robert Borden Junior High School opened
1970 Work begun on Colby Village development
1971 Housing Minister Scott MacNutt announced Forest Hills Housing Development
1971 Percy Baker retired from County Council to take over the administration of the Halifax County Hospital
1972 Community protests proposal to widen Cole Harbour Road to four lanes from Caldwell Road to Ross Road; widening deferred
1973 Cole Harbour Rural Heritage Society formed
1973 Pope John XXIII Parish established
1976 Giles House relocated to Stuart Harris farm; start of Heritage Farm Museum
1976 Cole Harbour Road widened to four lanes from Caldwell Road to Bissett Road
1978 Baptist Fellowship Church opened
1982 St. Andrew's Anglican Church became a separate parish
1983 Planning begun on Bissett Lake Park
1987 New St. Andrew's Church built on Circassion Drive
1987 St. Vincent de Paul Church officially opened
1988 Cole Harbour Place opened
1996 Cole Harbour became part of the Halifax Regional Municipality
1997 Residents joined forces to stop ring road through community
1999 Mormon Temple opened
2002 Darrell Dexter, MLA for Cole Harbour, elected leader of the Nova Scotia New Democratic Party
2003 Cole Harbour Rural Heritage Society celebrated 30th anniversary

SELECTED SOURCES

NSARM = Nova Scotia Archives and Records Management

BOOKS

Blakeley, Phyllis. *Glimpses of Halifax from 1867 to 1900*
Campbell, Margaret Kuhn. *A Tale of Two Dykes*
Chapman, Harry. *The Mustard Seeds*
_____. *In The Wake of the* Alderney
Collins, Louisa. *Louisa's Diary*, NSARM
Dictionary of Canadian Biography
Harris, Rev. Emery *History of St. Andrew's Anglican Church, Cole Harbour*

Kilcup, Fred, ed. *Halifax Farmers Market – Chasing the Dawn*
Kuhn, Bernard. "The Life and Times of Peter Max Kuhn 1887–1938" (unpublished)
Lawson, Mary. *History of the Townships of Dartmouth, Preston, and Lawrencetown*
Lowe, Barry. *Ira Settle, Gentleman Farmer*
MacKenzie, A. A. *The Harvest Train*
Martin, John P. *The Story of Dartmouth*
Ruck, Calvin. *Canada's Black Battalion*
Settle, Marion. "When Farview was a Farm" (unpublished)
St. John's Anglican Church History (1989)
Whitehead, Ruth Holmes. *The Old Man Told Us – Excerpts from Micmac History*

PAPERS AND FILES

Bishop Inglis Letter to Governor Kempt, NSARM RGI Vol 433 #34
"Chronological Table of Events That Shaped Early Cole Harbour," Cole Harbour Rural Heritage Society
"Cole Harbour Earlier Days," Rosemary Eaton, NS *Conservation Summer*, newsletter
Cole Harbour Place brochure
Cole Harbour Rural Heritage Society newsletters and reports
"County Home 1887–1929," Howard S. Leonard
Fellowship Baptist Church 30th Anniversary brochure
Forest Hills United Church files
Gammon Land Sale, NSARM microfilm 17815, 1828, Book 51, pg 83
Gary Gibson files
Grace Lutheran Church reports
Hillside Wesleyan Church files
"History of the Anchor Lodge and the Cole Harbour Community," Shauna Whyte, honours thesis
"In the beginning Mi'kmaq," Dan Paul, *The Chronicle-Herald*, December 31, 1999
Methodist Church Minutes Books
"Mi'kmaq Past and Present: A Resource Guide"
Minutes Books of the Cole Harbour Women's Institute
Minutes of the Dartmouth Agricultural Society
Mormon Church brochures
Petition to Governor Kempt, NSARM RGI Vol 433 #34
Poor Farm files, NSARM
Royal Commission on the Operation of the Halifax County Hospital
United Church of Canada Maritime Conference archives, Microfilm 316

ORAL HISTORIES
Eugene Bellefontaine
Wilfred Bissett
Annie Bissett
Dorothy Bissett
Gordon Eisener
Murray Elliott
John Giles
Florence (Bissett) Hartlen
Helen Horne
Jessie Joslin
Joan Langille
Effie Nieforth
Harvey Patterson
Vinie Patterson
Rev. George Russell
Ira Settle
Maurice Strum

NEWSPAPERS
Acadian Recorder
Atlantic Weekly
The Chronicle-Herald/Mail-Star
The Daily News
Dartmouth Free Press
Dartmouth Patriot
Dartmouth Times
Provincial Wesleyan

INTERNET
The Antigonish Movement

END NOTES

1 "Chronological Table of Events That Shaped Early Cole Harbour," Gary Gibson
2 "Chronological Table of Events"
3 "Chronological Table of Events"
4 Heather Clarke, "Research Project: Giles House, Cole Harbour Heritage Farm Museum," September 29, 1995
5 "Maroon Legacy," Sunday Herald, February 24, 2002
6 Fred Kilcup, ed., *Halifax Farmers Market – Chasing the Dawn*
7 Rosemary Eaton, an article in The Voice, June 1986
8 The Rev. Emery Harris, *History of St. Andrew's Anglican Church, Cole Harbour*
9 Shauna Whyte, "History of the Anchor Lodge and the Cole Harbour Community"
10 Shauna Whyte, "History of the Anchor Lodge and the Cole Harbour Community"
11 Margaret Kuhn Campbell, *A Tale of Two Dykes*
12 Howard Leonard, "County Home Cole Harbour – A Brief History of the Building, Construction, and Expansion," February 1996.
13 Leonard, "County Home Cole Harbour"

INDEX

Italic page numbers indicate that the index topic appears in a photo or photo caption. Consecutive Roman numerals have been used to distinguish among some people with the same names; the numerals do not indicate lineal descent among those people.

A

Abenaki Canoe Club 251, 323
Acadia Sugar Refinery 166
Acadians 26–30
    Beausoleil, 33
    Tatamagouche 46
    West Chezzetcook 150–152
Agriculture Extension Services 224
Agriculture, Department reps 224
agriculture statistics (1827) 84
agricultural exhibition 216, *217*, 218
agricultural literary society 156
agricultural society *see* Dartmouth Agricultural Society
Akerlund, Norwood (Akie) 263, 269, 270
Akins, Thomas 62
Albyn (poet) 96
Alderney Drive 177
Allen, Mrs. (Eben[ezer]) 88–90, 92, 93
Allen, Miss E. 92
Allen, Ebenezer (Mr.) 49, 51, 65, 94, 95
Allen, Edward 94
Allen, Jim *305*
Allen, John 65
Allemand, Jane Elizabeth 66
Alexander 25
Alexander, Kerry *306*
Allison, J.W. 141
Almon, Mather B. 128
amalgamation, Dartmouth 236
amalgamation, HRM 310, 311, 323
Anchor Lodge
    president of 116
    formed under IOGT117
    in the community 121, 122
    Lodge Hall 118, *120*, 191, 216
    pledge card *119*
Anglican Church, firsts 110
Anglican Church of Eastern Passage and Cole Harbour 154
Angwin, W.K. 215
Ann 43, 66
Anne 56
Antigonish Movement 192
Armstrongs *279*
Ashgrove Drive 73, 247
Asia 58
Astral Drive 251
Auburn Drive High School 300, *320*
Audson, Sylvia 288

B

Babes in the Woods 113, *114*, 321
Baker, H.J. 245
Baker, Henry 218, 219
Baker, Joe 284
Baker, Judson 155, 218, 293
Baker, Percy 253–255, 290 323
Baker, Scott *305*
Bambridge, Thomas 65
Band of Hope for Children 117
baptisms 36, 51, 66, 67, 81, 82, 93, 107, 110, 201
Baptist Fellowship Church 323
Barker, John 33, 34
Barnard, Matthew 33
barrel-makers 98
Barry, John A. 77, 78
Barteaux, Dr. J.W. 253
baseball 310
Bates, Ben 294, 296

Bathic, William 85
Beamish, Miss 87
Beamish, Amelia Mason 62, 63
Beamish, Charles Ott 62
Beamish, Elizabeth Ott 62
Beamish, Frederick Ott 62
Beamish Lake *see* Bisett Lake
Beamish, Margaret Ott 62
Beamish, Sarah Catherine Ott 62
Beamish, Thomas 62, 63
Beamish, Thomas Ott 62, 88–94
Beausoleil 33
Beaver, Allen *305*
Beazley, Cyril (Todds) 242
Beck, Arthur *72*
Beck, Catherine Ann 66
Beck, J.G. 124
Beck, Jacob 69
Beck, James 69, 98, *109*
Beck, James A. (Jim) 215, 285
Beck, Jim *222*
Beck, Johanna 69
Beck, John 216
Beck, Martin 69, 71
Beck, Martin Jr. 69, 84
Beck, Mary 69
Beck, Michael 69
Beck, Sophia 69
Beck's Hill 11, *267, 295*
Beck's plow *98*
Bedford Magazine Explosion 207, 208, 322
Bel Ayr Elementary School 301
Bel Ayr subdivision *268,* 237
Bell, Barbara 261, *262,* 263
Bell farm 237, *268,* 322
Bell, George I 69
Bell, George II 69
Bell, George III 69, 122
Bell, Hugh 106
Bell K Calf Club *224,* 225
Bell Lake 35, 67, 323
Bell Lake Radar Station *203, 205,* 322
Bell, Laurie *224,* 225
Bell, Mary (Mame) *72*
Bell, Percy *72*
Bell, Williams 65
Bell's Hill 11

Bellefontaine, Dennis 105
Bellefontaine, Eugene 284, 325
Bellefontaine, Mrs. Lawrence 175
Bellefontaine, Michael 175
Bennett, James 71
Ben's Bakery 213
Bergengren, Roy F. 192
Beseter, John 33
Betty 43, 45
Big Leagues Beverage Room 317, 318
Binney, Bishop 110
Biset, Jacques *see* Bissett, Jacques
Bishop, Benjamin 82
Bishop, Margaret *309*
Bishop, property 263
Bissett, Agnes Davidson 83
Bissett, Alex 124
Bissett, Anna Catherine 46
Bissett, Annie 325
Bissett, Austin *320*
Bissett, Benjamin 79, 84
Bissett, Bradley *300*
Bissett, Bryden *72,* 225
Bissett, Catherine (1781) 47
Bissett, Catherine (1846) 134
Bissett, Charles 84, 124, 215, 216, *295*
Bissett, Claudine 46
Bissett, Cyril *214*
Bissett, Dorothy 325
Bissett, Eleanor 86
Bissett, Ethel *72*
Bissett farm *47,* 225
Bissett, Florence *46, 320*
Bissett, Francis 124
Bissett, Frank 237, *277*
Bissett, Fred *222*
Bissett, George Sr. 79, 84, 124
Bissett, Hattie *186, 197*
Bissett, Hezekiah *287*
Bissett, Jacques (Jean) George 45, 46
Bissett, James (1827) 84
Bissett, James Frederick 66, 67, 69, 96, *97,* 124, 300
Bissett, James, Frederick *72, 300*
Bissett, James Jr. (1835) 108
Bissett, Jane 66
Bissett, Jean George 46, 47, 83, 123
Bissett, John 110

Bissett, John George (Squire)
   great-grandson of Jean George Jr.123
   chaired dyke meeting 1842 123, 124
   managed dyke lands *128*, 132
   becomes councillor 132, 282, 293
   buys 10 acres salt marsh 133
   visits Poor Home at Christmas 140
   delegate to Tariff Commission 155
   first president, Dartmouth Agricultural Society 215
   dies 282, 283
   school named in his memory *300*
Bissett, John Sr.124
Bissett, Joseph 71, 84, 134
Bissett, Joseph Jr. 124
Bissett Lake 35, 62
Bissett Lake Park 323
Bissett Lake Park Development Committee 305, 306
Bissett, Louisa Giles 64
Bissett, Margaret *130*
Bissett, Mary Ann 66, 77, 81, 108
Bissett Road
   early schools on 14, 73
   County Home built on 195, 206
   farming on 226
   church was built on 242, 322
   Cole Harbour Road widens to 267, 291, 323
Bissett, Robert 72
Bissett Rose *309*
Bissett, Samuel 84, 124
Bissett, Sophie *244*
Bissett, Stewart *46*, *214*, 226, *320*
Bissett, Mrs. Thomas 191
Bissett, Thomas 72, *214*, 222
Bissett, Wilfred 170, 263, *265*, 282, 325
Bissett, William 124
Bizette, Jacques (Jean) George *see* Bissett, Jacques
Black, John 141
Black Labour Battalion 169, 170, 316, 322

Black Loyalists *see* settlers
Black, William 75, 77, 78, 81
blacksmith 96, 97, 98
Blakeley, Phyllis 103
Blakeney, Blair 309
Blindman's Bluff, game 92
Blueberry Express 240
Board of Home Missions 242
boat-building 47, 97, 276
Boggs, Elizabeth 73 *see also* Elizabeth Stuart
Boggs, Dr. James 73
Boggs, Thomas 50
Bonan 151
Bonn, Bill 251
Bonn, William 248
Bonnevie 34
Booth, Ann 139
Booth, John Wilkes 285
bootlegging 181, 322 *see also* Prohibition
Bourgeois, Henry 254
Bowes, George Jr. 110
box socials 191
Box, The *247*, 299
Breakheart Hill 11, 13, 83, 87, 204
Bremner, Daniel 85
Breynton, Rev. John 33
Bridge, Benjamin 35, 36, *37*
Brinley, Mrs. 92, 94
British Board of Trade and Plantations 42
Bromley, Walter 70–72
Brook House 71, 94, 216
Brooks, Randy *305*
brooms, making 263
Broussard (town of) 33
Broussard, Joseph 33
Broussard, Walter 70–72
Brown, Garnet 291, 297
Brown, Uncle 94
Bruce, Gerry *306*
Bruce, Stephanie *306*
Brucha, Beverly 313
Brule Point 47
Brunelle, Paul *272*
Brunswick Street Church 82
Buchanan, John 297

Bulkeley, Richard 32, 34
Burns, Rev. Charles 110
Bundy, Henry 170
Bundy, William H. 170
businesses, early years 97, 98
butter making 89, 91
buyer's club 233, 234

C

cairn 248, 249
Caldwell, Rev. Blake C. 304
Caldwell Road 15, 118, *153*, 286, 302, 323
Caldwell Road School 201, 231, 300
Calvin United Church 110
Campbell, Janice 310
Campbell, Mollie Kuhn *275*
Campbell, Margaret Kuhn 123, 124, 126, 132, *249*
    see also Kuhn, Margaret
Canadian National Railway 238, 239
Canadian Plant and Process Engineering Ltd. 288
carding 88, *271*
carding mill 96
Casely, Rev. Garth 301
Cauldwell, Thomas 84
cemeteries 51, 65, 69, 95, 108, 111, 113, 114, 201, 219, 291
census
    (1827) 83–86
    (1939) 97
Centennial project 248, 249, 322
Chaddock, Christian *271*
Chamberlain, Anne 52
Chamberlain, Ephraim 52
Chamberlain, John 124
Chamberlain, Theophilus 50–52, *53*, 54, 63
Champlain, Samuel de 26
CHCN radio 314
Cherry Brook 169, 170, 322
Chezzetcook 27–30, 243, 321
Chezzetcook Inlet 30
Chezzetcook River 33
Choyce, Leslie *149*
Christ Church, Dartmouth 77, 110
Church of England 51, 70, 71, 72, 74, 76, 84
Church of the Holy Spirit 301
Church of Jesus Christ of the Latter-Day Saints 303, *303*, 323
Church of Scotland 112
Circassion Drive 110, 301, 323
clam-digging 284
Clark, Ernie 266, 267
Clark, Hartland 254
Clark, Mike *305*
Clayton Developments Ltd. 287
Clayton, Ervin *225*
Clifford, Aunt 87
Clifford, Hood 95
Clifford Lake *see* Bell Lake
Clover Bank Dairy *257*
Coady, Father Moses 192
Coal Harbour 26, 34
Cogill, John 84
Colby Village 288, 290, 323
Colby Village Elementary School 302, *320*
Colby Village Mall 67, 96
Colchester County 47
Cole Harbour
    community 35–38, 45, 145–146, 321
    harbour 23–26, 34, 321
Cole Harbour Beach *148 see also* Rainbow Haven Beach)
Cole Harbour District High School 300, 302, 307, 311, 312
Cole Harbour dyke *see* dyke
Cole Harbour Dyke (district) *130*
Cole Harbour Dyke Company 123, 124, 125, 321, 322
Cole Harbour Environmental Committee 261
Cole Harbour Fire Chief *245*
Cole Harbour Fire Station *259*
Cole Harbour Heritage Farm Museum
    animals *30*
    buildings *64*, *264*, 269
    location of 67, 267, *268*
    artifacts 98, *272*, *280*
    archives 232, *283*
    preserves rural skills 265, *271*

preserves plants *272, 309*
Rose and Kettle Garden *277*
tea room and gift shop *280*
visitors *279, 280,298, 298*
Cole Harbour Heritage Park *273*
Cole Harbour Junior Colts (1976–77) *305*
Cole Harbour Kiwanis Club 258
Cole Harbour Land Company 126, 127, 128, 321, 322
Cole Harbour–Lawrencetown Coastal Heritage Park 270, 273, 274, 312
Cole Harbour Methodist Church
  petitions for meeting house 75, 76
  builds meeting house 79, 80, 106
  Syd Gosley *81*
  sizes of meeting houses 82
  fund-raising 107, 278
  first superintendent 122
  votes for union 165
  dedicates new church 242, 322
  becomes Cole Harbour United Church 184, 300, 301, 322
Cole Harbour Methodist Meeting House (old) 79–83, 321
  built on Long Hill, Cole Harbour Road 79, 82
  millstones 97
  and cemetery 108, 109
  pulpit and pews at St. Andrew's 112
  windows blown out *179*, 180
  heritage status 108, 278
  saved by the heritage society 263, 264, 300
  holds events 278
Cole Harbour Minor Baseball Association 310
Cole Harbour Parks and Trails Association 275
Cole Harbour Place 306, 307, *308*, 323
Cole Harbour Rehab Centre *see* Halifax County Regional Rehabilitation Centre
Cole Harbour Road 322, 323

early description 13, 32, 35, 38
in the 1930s *14*
first coat of asphalt 15, 299
built by settlers 32, 35, 38
divides land grants, map *37*
schools (1800s) 73
meeting house 109
community hall 184
Portland Street 223
tug-of-war on 223
paved 232
opposition to widening of 291
winter scene *295*
heritage society acts to preserve its name 313
Cole Harbour Rural Heritage Society 260–280
  its mission 12, 260, 261, 288–290
  organizing meeting 262, 323
  special church services 80, 278
  publishes *Louisa's Diary* 87, 88
  preserves meeting house 109, 263
  preserves Giles House *see* Giles House
  starts farm museum *see* Cole Harbour Heritage Farm Museum
  records traditional skills 264, 265, 271, 272, 277
  pushes coastal park idea 273–275
  owns public landing place 276
  20th anniversary 307, 309
  30th anniversary 319, 323
  two former presidents *81, 262, 263*
  first honourary member 266
  education 269
Cole Harbour schools *see* schools, early years *and individual namees*
Cole Harbour Temperance Society 321
Cole Harbour United Church *109*, 300, 301 *see also* Cole Harbour–Woodside United
Cole Harbour Volunteer Fire Department 243, 290

Cole Harbour–Westphal and Area Culture and Recreation Foundation 306
Cole Harbour–Westphal Kiwanis Club *317*
Cole Harbour–Westphal Recreation Advisory Council 309
Cole Harbour–Woodside United Church 276, 301, 318
Cole Harbour Women's Institute 231, 249
Cole, Joseph 25, 26
Cole Station *171*
Coleman, Miss 92
Coleman, Eliza 93
Coleman, Seth 71
Coleman, William 94
Cold Harbour 23, 24, 34
Colin Grove 67, 87, 95
Collier, John 33, 34
Collins, Betsy 87, 88, 92
Collins, Charlotte 87, 88–93
Collins, Georgina 87, 93
Collins, Jane 87, 88
Collins, Johanna 87, 89, 90, 93
Collins, John 65
Collins, Joseph 34
Collins, Louisa Sarah 62, 86
    diary excerpts 97–94
    diary published *88*
    marriage of 94
Collins, Mary Ann 87
Collins, Phebe 87, 88, 91
Collins, Phebe Coffin 62, 85, 87
Collins, Robert 87
Collins, Stephen 62, 85, 87
Colly's (old) 92
Colonel John Stuart Schools 249, 301, 302, 304
Community Central Commons 307
Community Enterprises 237
Community Hall of Cole Harbour Road Trustees 184
Congregationalists 322
Connors, Mike *305*
Conrad, Anna Catherine 51, 63, *64*
Conrad Brothers 282
Conrad, Donna *194*

Conrad, Elizabeth 45
Conrad, Enos 133
Conrad, Frank *265*
Conrad, Fraser 263, *273*, *296*
Conrad, Henry Jacob *130*, 132
Conrad, Jacob 1
    buys and sells land 45, 63, 266
    daughter marries 51
    dies 63
    Giles House *64*
    owns a vessel 276
Conrad, Jacob II 153
Conrad, Kenny 225
Conrad, Thomas Sr. 63, 124,197
Conrad, Thomas Jr. 124, 197
Conrod, Charles 152
Conrod, Irene *72*
Conrod, Mrs. James W. 187
Conrod, James W. 162, 164, 187
Conrod, Thomas 85
Cook, James 24, *25*
Cook, Thomas 71, 85
Coomber, Joan 200
Cooper, Ron 294, 296,*308*, 311, 318
Cope, Jean Baptiste 24
Cope's Harbour 24
Cornelius, Mr. *211*
Cornelius, Mrs. *211*
Cornwall, Amelia Marie 67
Cornwallis, Charles 49, 73
Cornwallis, Edward 23, 31, 32, 41, 101
Corser, Elizabeth 277, *297*, 313
Costley, Alice 285
Cottage industries 98
Council, municipal *see* Halifax County Council
Council municipal, positions of 293, 294
County Council *see* Halifax County Council
County Home
    formerly County Poor Farm 163
    Conrod as superintendent 164
    telephone service 166
    damaged by Halifax Explosion 179, 180
    damaged by fire; McIntosh

report 187, 188
closes doors in 1929 189
needs replacing; Special Committee on 206
new facility – Halifax County Home and Mental Hospital 207
in timeline 321, 322
see also Halifax County Home and Mental Hospital
County Poor Farm 321, 322
building and expanding 133–136, 137, 138
1887–1899 operations 138–139, 141, 157
1896 Christmas party 140–141
Farmkeeper Turner 136, 138, 141, 142
1900–1910 operations 162, 163
Henneberry as superintendent 162
re-named County Home 163
see also County Home
Cow Bay 235, 245
Cow Bay Beach 238
Cow Bay Ocean Park 245
Coyle, Catherine 318
Crawley, Eliza Inez *128, 132 see also* Pringle, Elizabeth
Crawley, George Baden 132, 321
credit unions 191, 192 *see also* Russell Credit Union
Creighton, Alexander 65
Creighton, Helen 249
Creighton, Jake 235
Cribby, Vince *279*
Cromwell, James Oliver 75
Cronan, Daniel 70
Crook, Andrew 254
Crook, John 97, 111
Crook, William 97, 111
Crooks, William 85
Crookshank, John 235
crops
working on 86
harvests 162, *225*
on marshlands 132, 164
marketing 211

at Exhibition 216, 218
blessing of *223*
threatened (1959) 238
specialization 242
Croscombe, Rev. William 80–82, *278*
Cross, E. 215, 218
Crowell, Ebenezer 85
Cub and Boy Scouts 204
Cumberland Drive 267, 303
Cummings, Alexander 85
Cummings, John 85
Cunningham, N.F. 139, 162
Curack, Major 216
Currie, Rev. Martin 302
Currie, Peter 114

D

daffodils, double *272*
dairy producers 213, 214, 215
Dakeyne Street Lads Club Farm 199
Daley, John 85
dances 92, 94, 191, 231, 281, 282
Dares, Norman 72
Darrach, Bill *305*
Dartmouth 24, 35, 70, 72, 230, 236, 240, 321
Dartmouth Agricultural Society
holds exhibition 216, *217*, 218
first president 128
first and last directors 215, 216, 218, 219
formed in 1880 122, 50
speaks for farmers189, 215–217, 218, 219
Dartmouth Cove 32
Dartmouth Engine Company 187
Dartmouth Fire Department 243
Dartmouth Kiwanis Club *224*, 235
Dartmouth Rod and Gun Club *234*, 322
Dartmouth Trap and Skeet Club 130, 241, 242, 322
Davies, Bob 234, *295*
Davies, Eric J. 252, 253, 254
Davis, Rev. 157
Dawson Street 202
Day, Charles *97*
Day, George H. 229

Day Nite Neon Signs Ltd. 241
deaths
    Russell 65
    census (1827) 84
    Minister 110
    Babes in the Woods 113, 114
    dyke workers 126
    Kuhn 174
    Rice 177
    McDonald 180
    Harris 197
    Giles 264
    Settle 256, 258, 260
    Strum 276
    Costley 285
de Goutin, Mathieu 22–24, 27, 28, 321
de l'Isle Dieu, Abbé 28
de Monts, Pierre Du Gua 26
de Villebon 27
de Saint-Père, Edme Rameau 29
Debrisay, Rev. M.B. 110
Deloughry, Dennis 133
DeRoche, Ray 294, *296*
desBarres, Joseph F.W. 46, 47
Detienne, David 310
Deveaux, Kevin 297
Devenport, Charles 196–198, *199*, 200, 201
Devenport, Ellen (Nellie) 197
Devil's Island 29
Dewolfe, Roy 251
Dexter, Darrell *297*, 318, 323
diary, Louisa Collins 86–95
domestic chores *see* women's rural skills
Dick, John 42, 43
Dickson subdivision 287
Diggs, Joe 263
District 14 Service Commission 247
Dineen Construction (Atlantic) Inc. 307
Donovan, Mrs. D. 218
Donovan Daniel 216, 293
Dover 56
DREE 287
dressmakers 98
Driscoll, Maria *271*
Drummond, Charles 170

Dunsworth, Dr. F.A. 254
dyke, the
    old, of stone 57, 58
    work begins 126, 321
    description of 126
    used for roadway 146
    gates dynamited 165, 174, 275, 322
    see also dyking the harbour
dykelands *128*, *129*, *130*, *132*, *133*
dyking the harbour
    by the Maroons 57, 58
    Cole Harbour Dyke Co. 1845 123–125
    Cole Harbour Land Co. 1877 126–128
    storm opens channel 163–164
    dynamite opens channel 174

E

Eagles and Radcliffe Limited 241
Eagles, Richard 241
Earle, Joyce *88*
early family names 70
East Chezzetcook 30, 150
East Dartmouth New Church Development Ministry 304
East Lawrencetown Beach 182
Eastern Halifax County Cooperative 234, 248, 251, 290, 323
East Preston 226, 276
Eastern Passage 110, 154, 221, 288
Eaton, Mike *274*
Eaton, Rosemary
    salt marsh photo 20
    holding a window *179*
    with visions for heritage society 263
    Rosemary's Way *274*
    the oral history project 277, 281, *282*, 284
Eaton, T., Company 212
Edwards, Rev. D. 169
eelgrass, gathering *265*
eel pots, weaving *265*
Eisener, Gerald *212*
Eisener, Gordon
    recalls Halifax Explosion 178

credit union member 193
market gardener 211, *212*
credits MacLaughlin 213
recalls road work 232, 325
wood-cutting *271*
Eisener, Grant 174
Eisener, Lloyd *194, 212, 296*
elections, federal 250, 297, 298
elections, municipal 234, 236, 242, 250, 294, 296, 311
elections, provincial 296, 297
Eliza 93, 94
Elizabeth, Aunt 89
Elkins Barracks 236, 240
Ellenvale 96
Elliot Almy (Green) 65
Elliot, Charles *72, 222*
Elliot, Edith 86
Elliot, Frank *72*
Elliot, Gertrude 88
Elliot, Harold *72*
Elliot, Harold Jr. *224*
Elliot, Harry *114, 119, 186, 222*
Elliot, Henry (architect) 218
Elliott, Hector 124
Elliott, John 85, 96
Elliott, Jonathan 65, 85
Elliott, Murray 243, 244, *245,* 325
Emino, James 174
epidemics 44, 46, 139, 162
Epworth League 165
Ernst, Arthur 174
Ernst, E. 174
Eskikewa'kik 21, 24
European Protestants 42, 48
Evans, Eli 135
Evans, John 85
Ewer, Robert 33
Eyland, Terry 277

F

Fahey, P. 135
Fairfield Estate 202
Fairview Farm 204
Falmouth *319*
Farm Days 277
Farm Forum 236, 237
farms (in 2003) 225, 226

Farmers' Federation
Farmer's Market *see* Halifax Farmer's Market
farmers protest Tariff protection 154, 155
farming, beef 225
farming, by settlers 47, 51 58, 95
farming, dairy
   Pattersons' 191, 214
   rank of 213
   Bissett's *214, 295*
   cattle fodder 214
   Kuhn's 214
   Morash's 215
   Geldart's 232
   Settle's 256, 257
farming, develops other industries 95–98
farming, market gardening 209–213
   market gardeners 175, 211, *225,* 226, 233, 257
   ranks first 190, 213
   selling produce *231*
   exhibition for 227
   history of 236
farming, mixed 226
farming, modernizations 209, 210, 211, 212, 213, 232
farming, pig 245
farming, poultry *233,* 232, 233, *268*
farming prospers 203, 204
farming, report on (1961) 242
Farquharson, Alex 65
Farquharson, James 216
Farquharson, Sandy *271*
Fassett, Joseph 294
Faucher, Rose 219
Faulkner's Field 202
Fellon, H.B. 137
fence viewers 293
ferry service 89, 103, *104,* 230, *265,* 299
fertilizer, sea manure 212, 213
fertilizer, sterilizing 213
Filmore, Murray 267
fires (major)
   Collins 94
   Presbyterian church 112
   Tullock homestead 156

Halifax explosion 179
County Home new wing 1929 187
Trongate 206
Bedford Magazine explosion 208
recycling depot, North Preston 316
Jack Settle's barn *244*
fishermen 95, 151
Fishon, William 65
Fitzgerald, Ann 36
Fletcher, Helen *273*
Flinn, Gerald 174
flowers *272, 309*
flour mills 96
Fly Island 19
Flying Point 127, *130*, 132
Foreign Protestant Monument *46*
Forest Hills Drive 304, 307
Forest Hills Fellowship Baptist Church 301, 302
Forest Hills Housing Development 323
Forest Hills Land Assembly 197, 267
Forest Hills Parkway *267*
Forest Hills United Church 304
Forestall, Michael 250, 297, 298
Forsyth, Ian 222
Fort Franklin 47
Foster, Miss 92
Foster, Miss A. 107
Foster, Edward 107, 215
4Cs Foundation *320*
Frances T. 182
Frank, Blye 312
Fraser, Daniel 85
Fraser, Darren *305*
Fraser, William 85
Fream, Rev. B 301
Freeman, Louise *306*
Free School Act (1926) 72
French Protestant settlers *see* settlers
Friesan, Moochie *305*
Fritten, Richard 34
Frontenac, Comte de 22, 27
Fullerton, Rev. Eric 242
furniture maker 97

Fyfe, Graham *266*

G

Gale 36
games 92
Gammon chairs *96*
Gammon, Ann 66
Gammon, George 34, 66, 79, *96*, 97, 124
Gammon, James 66
Gammon, James Jr. 66
Gammon, John 34, 66, 76, 77, 81, 85, 108, 124
  buys land 34
  his family 66
  petitions and deeds 75–77
  grand-daughter baptized 81
  in 1827 census 85
  is buried 108
  attends dyke meeting 124
Gammon, Mary Ann Bissett 81, 108
Gammon, Richard 66, 77, 78, 86
Gammon, Samuel 86
Gammon, William I 66
Gammon, William II 97, 124
Gammon, William A. III
Garrettson, Freeborn 75
Gaston Road 15, 234
Gates, John 86
Geary, Father Dennis 116
Geldart, Beatrice *279*
Geldart, Eric 232, *233*
Geldart farm *233*
Geldart, Gerry 312
Geldart, George *97*
Geldart, Walter 232
General Seafoods 284
George Bissett School *300*
George's Island 44
German settlers *see* settlers
Gerrish, Joseph 34
Gibson, Gary 106, *278*
Giffen, Ann 36
Giffen, Ron *308*
Giles, Miss 264
Giles, Alfie *224*
Giles, Arthur 145, 219
Giles, Catherine 64

335

Giles, Dora *224*
Giles, Edgar *72*
Giles, Everett *237*, 264, 266
Giles, Fred *105*, *237*, 264
Giles, Harold 234
Giles, Harry Joe 221
Giles House *64*,
    preservation of 264–265, *266*, *267*, 268
    fumigation of 269, *270*,
    in 1976 323
Giles, Isobel Glazebrook *163*
Giles, John 219, *222*, 234, 277, 325
Giles, Joseph 1
    arrives in Nova Scotia 49, 264
    marries 51, 63
    dies 64
    Giles House *64*
    in 1827 census 85
    descendants of *296*
    school named after 300
Giles, Joseph Jr. 64, 122, 124
Giles, Joseph II (d.1919) 264
Giles, Joseph III *296*
Giles, Kate 152
Giles, Louisa 64
Giles, Mary Ann 64
Giles, Percy 175
Giles, Ron *296*
Giles, Samuel 64
Giles, Sinclair *224*
Giles, Stanley *224*
Giles, William Jr. *224*
Giles, William Sr. 152
Glasgow Island 19
Glasgow, Joseph 63
Glazebrook, Jamie *114*
Glazebrook, Sandra *114*
gold mines 148, 321
Gomes, Lisa *306*
Gosley, Sid 26, *81*
Grace Lutheran Church 302, 303
Grace Methodist Church 65, 69, 83, 106 *see also* Grace United Church
Graham, Captain 140, 141
Graham Creighton School 250
Grand Desert 30, 34, 282
Grant, James 69

Grant, Robert 33
Grantham's Fair Faucets (1977–78) *306*
Gray, Rev. Benjamin 56
Gray, Jack *305*
Greatorex, Emily *279*
Green, Mrs. 77
Green, Anthony 314
Green, widow 63
Green, Benjamin Jr. *32–36*
Green, Benjamin Sr. 36, 37, 63
Green, Francis 34, 49, 50
Green, Henry 86
Green, Joseph 86
Green Market *102*, 103, 170 *see also* Halifax Farmer's Market
Green, Thomas 65
greenhouses 209, 213
Greer, Peter 254
gristmills 50, 96, *97*, *300*
Gross, Tamara *88*
Guildford 189, *270*
Gyles, Joseph *see* Giles, Joseph)

H

Haley, Martin D. 248
Haliburton, E.D. 246
Haliburton, Tim 224
Halifax 24, 25, 35, 29, 31, 33, 36, 43, 44, 321
Halifax City Market *see* Halifax Farmer's Market
Halifax County Council 292–294, 296, 323
    supports poor 133–142
    committee to discuss Market 189
    committees for Poor Home 206, 207
    welfare committee 235
    school expansion 251
    gives special designation 272
    negotiates water and sewer 286, 287
    abolished in 1996; becomes Halifax Regional Municipality HRM 311
    see also elections, municipal

337

Halifax County Home and Mental
Hospital
  on a map *172*
  opens 206, 252
  replaces County Home 207
  built on Bissett Road 195
  janitor 200
  overcrowding 235
  patient transfers 240
  quits farm operations 244, 245
  gets auditorium and chapel 246
  becomes Halifax County Hospital 252
  Davies as super 253, 254
  in timeline 322
Halifax County Hospital 252–255, 290
  see also Halifax County Home and Mental Hospital, County Poor Farm, *and* Halifax County Regional Rehabilitation Centre
Halifax County Regional Rehabilitation Centre 255, *315*
Halifax Farmer's Market 101–106
  market days 87
  on Market Street 170, *188*
  farmers critical of 189
  a way of life 219
  LaPierre, president of and sells at 226
  current location 226
Halifax Fire Department 187
Halifax Harbour Explosion
  number killed 208, 322
  oral histories of 176, 177, 178, 180
Halifax Herald Limited 185
Halifax Regional Municipality 275, 311
Hall, George A. 219
Hancock, L.T. 254
hanging 65
Harbour East Community Council 275, 313
hardware businesses 50
Harper, George 47
Harriet 89, 93
Harris, Brigid 200
Harris, Brogan 200

Harris, Donald 197, 208, *224*
Harris, Douglas 197, *224*, 233
Harris farm 267, *268, 223,* 323
Harris, Hattie Bissett 186, *197*
Harris house 268
Harris, Melvin
  family history 197, *200*, 201
  market gardening 226, 233
  wood-cutting *271*
Harris, Stuart
  home child 196, *200*
  with wife and friends *197*
  farm appropriated 197
  farmer 211, 233
  well house explodes 246
Harrison, Everett 189
Hart, Janice *306*
Hartlen, Florence Bissett 282, 283
Hartlen, Gary 311
Hartlen Point 236, 240
Hartlen Point Army Base 322
Hartshorne, Lawrence
  Loyalist 49–51
  enterprises 50 63, 67
  school trustee 71
  boundary 79
Hartshorne, Robert 71
harvest trains 221
Harvey, C.H. 141
Hatfield, Rev. L. F. 254
Hawkins, John 64
Hawkins, Joseph 85
Hawthorne, Elizabeth 66
Havers, Leslie 254
hay making 89, 263
hay rake *272*
Hayes, James M. 302
Hayes, John 133
Hazelhurst 202
Head of Chezzetcook 30
Heal, Rev. J.B. 165
Hemsley, Mrs. 198
Henderson, Graham *305*
Hendrie, Bob *305*
Henneberry, J.M. 142, 162, 219, *225*, 322
Hennigar, Rev. James 79
Henry, Andrew *320*

Heritage Farm *see* Cole Harbour Heritage Farm Museum
heritage properties 268, 278
Heustis, Rev. S.F. 107
Hillier, Craig 310
Hillside Wesleyan Church 304
Hiltz 145
Himmelman, Eleanor 67
Himmelman, Peter 110
Hinckley, Gordon B. 303
Historical Review of Cole Harbour 320
hockey *305*, 310
hog reeves 294
Holland, Connie 277, *280*
Holland, Samuel 24
home children 196–201
Hopson, Peregrine 31, 32, 44, 101
Horne, Harold 234
Horne, Helen *80*, 263, 285, 325
horse racing 219, *220*, 221
Horton's Tim 318
Hoskinson, W.C. 254
hotbeds 209, *210*, 213
Housing, Department of 266
Howe, Joseph 70
hucksters 103
Hudson, Sylvia 288
Hughallan Drive 301
Hughes, Governor 47
Huguenot *see* settlers, French
Humpraville, Lamira 54
Huntley, Brian *319*
Hupmobile *186*
Hussey, John 33

I

ice rinks *217*, 218, 223, 308
ice-cutting 284
IGA grocery 290
Illsley, Gary 305
Imo 176
Independent Order of Good Templars 117, 321
Indian Road 286 *see also* Caldwell Road
industries, of early years 61, 95, 97, 98
Inferior Court of Common Pleas 25, 26
Inglis, Charles 71, 76
Inglis, Rev. John 71, 72, 76
Ingles, Mr. 92, 93
Ingols, Elizabeth 36
Inner Harbour of Mouscoudabouet 22, 23, 27
Isle Rouge (now Devil's Island) 29

J

Jasch, Rev. Stephen 302, 303
Jamaican Maroons *see* settlers
Jefferson, Rev. P.C. 235
Jensen, L.B. *125*
Jensen, Jay E. 303
Jersey Jack 284, 285
John and James 93
Johnston and Caldwell 135
Jones, Colleen (sportscaster) *220*
Jones, Mark 65
Josedale Clansmen 220
Joseph Giles Elementary School 302
Joslin farm house *278*
Joslin, Jessie Way 178, 179, 284, 285, 325
Joudrey's, Mrs., Wax Works 107

K

Kazoo Kuties *279*
Keefe Contractor, M.E. 135
Keeler, C.J. 218, 219
Keeler, W.H. 215
Keilor, C.J. *see* Keeler
Keith's Brewery 226
kelp *see* sea manure
Kemp, Margaret 67
Kempt, Sir James 75, 76, 83
Kennedy Jones, W.S. 243
King, Sally 263
King's Daughters 141
Kiowa Medicine Show 285
Kiser, John 69
Kiser, Susannah (Keizer) 69
Kiwanian of the Year *317*
Kiwanis Centre Beach and Park *317*
Knickle, Gary *305*
Knickle, Rick *305*
Knock, John 124

Kuhn, Alexander 66, 113
Kuhn, David *275*
Kuhn, Donna *249*
Kuhn, Mrs. Eva Morash *96*
Kuhn, Fanny Foster *272*
Kuhn, Frank 169, 174
Kuhn, Mrs. G. 218
Kuhn, George 263, *265*
Kuhn, Henry 66, 132
Kuhn, Henry Jr. 66
Kuhn, Jane 176
Kuhn, John 95
Kuhn, Jacob 65, 66, 71, 85
Kuhn, M. 197
Kuhn, Margaret 176, 177, 178 *see also* Campbell, Margaret Kuhn
Kuhn, Mrs. Martha 174
Kuhn, Max 163, 174
Kuhn, Mollie 176, 177, 178 *see also* Campbell, Mollie Kuhn
Kuhn, Peter Max 214, 221, 222
Kuhn, Mrs. Peter McNab 177
Kuhn, Peter McNab
   owns dyke property 124, *128, 129, 130*, 132, 133
   farmer 155, 163–165, 218
   dyke dynamited beyond repair 174
   other occupations 175, 222
Kuhn, Peter McNab Wildlife Management Area 275, 276
Kuhn, Wilfred 163, 221

L

labour disputes 235, 315
ladder makers 98
Lady of the Lake 175
LaHave River 45
Lake Major 114
Lake Major Road 221
Lake Porter *see* Porter's Lake
land developments 230, 237, 238, 286, 287
Langille, Mrs. Joan 184, 325
Langille, Rev. Melvin 301
Langille, Shelly *306*
LaPierre, Mr. 165, 189
LaPierre boys (musicians) 282

LaPierre, Johnny 263
LaPierre, Leo 174
LaPierre, Mary Ann 226
laundresses 98
Lavergne, Françoise 28
Lawlor, Mrs. 123
Lawlor, Daniel 85
Lawlor, Henry 124
Lawlor House 58, *125*
Lawlor, James 124
Lawlor, Vella *72*
Lawlor, William 108, 124
Lawlor's Point 57
Lawrence, Charles 29, 31, 45, 69
Lawrence Town *see* Lawrencetown
Lawrencetown 321
   a ghost town 33
   early years 70, 84, 85
   Township of 23, 45
   in 1883 147, 148, 149
Lawrencetown Beach *149*
Lawrencetown Fire Department 243
Lawrencetown Lake 24
Lawrencetown Methodist Church 165, 321
   petitions for meeting house 75, 76
   builds on Lawrencetown Road 77, 321
   deed to land; preachers visit 78, 81
   meeting house closes 82, 83
   Society builds second chapel 111, 321
Lawrencetown Presbyterian Church 112, 321
Lawrencetown Road 13, 31, *32, 35, 38*, 77
Lawson, Mary 73, 125
Leslie Fairn and Associates 248
Levandier, Abraham 29
Levatte, George 254
Leverman, Gerald 242
Levine, Gilbert 254
Lewis, Captain 24
Lill, Wendy *298*, 319
Lisson Jim 304
Lisson, Sharon 304

339

Little Salmon River 19, 22, 147–149, 241, 242, 275
Livingston, Roderick 169
Livingstone, Dr. David 71
Lloy 215
Lloyd, David 33
Lloyd, William 86
loan credits 44
Lockhart, Edwin A 111
Lodge Road 286 *see also* Caldwell Road
Lonecloud, Abram 285
Lonecloud, Jerry 285, 286
Lonecloud, Mary Anne 285
Long Hill 11
    de Goutin's boundary 23, 24
    Ott's grant on 36
    Lawlor House at 58
    old meeting house on 79, 82, 83
    public landing place at 270, 276
Longard, George J. 133
Lord Cornwalllis (bull) 216
Louisa's Diary 86–94
Louisbourg (fortress) 47
Lower East Chezzetcook 30
Lower West Chezzetcook 150
lumbering 47, 174, 175
Lunenburg 36, 44–46
Lusher, Rev. L 78
Lydiard, C.(J.)156, 218
Lydiard, Samuel L. 293
Lydiard, S.W. 155, 218
Lynch, Mr. and Mrs. J.T. 241
Lynch, Rev. Wayne G. 301
Lyons, Charles 34

M

MacAskill, Ken 275
MacDonald, Angus 192
Macdonald, Angus L. (premier) 229
Macdonald Bridge, Angus L. 229, 230, 322
MacDonald, Gail *306*
MacDonald, Rev. J.D.N. 192, 235
MacDonald, Leslie *210*, 229
MacDonald, Rev. Peter 301
MacDonald, Rebecca *163*
MacDonald, Rebecca's son *163*
MacDonald, Ron 298
MacDonald, Shirley *306*
MacDonald's Hill 112
MacFawn Rogers 304
MacIntosh, Barbara 263
MacIntosh, Dr. G.A. 188
MacIntosh, James C. 128
MacIntosh, Suzie *306*
MacKenzie, A.A. 221
MacKenzie, Bill *222*
MacKenzie King 211
MacKinnon, D. Wayne 251
MacKinnon, Michael 316
Mackintosh, Barbara 263
MacLaughlin, Art 213, 224
MacLean, Rev. Ward 242
MacNamara, Edward 71, 321
MacNutt, Scott 290, 323
MacPhee, Richard Wayne 248
Macy, Miss 92
Macy, Mrs. 90
Madill 189
Maillard, L'Abbé Pierre 29
Mannette, Bill 105
maps, list of 9
Marie Thérèse 28
Maria 93
Maritime Sand and Gravel Co. 242, 243
Maritime Trap Shooting Championships 234
market *see* Halifax Farmer's Market
market gardening *see* farming, market gardening
Maroons, Jamaican *see* settlers
Martin, Sam 177
Mary 56
Maryann's Gift Shop *214*
Mason, Alexander 86
Mason, Charles 36
Mason, Margaret Mary 36
mat-makers 98
Matthews, John 234, 236
McDonald, Allen 96
McDonald, Andrew 139
McDonald, Catherine 180
McDonald, Donald 65
McDonald, John (1750) 25

McDonald, John (1917) 174
McDonald, Walter 174
McDow, Alex 174
McGee 34
McInroy, Harry
    elected to county council 294,
        296, 318
    at library opening *308*
    elected to HRM council 311, 318
    preserved name of Cole Harbour Road 313
    chair of Rehab Centre 315
McIntosh, Dawn *306*
McKeen, H.P. 254
McKeen Royal Commission 254, 255, 323
McKenna, John 97
McKenna, Peter 97
McKenzie, John 85
McKenzie, Keneth 85
McKeown, W.E. 254
McLaren, Donald 133
McNab, Peter 66, 215
McNamara, Edward 71, 321
McNeil, John 77, 78
Meagher, Jane Elizabeth 113, 114
Meagher, Mr. and Mrs. John 113, 114
Meagher, Margaret 113, 114
Mercier, Kelly *306*
Methodist circuits, 106, 107, 165
Methodist movement 74–79, 83, 111
Methodist Church *see individual names*
Middle Musquodoboit 225
Middlemore Home Children's Group 201
Mi'kmaq 19, 20, 21, 22, 24
    history of 19–22
    conflict with British 23, 24
    women 28, *152*
    at street market 108
    Morris Lake Reserve 152, *153*
    Lonecloud 285, 286
military installations 203, 203
militia 44, 45, 73, 92
Mill Cove 314
Millbrook band office 152
Miller Road 276

Miller, Russell, 288
Miller, Tobias 276
mills
    carding 96
    flour and snuff 96
    gristmill 96
    lumber 174
millstones 97
millwrights 97
Mineville 111, 165, 321
Miss Canada Girls 206
Mitchell, Alan 297
Mitchell, Dean *305*
model farm 50
Monavan, Daniel 86
Mont, Stephen 294, 307
Montague 165
Montague, Gerald 174
Montbéliard 43
Mont Blanc 176
Moor, Thomas 86
Mooy, C. 235
Morasch, Johannes Michael 69
Morash, Blanca 72
Morash Brothers Dairy 215
Morash, Daniel 72
Morash, David 262, 263
Morash, Ella 72
Morash, Ethel 72
Morash, Eusten 85
Morash, Foster 72
Morash, George M. 70, 108, 122, 124
Morash, Harold S. 248
Morash, Hazel 72
Morash, Hilda, 72
Morash, Hugh 138
Morash, J. 215
Moarsh, Mrs. J. 218
Morash, John (J.R.) 133, 215, 243
Morash, Justus 121, 122
Morash, Leonard 85
Morash, Marjorie *109*
Morash, Michael 70, 85
Morash, Muriel *249*
Morash, Norman (N.A.) 193, 215, 243, 262, 263, *295*
Morash, Phillip (1842) 124
Morash, Philip (1977) *234*

Morash, Stan 72
Morash, Scott 262, 263, *309*
Morehash 145
Mormon Temple *see* church of Jesus Christ of Latter-Day Saints
Morris, Charles (surveyor)
    maps the area 22–24, 28, 33, 34
    purchases land 63
Morris, Charles Jr. 34, 321
Morris Lake 152, *153*
Morris Lake Mi'kmaq Reserve 152, *153*
Morris, William, 33, 34
Morrison, Rev. James 72
Morton, Ruth 239
Mosher 145, 189
Mount Edward 91
Mount Edward Road 69
Mount Hope Asylum 134, 135, 139
mumming 94
murder 65
Murdock, Andrew 62
Murdock Beamish 23, 62
Murphy, Rev. Gerald B. 235
Murphy, Diana 30
Murray, John 52
Musquodoboit 23, 27–29 *see also* Inner Harbour of Mouscoudabouet
Musquodoboit Valley 171
Myrer, John 135

N

Nancy 63
Nantes, David 297, 307, *308*, *309*
Nantes, Dianne *309*
Nantes, Heather *309*
Nantucket Whalers 71, 74, 87
Naval Armament Depot 202
Neagee, William 33
Negus, Charlie 221
Nelson, Steve 310
New York Herald 71
Newell, Thomas 35, 36, *37*, 45
Nicholson, Francis 28
Nieforth, Mrs. Effie 182–183, 281, 282, 325
Nisbeth, William 33
Nixon, Frances 263

Noiles, Ron (fiddler) 279
North Preston 301, 316
Nova Scotia Farmer's Association 216
Nova Scotia Historical Society 62
Nova Scotia Housing Commission 302
Nova Scotia Museum 88, 277
Nova Scotia Telephone Company 162
Nova Scotia Trap Shooting Championships 234
Nova Scotia Water Resource Commission 288
Nova Terrace 251
No. 2 Construction Battalion *see* Black Labour Battalion

O

occupations (1800s) 95–98
Ocean View Manor 240, 252, 322
Ochterloney, Alexander 56
Oland, Victor deB. 259
Old Preston Road 69
O'Leary, Jeff *319*
one-room school 191
open-air market *see* Green Market
oral history project 281, *282*, *283*, 284, 285, 325
organ, pump 80, 263
Osborne, Mary Kuhn 275
Osborne, Ron 98
Osborne, Ross *194*, 238, 291
Osborne, Verna Giles 279
Osborne, William 64, 85
Ostrea Lake 314
Ott, George Frederick 35, 36, *37*, 62, 63
Owen, Dick 222, 223

P

Palatinate 43
Patterson, Alex *319*
Patterson, Andrew *319*
Patterson, Arnie 250, 297
Patterson, Gordon *319*
Patterson, Harvey
    works at blacksmith shop 170
    recalls Halifax Explosion 176–177, 325

rode harvest trains 221
   in tug-of-war 222, 223
Patterson, Ian *319*
Patterson, Nat 214
Patterson, Vinnie 284, 325
Patterson, Mrs. Vinnie McKay 191
Paul, Elizabeth 285
Payzant, Mike *319*
Payzant, Randy *319*
Peach, Darren *319*
Pearl 45
Pearson, Don *305*
Pense, George 86
Peter McNab Kuhn Wildlife Management Area 275
Peters, Thomas 54, 55
Pettipas, A.C. 235
Pettipas, Claude 28
Pettipas, Jacques 29
Pettipas, Jean Baptiste 29
Pettipas, Joseph 29
Pettipas, Louis 29
Pettipas, Marie Thérèse 28
Peverell, Wallace (W.W.) 189, 197, 219, 294
Phelon, John 65
Phillips, Mrs. Margaret Ann *152*
Phinney, E.H. 174
Phippens, Mary 36
Phipps, William 27
Pinsent, Gordon *280*
Pitcher, Moses 65
Players Tobacco Company 199
plowing match 216
Pollach, Barbara 249
Poor Farm *see* County Poor Farm
Pope John XXIII parish 302, 323
Poplar Hill 50
population, general
   (1745) and (1748) 28
   (1792) 74
   (1827) 83, 84
   (2003) 15, 299, 313, 318
population, schools (1989) 300
Port Wallace 230
Port Wallace Ratepayer's Association 236
Porter, William 27

Porter's Lake 24, 35, 245
Portland Estates 37
Portland Street 66, 223
postal service 195, 201
Pottie, Rev. Joseph 302
Potts, Edward H. 71, 321
poultry *see* farming, poultry
pound keepers 293
Presbyterian Church of Nova Scotia 112, 321
Prescott, Mrs. 88
Preston
   the road to 32, 38
   Loyalist grants 51–54, 64
   Maroons at 55, 58
   governor's estate at 56
   first Anglican church in area 74, 110
   Settles purchase land 68
   residents enlist 169, 322
Preston Road 174, 230
Preston, Robert 54
Price, Arthur 33
Prince Andrew High School 312
Pringle, Elizabeth Inez 132, 133 *see also* Crawley, Eliza Inez
Pringle, John Elliot 132
Proctor, Abigail 71
Prohibition 180–184, 190, 322
Provincial Heritage Property 268
Provincial Parks 274
public education *see* schools
public landing place 276

Q

Quakers *see* settlers, United Empire Loyalists
Quaker Meeting House 71
quarantine 44
Quarrell, William 56, 79
Quebec gale 93
Queen Street 71

R

racial tensions 311
racism 169
radar station *203, 205,* 322
Radcliffe, Geoffrey 241

radio 206
rail service 166, *167*, *239*, *322*
railway bridge 166, 170, 171, *172*
Rainbow Haven Fresh Air Camp 184, 185, 186, 322
Rainbow Haven Beach *130*, *148*, *229*, *270*
Ramsay, Alexander 128, 132
Ratepayers Associations 236
recreational facilities *247*, *307*, *308*
Reid, Canon David 301
Regan, Gerald *259*
Regan, Mrs. Gerald *259*
Regional and Economic Expansion, Department of 287
Rice, Mr. 177
Rice, Clara Evelyn 177
Richards, Dennis 294, 297
Richards, Lois *88*
Richardson, Josiah 36
ring road, opposition to 312, 313, 323
ringette *306*
Rippon, Hannah 67
Ritcey, David W. 260
Ritcey, Lorne *211*
Ritcey, Murray
    recalls Halifax Explosion 178
    member of the credit union 193
    on his farm *211*, *231*
    member of buyers club 233
    president of farmers' federation 238
    thwarts a robbery 248
    promotes farm museum 263
    heritage society member 267, 277
    fights four-lane 291
Ritcey, Robert (Bob) *211*, *224*
Ritcey, Stanley *211*, *295*
Roach. Freeman 315
Roache, Henry James 248
road overseer 293
roads, condition of 13, 35, 101, 203, 232
roads early construction of 32, 35
roads maintenance of *14*, 232, *295*
roads, ring *see* ring road
roads, snow removal *295*
Roast, Christopher 85

Roast, Gasper 80
Roast, Leonard, 85
Robb, Ken 288
Robb, Walter 82
Robert Kemp Turner Elementary School 304
Robertson, James 66, 124
Robertson, John 124
Robinson, Andrew 97
Robinson, James 77, 86
Robinson Road 276
Roche 215
Roche, Harriet 134, 321
Roche, Michael 134
Rogation Service *223*
Roma 34
Romans, John D. 254
Romeau 151
Rose and Kettle Garden 277
Rosemary's Way *274*
Ross, Eunice 256
Ross Road 323
Roy, Rev. E 154
Royal Acadian School 70–72
Ruddock, Rick *305*
Rudland, J.A. 187
Rudolphe *295*
rugby 310
rum-running 181, *182*, 183, 184, 322
Runt, Henry 65
Russell Credit Union
    organizing days of 192, 193
    makes a presentation *194*
    locates in Victoria Hall 236, 248
    manager of 238, 291, 322
Russell, Rev. George
    promotes and organizes credit unions 191–*194*
    helps get rural postal service 195
    speaks of changes 203, 325
    leaves Cole Harbour 204
    returns for a special service *278*
Russell, John 310
Russell Lake 35, *37*, 51, 64, 89, 96
Russell, Mary (daughter of Nathaniel) 65
Russell, Mary (wife of Nathaniel) 64

Russell, Mary (wife of Nathaniel Jr.) 65
Russell, Nathaniel
    early settler 13, 49, 51, 85
    buys land 36
    joined Sandemanian sect 64
    daughter Mary murdered 65
    sells land 96
Russell, Nathaniel Jr. 65, 83, 106
Rutherford, Bert 72

S

St. Andrew's Anglican Church
    on Cole Harbour Road 111, *112*, 224, *267*, 321
    first superintendent 122
    holds special services 169, *223*, 224
    donates heritage land 276
    becomes a parish; builds on Circassion Drive 301, 322, 323
St. Clement's Catholic Parish 302
St. George's Anglican Church 63
St. John's Anglican Church (Lunenburg) 36
St. John's Anglican Church (Preston) 74, 110
St. Matthew's Presbyterian Church 36, 66, 67
St. Paul's Church (Halifax) 33, 36, 66
St. Peter's Roman Catholic Church 116
St. Peter's Total Abstinence Society 116
St. Thomas More Catholic Parish 246, 302
St. Thomas More Men's Club 301
St. Vincent de Paul Catholic Church 302, 323
Sally A. 91, 92
salt marshes
    birds 19, 288, *289*
    peaceful waters of 20, *127*, *263*
    crops 164
    map of *172*
    threatened 12, 260, 288
    residents act to preserve 260, 261, 275, 276, 288
Salt Marsh Trail *239*, *274*, 276
Salmon River 148
sampler, sewing of *68*
Sandeman, Robert 53
Sandemanian sect 53, 64
sauerkraut, making *265*
Saul, George 33
Savage, Dr. John 297
Sawler, George 98
Sawler, William 98
schools, early years 14, 70–73, 247, 321
schools, later years *see individual names*
Scotia Stadium 307
Scott, Abigail 79, 82
Scott, John 79, 85
sea manure 147, 212, 213, 153, *154*
Seaforth 150, 183, 281
seamstresses 98, 139
Seatle, Mary *see* Settle, Mary
seaweed 153
2nd Construction Battalion *see* Black Labour Battalion
Sellars, Russell *282*
Sellers, Elizabeth 111
Sellers, Henry 111, 124
Sellers, James T. 111
Sellers, William 111
Settle, Alexander 69
Settle, Andrew, 69, 197
Settle, Andrew Mrs. *268*
Settle, Beatrice 204
Settle, Bernice *249*
Settle, Charles 214, *222*, 246, 256, *257*
Settle, Clara *197*, *244*, 256
Settle, David *168*, 169, *244*, *320*
Settle, Doll 72
Settle, Edith Turner 256
Settle, Eunice 256
Settle, Frank 204
Settle, Fred 258, 294
Settle, Hannah 67, 68, 69
Settle, Hattie 197
Settle, Ira
    remembers Anchor Lodge 122
    sells to Eaton's 212
    dairy farming 214

recalls tug-of-war 223
is elected to council 234, 236, 242, 250, 264, 288, 294
as deputy warden and warden 246, *259, 289*
gets Little Salmon River project 241
in younger years 256–257
receives citizen's award 258
chairs Planning Board 258
his house and the fire station 259
"Mr. Cole Harbour" 260
retired, in his garden *260*
does heritage work 264, 277, *296*, 325
at library opening *308*
Settle, Jack *129, 197, 244*
Settle, James 67, 98
Settle, James (son of Robert Sr.) 69
Settle, John (b. 1776) 67–69, 108, 124, 140, *244*
Sett.e, John (b. 1810) 67
Settle, John Daniel 69
Settle, John E. 256
Settle, Judson 69, 294
Settle, Keith *224*
Settle Lake 35, 69
Settle, Rev. Lester *278*
Settle, Marion L. 204, 205, 206
Settle, Mary 67, *68*, 69
Settle, Mary Ann 69
Settle, Melvina 69
Settle, R. (buys bull) 216
Settle, Ralph *194*
Settle, Robert Sr. 67, 69, 124, 218
Settle, Robert Jr. 69, 95, 197, 216, 219, 256
Settle, Robert (Rippon) (father of Ira) 110, 214, 256, *257*
Settle, Robert (Bob) (brother of Ira) *222*, 256
Settle, Sadie *72*
Settle, Sophia 69
Settle, Susannah Emma 69
Settle, Thomas 68
Settle, Victor *72*
Settle, William 256

settlers 321
  Black Loyalists 51–55
  British 33, 41
  French Protestant 42, 43, 45, 47
  German Protestant 36, 37, 41–45, 51, 145
  Jamaican Maroons 51, 55–58, 79, 125, 321
  Quakers 50, 51, 87
  recruitment of 42, 43, 44
  Swiss Protestant 41, 42, 43, 132
  United Empire Loyalists 35, *37*, 48–51, 72, 321
sewer and water lines 261, 288–290
sewing *68, 89*
shallops 47
Sharp, Granville 55
Shattered City 315
Shaw, John 86
sheep valuers 294
Shelton, Ebenezer 63
Sherbrooke, John 71
Shields, Andrew 96, 116, 117
shoemakers 97
Shubenacadie Canal 21
Shubenacadie River 54
Sierra Leone 55, 79
Silver Sands Beach 234, 322
Silver Sands Company 234, 235, 238
Simms, Mrs. *72*
Sinma Investments Ltd. 301
Sir Robert Borden Junior High School 252, 323
Slack, Joan 263
Slade, Arthur 197
Slater, John 263, *266*
slavery 51, 52, 55
Smelt Brook 19, 24, 33, 79, 276
Smith, Alex W. 133
Smith, Rev. D.K. 157
Smith, E.V. 235
Smith, Nathan 314
Smith, Sean 277
Smith subdivision 287
Smith, Titus 50
Smothers, Richard 77
snuff mill 96
soccer 310

softball 310
Sons of Temperance 117
Southland 170
Sparks, Bertha 258
Speedwell 43
Sperry/MacLennan 307
Spike, William Drake 33, 34
spinning 88, 89
sport and recreation 305–310
sports, local championships 310
sports, minor stats 310
sports teams *305, 306*
Spring Avenue 87
Stanfield, Robert L. 250
Stanley, Henry 71
Starr, John 77
Starr Manufacturing Company 175
Steel, Wanda *306*
Stevens Construction Ltd., D.B. 304
Stevens, Edmund 80, 82
Stewart, Bernetta *306*
Stewart, Charles 77
Stewart, Melanie *306*
Stewart, Peter 224
Stewart, Rick 294
Stewiacke Valley *319*
Stirling, George 77
Stomford, Robert 235
Storey, Steve *305*
Story, John 34
Stowell, William 86
Stratton, Bill *317*
Strawberry Island 234
street market *see* Green Market *and* Halifax Farmer's Market
Strum, Gerald *279*
Strum, Maurice
    shares oral history 212, 213, 219, 223, 325
    and Willow 225
    honourary member *266*
    with Rosie *283*
    shovelling snow *295*
Strum, Robie *80,* 276
Strum, Willow Henneberry 225
Stuart, Elizabeth 73, 79, 91
Stuart, John (Col.) 73, 79, 91, 300
Stubbs, Eileen 236, 254

student violence 311, 312
sugar refineries 166, 213
Sullers, George 86
Sullivan, Allan 289
Sunnyside 284
Sunshine Manor 315
surfing, Lawrencetown Beach *149*
Sutherland, Colonel 45
Sutherland, Daniel H. 169
Swiss *see* settlers

T

Taggart, John 33
Tallahassee School 251
tannery 51, 71, 95
Tariff Commission 154, 155
Tatamagouche 46, 47
tavern 96
Taylor, Henry Ramsay 126
telephone service, first 166
Temperance Hall *32,* 108, 154
temperance movement 115–118, *119, 120–123*
temperance societies 115, 116, 117, 121, 321 *see also* Anchor Lodge
Temple, Rev. William 78
Thompsons of Petpeswick 98
Thomson, Eric *305*
Thoms, W.M.M. 254
Thornham, John 294
Three Fathom Harbour 165, 182, 245
Thurston-Neeley, Linda 315
timeline 321–323
Tingley, D.W. 254
Titanic 165
tobacco 96, 199
Tobin, Russell 174
Tompkins, Father James J. 192
Tonks, Thomas 251, 288
Topple, Wes 294
Tourism and Culture, Department of 269
traditional rural skills 263, *265, 271, 272*
Trans-Canada Trail 239, 312
Trelawney 56
Tremaine, Abigail 50
Tremaine, Johnathan 49, 50, 71
Trider, Chris *273*

Trider, Donald 311
Trongate 205, 206
Troop, G.J. 216, 218
Trynor Construction Company 235
Tuft's Cove 207, 230
Tuft's Cove Ratepayer's Association 236
tug-of-war 222, 223, *319*
Tulloch, Edith 66
Tulloch, George 155
Tulloch, Maynard 66, 218, 219
Tulloch, Robert 66, 248, 277
Turnbull, Chris *319*
Turner, Andrew 121, 122, 184
Turner, Ann 66
Turner, Bessie 184
Turner, Clara 139
Turner, Daniel 124
Turner, Donald (Donnie) 174, 219
Turner, Eunice Ross *138*, 256
Turner, Florence 139
Turner, Frances 230
Turner, George 219, *220*, 221
Turner, Harold *224*
Turner, Isabella 184
Turner, James
  Farmkeeper at Poor Farm 135–142, *138*, 162, 322
  obituary of 141, 142
  ancestor of Ira Settle 256
  fence viewer 293
Turner, Percy 174
Turner, Ralph 174
Turner, Robert Kemp Sr. 1 67, 85, 124
Turner, Robert Kemp Jr. 11 7, 124
Turner, Robert Kemp III 184
Turner, Robert Kemp IV 184, 300
Turner, Sophia 184
Turner, Walter J. 184
Turner, William 67, 85, 124
Turner, William Jr. 67, 85
Turner farm 67
Turner's Lake *see* Settle Lake
Twin Cities Cooperative Dairy 215
two-room school 299

U

United Church of Canada
  is formed 184, 186, 187
  dedicates new church 242, 263, 322
  deeds old chapel 264
United Empire Loyalists *see* settlers
Upper Lawrencetown 19, 108
Upper Musquodoboit 239
Ustick, Elizabeth 50
Ustick, William 50

V

Van Buskirk, James 126
Verge, Dr. Wylie 242
Victoria Hall (community centre)
  as a landmark 14, 191, *194*, 233
  land obtained for 184, 322
  group on balcony *185*
  used by 191, 193, 204, 236
  replaced and sold 247, 248
Victory Bonds 206

W

Wakefield, Benjamin 35, 36, 37
Wakefield, James 35, 36, 37
Wakefield, Joseph 36
Walker, Robert T. 33
Wallace, Michael 49, 55, 71, 79
Walsh, Peter Daniel 248
Walsh, Michael 200
Walton, Isaac 146
Wampawk 19, 23, 24
War Saving Stamps 206
Ward, Lerosa 69
water and sewer lines 230, 251, 261, 288–290
Water Street *see* Alderney Drive
Waterbury, David 254
Watson, John 126, 128
Watson, Thomas 126
Waverly Methodist mission 108
Wax Works 107
Way, Jessie 178
Weagle, Anna Catherine 45
weavers 98
Weeks, Rev. Joshua Wingate 110
Weigle, Anna Catherine 45
Weir, Rev. John 107
Welsham, James 85
Wenman, Richard 33, 36

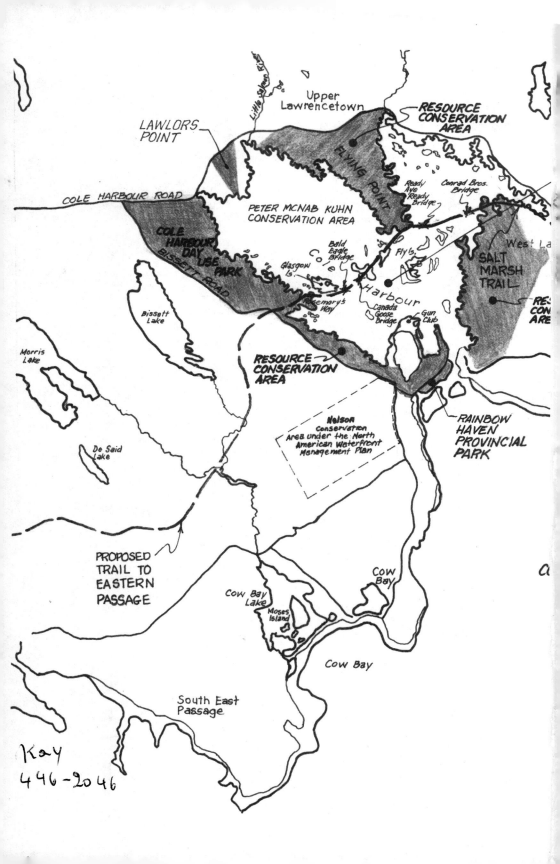

Wenman, Susannah 36
Wentworth, John
    came to Nova Scotia 49
    became governor 50
    employed Maroons 56, 58
    owned land in Preston 63, 74, 276
Wentworth Road 276
Wentzell 111
Wesley, Charles 74, 75
Wesley, John 74, 75
Wesleyan Methodist Missions of Nova Scotia 78
West Chezzetcook 30, 150–153
West Lawrencetown Road 32
Westphal 79, 230
Westphal, George 230
Westphal, Philip 230
Westphal Ratepayers Association 236
Westphal Women's Institute 230
wheat 50
wheelwrights 98
White, Editha 53
White Ribbon Army of the Nova Scotia Sabbath School Association *119*
White, William Andrew 169
White, Father Thomas 302
Whitehead, Ruth Holmes 286
Whitehouse, Mike 315
Whitehouse, Sophie Bissett *244*
Whyte, Shauna 118
Williams, John (trader) 25, 26
Williams, John 170
Williams, Morgan 310
Williams, Rev. Robert 108
Willis, John 34
Wilson, Rev. H.C. 304
Wilson, John 135
Winchester, Joe *305*
wine making 89
Winfield, I.A. 154
Wisdom, Henry 65
Wiseman, John 86
Wiswell, Joseph 76–78
Wiswell, Mary 66, 78
Wisell, W.H. 134, 135
witherod 263, *265*

Wolfe, A.S. 218
Women's Christian Temperance Union 117
Women's Missionary Society 122
Women's Institute of Nova Scotia 230–232
women's rural skills 68, 98, 103, 151, 218, *271 see also* Louisa's Diary
wood cutting *271*
Wood, Daniel 65
Wood, Harry 86
Woodlawn 32, 51, 70, 230, 232
Woodlawn Cemetery 65, 95, 113, 114
Woodlawn Dairy 191, 215, 243
Woodlawn Forks 205
Woodlawn Methodist Church
    mission 83, 108, 112, 113, 165
    votes for union 165
Woodlawn Ratepayers Association 236
Woodlawn United Church 71
Woodside 230
Woodside Ratepayers Association 236
Woodside–Imperoyal United Church 301
Woodside sugar refinery 213
wool carding *271*
World War One
    begins 166–168
    enlisting in *168*, 169
    Black Battalion sails 170
    men serving 174, 175
    Halifax Explosion 175–180
    ends 180, 322
World War Two 199, 202–208, 240, 322
Worral, M. 145
Wright, Esther Clark 69
Wyman, Ephraim 36

Y

Yates, Jamie *305*
Yorke, William 85
Young People's Union 205

Z

Zinck, Dorothy Covert *88*